Cracking the
AP*
ENGLISH
LITERATURE
& COMPOSITION
Exam

The Princeton Review

Cracking the
AP*
ENGLISH
LITERATURE
& COMPOSITION
Exam
2009 Edition

Douglas McMullen, Jr.
Updated by Stephen Mounkhall

PrincetonReview.com

Random House, Inc. New York

The Princeton Review

The Independent Education Consultants Association recognizes The Princeton Review as a valuable resource for high school and college students applying to college and graduate school.

The Princeton Review, Inc.
2315 Broadway
New York, NY 10024
E-mail: editorialsupport@review.com

ISBN: 978-0-375-42889-0
ISSN: 1092-0099

*AP and Advanced Placement Program are registered trademarks of the College Entrance Examination Board.

Editor: Selena Coppock
Production Editor: Emmeline Parker
Production Coordinator: Effie Hadjiioannou

Printed in the United States of America.

10 9 8 7 6 5 4 3 2 1

2009 Edition

Acknowledgment

The Princeton Review would like to thank Blake Taylor for doing a fantastic review of this title.

Contents

Introduction

WHAT IS THE PRINCETON REVIEW?

The Princeton Review is an international test preparation company with branches in all major U.S. cities and several cities abroad. In 1981, John Katzman started teaching an SAT prep course in his parents' living room. Within five years, The Princeton Review had become the largest SAT prep program in the country.

Our phenomenal success in improving students' scores on standardized tests is due to a simple, innovative, and radically effective philosophy: Study the test, not just what the test *claims* to test. This approach has led to the development of techniques for taking standardized tests based on the principles the test writers themselves use to write the tests.

The Princeton Review has found that its methods work not just for cracking the SAT, but for any standardized test. We've already successfully applied our system to the GMAT, LSAT, MCAT, and GRE, to name a few. Obviously, you need to be well versed in English literature to do well on the AP English Literature and Composition Exam, but you should remember that any standardized test is partly a measure of your ability to think like the people who write standardized tests. This book will help you brush up on your AP English Literature and Composition and prepare for the exam using our time-tested principle: Crack the system based on how the test is created.

We also offer books and online services that cover an enormous variety of education and career-related topics. If you're interested, check out our website at **PrincetonReview.com**.

Author's Foreword

Throughout this book you'll notice that when I refer to myself, I say "we." I'm not the Queen of England, and this isn't the "royal 'we'"—it's just that The Princeton Review's test-taking techniques are the refined product of hundreds of smart people spending thousands of hours figuring out how best to teach standardized tests. Saying "we" is a matter of giving credit where it's due. Just this once, though, I'd like to step out of the collective shadows and say a few personal things about the book you're reading.

Because you're reading this book, chances are good that you're a high school student studying English literature. I was once where you are, and I never thought I'd be here on the other side of the page, writing about English. In high school, I loved reading (that is, the books I wanted to read) and I even sometimes liked writing, but I definitely wasn't sure I liked studying English. It seemed to me that my teachers were bent on ripping literature into tiny little pieces so they could squint at the wreckage. My English teachers seemed like maniacs who spent their time shooting birds out of trees so that they could take a bird's body, pluck its feathers, cut it open, and talk about its intestines. I just wanted to listen to the birds sing. At the time, I was sure I had the better attitude. But now look at me: carving into books and poems as if they were cooked turkeys and serving them up, supposedly for your benefit.

Well, it is for your benefit: first and foremost to help you on this test—but there's much more than that. Reading poetry and fiction is an art—not a skill, *an art*. If you'd told me when I was 15 that I didn't really know how to read fiction I would have laughed at you. But, if you'd told me I didn't know how to read music or how to play the violin, well, it would obviously have been true.

When it comes to literature, great authors are great composers, and you, the reader, are the violinist, the pianist, the conductor—the whole orchestra. The difference is that the performance is one only you can hear, and only you can really know how well you've played the piece. It takes years of practice and study to read (or write) truly well, just as it does to master a musical instrument. There's no shame in being less than perfect. You'll know when you get it right—it will sound right inside. That maniac English teacher is just a stern piano instructor, making you practice your scales over and over again. Does it get boring? Yes. Does it seem totally pointless at least half the time? Yes! Is it fun? No, not really—except that every now and then you discover that you can play a new, harder piece just right. When you realize, "Hey, all this practice is starting to pay off!" it's exiting. I'll bet you've already come across a piece of literature that's made you sit up and say, "Wow, there really *is* something special about this book." I want to remind you that English teachers are not part of a secret conspiracy to drive students crazy, and that there's a method (and a love of literature) behind your English teacher's and my madness. When you get bogged down, remind yourself that the point of all this study is the mastery of an art— intelligent reading and writing—an art you'll be able to use every day of your life.

This book is my small contribution to your career as a concert soloist in literature. Good luck. Who knows? Maybe I'll see you reading in Carnegie Hall some day.

—Douglas McMullen, Jr.

PART I

Orientation

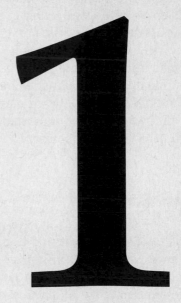

A Brief Introduction to the AP English Literature and Composition Exam

WHY DO YOU NEED THIS BOOK?

The book you hold in your hands has been designed to meet the differing needs of English students across the country. Above all, this book is for the student whose goal is to achieve the best possible score on the AP English Literature and Composition Exam. The Princeton Review believes that the best way to achieve this goal is to better understand the test itself, especially how the test is written. By understanding the limitations that test writers (and essay readers) face, you will know how to approach the test for the maximum score—that's what matters most here. If, like many students, you have had excellent English instruction in a course specifically designated as AP English, then you primarily want a book that will help ensure that you ace the test. We provide that.

This book is also for students who aren't confident about the course they took or who haven't taken an AP English course at all. For these students, we go into depth on many topics, especially in the essay-writing portion of the book. Although no book can replace several semesters with a good teacher, motivated students are their own best teachers and can accomplish amazing things. This book offers instruction and points the way to further learning for these kinds of students.

Finally, this book is for the not-so-uncommon student who loves literature and writing and can't get enough of it; we aren't saying this book is fine literature itself, but we think it can help you toward greater understanding, appreciation, and yes, love of literature, all the while helping you ace the test, of course.

AP ENGLISH

In May 2006, roughly 281,000 students took the AP English Literature and Composition Exam. The AP English Literature and Composition Exam has a sister test, the English Language and Composition Exam, which is also given in May and is taken by about 257,000 students a year. (This book is for students who intend to take the Literature Exam. Near the end of this chapter, there is a brief description of the AP Language Exam and how it differs from the Literature Exam.)

Almost all of these 538,000 students have at some point taken a class structured, at least partially, with an AP English Exam in mind. Most often this course is called, naturally enough, AP English. Some schools do not have specifically titled AP courses, but do have accelerated courses which can be adequate preparation for the AP exams. There is no prerequisite for either AP exam. Anyone who wants to take the tests can.

AP English courses (in fact *all* AP courses) are essentially first-year college courses. AP English could very easily be called College English on the High School Level (if it sounds challenging, that's because it is). So, if AP English is available at your school, seriously consider taking it. It looks great on your high school transcript when you're applying to college. Moreover, when you get to college, you can probably skip some introductory courses and start with the more interesting ones.

GETTING CREDIT

Getting AP English credit is harder than simply passing freshman English, which takes only a C or higher. To get credit for AP English you need to meet two requirements. You need to attend a college that recognizes the AP Program, and you need a good score on one of the two AP English tests (Literature and Composition or Language and Composition). Your guidance counselor (or AP teacher) might be able to provide information on whether the schools you are applying to award AP credit, how much credit, and just what scores you need. Chances are they won't know exactly, and you'll want to know—exactly. The easiest way to find out about a particular school's AP English policy is to check the school's website. The most reliable way, however, is to write or e-mail (not call) the admissions office of the school or schools you are interested in and ask. When they write back, *keep the letter and take it with you when you register for courses.*

In general, the AP exams are widely accepted, but which test is preferred, what score is necessary to earn credit, and how much credit is awarded can vary widely from school to school or even within colleges at a school. A 5 will always get you credit when it's available. Most of the time, a 4 will work equally well. A 3 is considered borderline, but two of the largest state university systems (the Universities of California and Texas) grant some credit for a 3.

AP ENGLISH CURRICULUM AND ITS TEACHERS

It may come as a surprise to some students that there is no standard AP English curriculum. The course you take is undoubtedly different from the one given at the high school across town, and both are different from the course given ten states away. What you study is up to your teacher and, to a lesser extent, the English department faculty of your school. Despite all this current diversity, however, the courses share a common task: *to teach you to read and write about English Literature at a college level.* In college, you will be expected to read difficult texts for meaning. You will also be expected to formulate ideas about what you read and to express those ideas in clear, grammatically correct writing. AP courses share these same goals. But because so much leeway is given to the teacher, and individual teachers have their own likes and dislikes, the emphases of one course will differ from those of another. Some courses spend half the year on Shakespeare, others focus on personal and creative writing, some deal almost exclusively with nineteenth- and twentieth-century novels, while others focus on ancient texts. Finally, many of the best teachers do not teach AP English with the test in mind at all. They believe that maintaining and building your enthusiasm for the subject is more important than any test score (and they're probably right). In general, an English teacher's expertise is in English Literature, not the AP English Literature Exam.

Well, our expertise is test taking. As we discuss what you can expect to see on the AP English Literature Exam, keep a lookout for what you haven't studied and for your weaknesses. A little extra study in those areas will go a long way.

THE FORMAT OF THE AP ENGLISH LITERATURE EXAM

Test Date: Early May
Total Time: 3 hours (usually administered at 8:00 A.M.)

Section I: Multiple Choice (60 minutes)—45 percent of your grade
Total number of questions: 55
Four or five prose and poetry passages: 10–15 questions per passage

Section II: Essay (120 minutes)—55 percent of your grade
Three Essays:
1. Analysis of poetry (40-minute essay on a single poem or comparison of two poems that ETS provides)
2. Analysis of prose (40-minute essay on a story, novel excerpt, or essay that ETS provides)
3. Open essay (40-minute essay on a literary topic that ETS provides, supported by the student's own reading)

WHO WRITES THE AP ENGLISH EXAM?

The test is written by the AP English Development Committee. The committee is assisted by ETS (Educational Testing Service), the folks who write the SATs, as well as other tests you'll no doubt take if you head for graduate school. The AP people (there are eight on the committee, all English teachers, either high school or college) pick the passages and write first drafts of the test questions—but then the ETS people step in. They fine-tune the test. ETS's primary concern is to ensure that the test, especially the multiple-choice section, is similar to previous administrations and tests a broad spectrum of student ability. The ETS contribution is what concerns us and you. ETS has predictable ways of shaping questions and creating wrong answers. On multiple-choice tests, knowing how the wrong answers are written and how they can be eliminated is always key. We'll discuss this topic in detail in Chapter 5, "Cracking the System: Multiple-Choice Questions."

SCORING

WHAT YOUR FINAL SCORE MEANS

After taking the test in early May, you will receive your scores sometime around the first week of July, which is right about when you've just started to forget about the whole experience. Your score will be, simply enough, a single number from 1 to 5. Here is what those numbers mean:

Score Meaning	Approximate percentage of all test takers receiving this score at participating colleges	Equivalent first-year college course grade	Will a student with this score receive credit?
5—Extremely Well Qualified	10.6%	A	Usually
4—Well Qualified	22.4%	A–, B+	Usually
3—Qualified	35.8%	B–, C	Maybe
2—Possibly Qualified	25.1%	C, D	Very Rarely
1—No Recommendation	6.2%	D	No

YOUR MULTIPLE-CHOICE SCORE

In the multiple-choice section of the test, you receive one point for each question you answer correctly. You receive no points for a question left blank. You receive a deduction of a quarter of a point for each question you answer incorrectly. This quarter point deduction is the infamous "guessing penalty." (You might be familiar with this scoring method from the SAT.) We'll discuss that so-called penalty in detail in Chapter 3.

YOUR ESSAY SCORE

Each AP essay is scored on a scale from 0 to 9, with 9 being the highest score. The scores of each essay are added together and this total, anywhere from 0 to 27, is your Essay section score. A Reader (a high school or college level English teacher) goes through your essay and gives you a score based on an overall evaluation. This process is called "holistic" scoring. We will go into the details of essay scoring in the "Cracking the System: The Essays" part of this book, but here is the general outline of the 0 to 9 system: A "9" essay answers all facets of the question completely, making good use of the passage to support its points, and is "well written," which is a catch-all phrase that means sentences are complete, properly punctuated, clear in meaning, show an educated vocabulary, and are spelled correctly. Lower scoring essays are deficient in these qualities to a greater or lesser degree. At the zero level, the student has written what amounts to gibberish (misspelled gibberish). If you write in perfect medieval Latin, or Esperanto, or perhaps write a funny, publishable, prize-worthy story about your AP teacher, you will receive a "—." This score is the equivalent of 0.

The essay Readers do not award points according to a standardized predetermined checklist. The essays are scored individually by individual Readers. Each Reader scores essays for only one type of question. ETS says (and we have no reason to doubt them) that the Reader of your open essay will be familiar with the work about which you write. If, for your open essay on mistaken identity, you chose to write about Sophocles' *Oedipus Rex*, then your essay Reader would have read that work. (Of course, you could choose something stunningly obscure and mess with their heads, but we don't recommend it.) If a certain test has an essay on a poem by John Donne, an essay on a prose extract by Jean Toomer, and an open essay on the topic of mistaken identity in a novel or play of your choice, there will be three distinct Readers: a Reader for your Donne essay, a Reader for your Toomer essay, and a Reader for your open essay. Each will give you a score based solely on the essay she or he reads. The other Readers will not see your other essays or know how you were scored on them, nor will they know how you performed on the multiple-choice section.

YOUR FINAL SCORE

Your final 1 to 5 score is a combination of your section scores. Remember that the multiple-choice section counts for 45 percent of the total and the essays count for 55 percent. While this proportion makes them almost equal, they are not entirely equal. ETS adopts a somewhat convoluted mathematical formula to arrive at your score. This formula involves a 150-point scale, but first you multiply your essay score by 3.0556, and your multiple-choice score by slightly less than 1.3.

Neither you, nor the colleges you apply to, will ever know what your individual section scores are. ETS doesn't tell. You get a final score between 1 and 5, and that's it.

Does this mean you don't need to think about how your multiple-choice and essay scores combine? No. You should get a feel for how your multiple-choice score affects your final, total score. Look at the overall test as two separate assessments:

Multiple Choice = 55 questions for a total of 45 percent of the score.
Three Essays = 3 questions, each scored on a 0 to 9 scale, for a total of 55 percent of the score.

The cutoff point for each grade varies from year to year and is set only after all the multiple-choice sections and essays have been scored. Regardless, a good bottom-line goal is to get at least 30 questions right on the multiple-choice sections and to earn at least 15 points on the essays. These two scores will net you a final passing grade of 3. Increases in either category can increase your final scores. The grading scale for the AP English Literature Exam looks something like this:

Essay Points	15	18	21	24	27
MC Points					
20	2	3	3	4	5
25	3	3	4	4	5
30	3	4	4	5	5
35	3	4	4	5	5
40	4	4	5	5	5
45	4	5	5	5	5
50	5	5	5	5	5
55	5	5	5	5	5

CONCLUSIONS

1. The bottom-line goal on the multiple-choice section is 30, or little more than half. The bottom-line goal on the essays is the minimum passing score on each essay, 5 (3 × 5 = 15).

2. Set realistic goals for yourself. Look what happens if your multiple-choice score stays at 30 while you raise your essays one point each (from a 15 to an 18): You go from a 3 to a 4!

The odds are long, but earning a 5 is possible, even if you only scored within the 20 to 35 range on the multiple-choice section.

Now let's start practicing ways for you to get your best possible score.

Pacing Chart for AP English Literature and Composition Exam				
My Score on Practice	Shooting for Minimum of	Time Spent	Must Get Right	Guess or Leave Out
_____	30 of 55	60 mins	30	25

There are two ways to get 30 points:

1. Answer 30 questions and get every one of them right.

2. Answer more than 30, to adjust for the ones missed and for the $\frac{1}{4}$ right-wrong penalty (or $\frac{3}{4}$ right-wrong bonus!).

   Roughly: answer 40 questions, miss 8 = penalty of 2 points
   $$40 - 8 = 32$$
   $$32 - 2 = 30$$

   answer 55 questions, miss 20 = penalty of 5
   $$55 - 20 = 35$$
   $$35 - 5 = 30$$

CONCLUSION

You do not have to get every answer right to get a good score! Use the chart below to map out how many guesses you can afford. Use a set of our questions in the practice sets (Chapters 6 and 7) to give yourself Before and After scores. The Before score reflects how you did when taking the practice set cold, and the After score shows what you can do after you've tried our strategies. Look at it this way:

The Numbers Game				
Number Right	Penalized Answered	Number Guessed	Number Omitted	Number Penalized Right-Wrong
Before: _____	_____	_____	_____	_____
After: _____	_____	_____	_____	_____

The AP English Literature and Composition Exam is unlike other AP exams in one other factor: time. The multiple-choice section is always one hour long and contains 4 or 5 passages with a total of 55 questions. Obviously, you could evenly divide your time, say 15 minutes each for 4 passages or 12 minutes each for 5 passages.

When you are getting the feel of the passage and the kinds of questions, take all the time you need. Your purpose, after all, is different at this stage, as you are familiarizing yourself with the process. Later, when you are practicing for the real experience, limit your time to precisely one hour.

Remember—you can guess (with right-wrong bonus!) and you can omit. Look at it this way:

Time: 1 hour
Practice Test of 55 questions

Passage	Number of Questions	Number To Get Right	Number To Omit or Guess On
1	15	8	25 (from any section)
2	14	8	
3	11	6	
4	15	8	
		30	

Use a chart like this one to evaluate your performance when practicing:

The Time Factor				
Time Evenly Divided	Time I Spent	Time Shooting For	Number to Get Right	Number to Omit
_____	_____	_____	_____	_____

THREE STUDY NOTES FOR THE AP ENGLISH EXAM

You'll see a total of 6 or 7 reading passages on the AP exam: 4 or 5 multiple-choice passages plus a passage each for the first 2 essays. ETS is careful to draw these passages from different time periods, from male and female authors, from racially diverse authors, and from both English and American literature. Among these 6 passages (there actually could be 7 if one of the essays asks you to compare and contrast two poems or short prose works), chances are very good that there will be at least one passage from each of the following periods: 1558–1659; 1660–1798; 1799–1917; 1918–present. Whether you're on a multiple-choice or essay section, comprehension of these passages, both in detail and in an overall sense, is critical. Typically, students find prose easier to understand than poetry, and modern writing easier to comprehend than that of earlier periods. Furthermore, students do better on material they've studied previously than on material they haven't studied. Stick to these general rules:

First, study to eliminate weaknesses, but on the test itself, emphasize your strengths. We will discuss in detail how to do both these things in the chapters that follow.

Second, notice that although two-thirds of the test-taking time is devoted to essays, the multiple-choice section is almost its equal in terms of your score. Many students fixate on the essay questions and act as though the multiple-choice section is just extra. It isn't. **Don't blow off the multiple-choice section.** You can and should study for this part.

Third, **prepare for the whole test, don't just fixate on the open essay.** The essays are all weighted equally. The open essay is about 18 percent of your score.

THE ENGLISH LANGUAGE AND COMPOSITION EXAM

As we mentioned above, there are two AP English exams: the English Literature and Composition Exam and the English Language and Composition Exam. The reason for this distinction is the differing emphases of freshman college English courses. The literature test, which is the more popular of the two tests, is meant to assess the knowledge and skills that are developed by first-year English courses. The language test assesses the knowledge and skills developed by courses with titles like Expository Writing or Rhetoric. In such courses, the emphasis is distinctly on nonfiction writing. Students study the means by which an author develops an argument in writing and then produce persuasive writing of their own.

In keeping with these differences, the AP English Language and Composition Exam uses a format similar to the English Literature Exam, with multiple-choice questions on 4 or 5 different passages and a second section that calls for 3 essays. The difference is that the language test's passages are drawn from critical writing and other kinds of nonfiction, rather than from the fiction and poetry that make up most or all of the literature test. The emphases of the multiple-choice questions and the essay topics on the language test are also somewhat different from those of the literature test. The language test focuses on the student's ability to grasp the overall structure of an argument, to identify the rhetorical devices the author has used, and to discern the important elements of logical reasoning that are present in any argument.

The tests are scheduled on separate days and one can take both in the same year. Whether this is practical depends on the course work you have done in English, the workload from your other courses, and the schools to which you are applying. Some schools prefer one test; some, the other. If you write well and think logically, but hate (and cannot make sense of) poetry, the language test is worth investigating.

BUT WHAT'S IN IT FOR ME?

There's a mysterious little box on the form you'll be given on the AP exam you take. It asks your permission to use your writing as a sample for research. Checking the box will not affect your score. It simply means that when ETS publishes samples of student writing, it makes sure it only chooses from students that have given their permission.

HOW TO USE THIS BOOK

We strongly recommend that you read the chapters on test-taking techniques before you take the practice tests at the end of this book. You'll have a better idea of what you're doing, and you will be able to apply the techniques we've taught you. After you've taken the practice tests, we suggest that you read all the explanations, even the explanations to the questions you've answered correctly. You'll often find that your understanding of a question and the best way to have gone about answering it will be much clearer after you've read the explanation. You'll also catch some instances in which you got the question right, but for all the wrong reasons. Finally, some of the explanations have tidbits of information you won't find elsewhere in the book.

STILL HAVE QUESTIONS?

The fee for this exam is $84. Fee reductions are available from the College Board for students with financial need. These reductions take the price of the AP exam down to $54 per exam. That's the bare bones of the AP English Literature and Composition Exam. We hope you still have questions, because we still have lots of answers. What are the passages like? What kinds of questions are on the multiple-choice section? What book(s) should you read to prepare for the open essay? Does handwriting count? When should you guess? How do you ace the essays? We'll answer all of these questions and much more in the chapters that follow.

HOW TO GET MORE INFORMATION

Additional information on AP policies and the AP English Literature and Composition Exam is available on the College Board's website at **www.collegeboard.com/student/testing/ap/sub_englit. html?englit** or by contacting:

AP Services
PO Box 6671
Princeton, NJ 08541-6671
609-771-7300 or toll free 888-225-5427 in the U.S. and Canada
E-mail: apexams@info.collegeboard.org

An Overview of Literary Movements

USING THIS OVERVIEW

If you are reading this book months before you are to take the test, you can use this section in a methodical, poem-by-poem manner. By reading the 200 representative poems listed in this section, you will gain a thorough sense of the kinds of poems that the College Board chooses from when writing their tests. If you are using this book during crunch time and the test is a few weeks away, our suggestion is to read a poem or two from under each heading and to familiarize yourself more broadly with the ideas associated with each movement. If you are picking up this book for the first time when you have only a few days left to study for the exam, then skip this section and go straight to Part II and Part III of this book, which address cracking the test. This section gives you the opportunity, if you have allotted yourself enough time, to familiarize yourself with the potential content of the exam. Before getting into the overview, let's answer some questions you might have.

Does the AP English Exam Require Certain Readings?

Though the Advanced Placement English curriculum avoids requiring any specific list of authors or texts to be taught, it does offer a *suggested* authors list. W. H. Auden, Elizabeth Bishop, William Blake, Gwendolyn Brooks, Samuel Taylor Coleridge, H. D. (Hilda Doolittle), Emily Dickinson, John Donne, T. S. Eliot, Robert Frost, Seamus Heaney, George Herbert, Langston Hughes, John Keats, Robert Lowell, Andrew Marvel, Marianne Moore, Sylvia Plath, Alexander Pope, Adrienne Rich, Anne Sexton, Percy Shelley, Walt Whitman, William Carlos Williams, William Wordsworth, and W. B. Yeats all show up on the representative author list for the English literature exam and in the chapter below. Just because the College Board lists these poets as representative does not necessarily mean that these are the poets you will find on the exam. Getting to know the work of these poets, however, will give you a solid background with which to approach the poems the test makers *do* choose.

How Can a List of Representative Authors Help Me Prepare for the Exam?

By itself, a list of representative authors will not help you. To someone who doesn't know much about poetry, it will be more daunting than illustrative. When the list is reformatted, however, grouping writers by literary movement rather than listing them alphabetically, you may find that the once daunting list has become much more understandable and helpful. You will still need to do a good deal of reading in order to apply literary movements to this exam, as no shortcut exists for becoming well read. This chapter, however, will give you an efficient and organized method to follow, and a good overview of each movement.

What Is a Literary Movement?

A literary movement (or school of literature or poetry) is a grouping of writers who share similar aims, similar years of publication, and a similar base of operations. Some writers acknowledge or even encourage the idea of being seen as members of a single group, such as William Wordsworth and Samuel Taylor Coleridge, who consciously published some of their earlier poems in a volume that also included essays about their shared aesthetic ideals. Other writers actively reject the notion of being grouped, such as John Ashbery, who often maintains a bemused wariness when the term "New York school of poetry" is applied to his work.

How Can Knowing the Literary Movement of a Poem Help Me?

Regardless of whether or not the poets acknowledge their participation in a movement, you can put the following information to good use. For example, if you recognize that a poem is in the metaphysical tradition, you will have some immediate, ready-made ideas about form, content, figurative language, and overall meaning. You will know to look for witty, surprising pairings of concrete and abstract ideas. You will expect irony and paradox to percolate beneath even the most religious content. And you will pay special attention to the ornate quality of the conceits. The moment you recognize that a poem is from the romantic tradition, you will be able to call up the phrases "sublime transcendence," "redemptive nature," and "imaginative power." If you have practiced using these phrases, you can use them appropriately as part of a meaningful and attentive analysis of the concrete particulars of a poem. Studying these poems within the framework of literary movements may also help you on the multiple-choice section, because knowing these bodies of work will help you recognize the kinds of questions and answers typically related to particular kinds of poems.

LITERARY MOVEMENT OVERVIEW

In the overview below, you will find some of the most important poets and poems of each movement. You will also find a list of what to look for in these poems as well as a website that may help you with further study. The best way to use these lists to help you crack the exam is to read some of the suggested poems and to note where specific examples of these movement features show up in the poems. Practice writing an analytical essay on one poem from each movement, using at least two of the features from the list somewhere in your essay, and you'll be off to a great start. The more familiar you are with such phrases, the more likely you'll be to smoothly incorporate them into your analytical prose. Be warned: if you only adopt them without actually considering what they mean or without practicing using them, they are likely to seem artificial and may even hurt your score.

The following list concentrates on the schools of literature that are most commonly included on AP English Literature exams, and ignores many other important movements that the College Board is less likely to emphasize. An excellent website for further study of the whole idea of literary movements is **www.poets.org**. It includes many links to brief poet biographies and sample poems from the movements listed in our overview. In fact, many of the representative poems in our overview were chosen because they are easily accessible through links from this website.

METAPHYSICAL POETRY

Representative Metaphysical Poets and Poems

- John Donne (1572–1631)—"A Valediction Forbidding Mourning"; "The Sun Rising"; "Death Be Not Proud—Holy Sonnet X"; "Woman's Constancy"; "Love's Alchemy"

- George Herbert (1593–1633)—"Easter Wings"; "The Collar"; "Jordan (I)"; "Love (III)"; "The Windows"

- Andrew Marvell (1621–1678)—"The Mower's Song"; "The Mower to the Glo-Worms"; "The Mower Against Gardens"; "The Garden"; "To His Coy Mistress"

A Quick Definition

Metaphysical poetry is a mostly seventeenth-century English poetic mode that breaks with earlier Renaissance ideas about romantic poetry. Instead of following in the footsteps of the troubadours and Petrarch and Shakespeare, who often wrote love poetry that placed the object of their poems on a pedestal, metaphysical poems often exhibit introspective meditations on love, death, God, and human frailty. The poems of John Donne, for example, are much more realistic about sexual relationships. Metaphysical poetry is famous for its difficulty and obscurity (and therefore a favorite choice of the College Board).

What to Look for in Metaphysical Poetry

- Wit, irony, and paradox are paramount—wit is often seen in the pairing of dissimilar objects into the service of a clever, ironic analogy or paradoxical conceit. For example, see how Donne's speaker in "A Valediction Forbidding Mourning" uses astronomy and math to illustrate his deep abiding love for his wife.

- Elaborate stylistic maneuvers (ornamental conceits, dazzling rhymes) are pulled off with aplomb. For example, look at how Herbert in "Easter Wings" uses relative line length, stanza shape, rhyme, and repetition to underscore the importance of human humility.

- Huge shifts in scale proliferate (e.g., ants to planets). Consider how Marvell's speaker in "The Mower's Song" conflates glo-worms and comets, for example.

- These formal tendencies are used by metaphysical poets to talk about deep philosophical issues: the passage of time; the difficulty of ever being sure of any one thing; the uneasy relationship of human beings to each other and to God; the fearful, obsessive qualities that death often inspires in human consciousness. Sometimes, after all of the elaborate style is reduced and its content summarized, the truism that is left can seem clichéd. Most of the beauty of metaphysical poetry is in the dramatic unfolding of that truth through irony, conceits, and scale shifts.

AUGUSTANS

Representative English Augustan Poets and Poems

- John Dryden (1631–1700)—"Mac Flecknoe"; "Marriage a-la-mode"; "Absalom and Achitophel"

- Alexander Pope (1688–1744)—"The Rape of the Lock"; "Windsor Forest"; "Epitaph on Sir Isaac Newton"

Related Prose and Plays

Gulliver's Travels and *A Modest Proposal* by Jonathan Swift (1667–1745), and *A Beggar's Opera* by John Gay (1685–1732)

A Quick Definition

Augustan poetry is best known for its rhymed, heroic-couplet satire. These pairs of lines in iambic pentameter often produce great forward propulsion, and most students report that reading them aloud helps with comprehension. Coming between the baroque metaphysical poets and the enthusiastically sincere romantic poets, the wickedly funny Augustan poets went back to antiquity for their inspiration. They translated Greek and Roman epics into English using heroic couplets, and wrote their own original work based on classical forms.

What to Look for in Augustan Poetry

- Wit, irony, and paradox are still as important as they were for the metaphysical poets, but one must also add brevity to the list when discussing the Augustans. Their poems can be quite long, but because they employ the heroic couplet so pointedly, their observations are often quite pithy. As Pope put it in his poem "Essay on Criticism," "True wit is nature to advantage dress'd, / What oft was thought, but ne'er so well express'd."

- The ongoing subject of Augustan poetry is human frailty. Even when these poets used biblical subjects for their plots, as Dryden does in "Absalom and Achitophel," the tone taken often mocks human behavior: "What cannot praise effect in mighty minds, / When flattery soothes, and when ambition blinds!"

- These poets were also likely to dress absurdly mundane plots (such as the secret cutting of a noble maiden's hair in "Rape of the Lock"), in the outward appearance of heroic epic poetry, for comic effect.

- Current events figure in these poems, either allegorically or directly. Pope, in his famous epitaph for Sir Isaac Newton, wrote: "Nature and nature's laws lay hid in night; God said 'Let Newton be' and all was light," which addresses the ongoing controversies between the forces of religion and science in Europe's eighteenth century. Dryden's poem "Mac Flecknoe" satirizes another prominent poet of his day and takes sides in contemporary political debates, similar to how a present-day poet with Democratic leanings might make fun of Republican leaders.

ROMANTIC POETRY

Representative English Romantic Poets and Poems

- William Wordsworth (1770–1850)—"I Wandered Lonely as a Cloud"; "Composed Upon Westminster Bridge Sept. 3, 1802"; "Lines Composed a Few Miles Above Tintern Abbey"; "My Heart Leaps Up When I Behold"; "Lucy"

- Percy Shelley (1792–1822)—"Ozymandias"; "Ode to the West Wind"; "Adonais—An Elegy on the Death of John Keats"; "The Cloud"; "Hymn to Intellectual Beauty"

- John Keats (1795–1821)—"Ode on a Grecian Urn"; "When I Have Fears that I May Cease to Be"; "To Autumn"; "La Belle Dame Sans Merci"; "Ode to a Nightingale"

Representative American Transcendental Poets and Poems

- Ralph Waldo Emerson (1803–1882)—"Ode to Beauty"; "The World-Soul"; "Song of Nature"

- Walt Whitman (1819–1892)—"When I Heard the Learn'd Astronomer"; "A Noiseless Patient Spider"; "Crossing Brooklyn Ferry"; "There Was a Child Went Forth"; "Song of the Open Road"

Related European Prose
Ivanhoe by Sir Walter Scott (1771–1832) and *Les Miserables* by Victor Hugo (1802–1885)

Related American Prose
The Scarlet Letter by Nathaniel Hawthorne (1804–1864); *The Poet*, an essay by Ralph Waldo Emerson that inspired Whitman to become a poet; and *Walking*, an essay by Henry David Thoreau (1817–1862)

A Quick Definition
Romantic poetry written in English is a (mostly) nineteenth-century English and American poetic mode that breaks with earlier neoclassical ideas about poetry by specifically emphasizing that these poems were written in, as Wordsworth calls it, "the real language of men" and about "common life." This poetry is emotional and often enthusiastic in its embracing of the large, impressive forces of nature and the infinite resources of the human imagination. Famous for having given us the image of tormented poets idly strolling over moors, looking through their wind-whipped hair at a tulip, these poems are often used on AP exams because of their strong thematic content.

What to Look for in Romantic Poetry

* Natural imagery redeems the imagination of the individual stuck in the crowded, industrial torment of the city. See Wordsworth's *I Wandered Lonely as a Cloud*, where the speaker, on a couch, imagines himself floating above a chorus of daffodils.

* The human imagination empowers the individual to escape from society's strictures, established authority, and even from fear of death. Think about how Whitman's speaker in *When I Heard the Learn'd Astronomer* needs to leave the room where the lecture is happening in order to better understand the perfect silence of the stars.

* The sublime (impressively big, obscure or scary) is the main descriptive mode, rather than the "merely beautiful." Look at how the speaker in Shelley's *Ozymandias* relies on words such as "vast," "colossal," and "boundless" to create a sense of how intimidating the statue must have been, and actually is.

* Transcendence is the ultimate goal of all the romantic poets. Wordsworth turns a city into a beating heart in *Composed Upon Westminster Bridge Sept. 3, 1802*; Shelley in *Ode to the West Wind* turns the west wind into poetic inspiration; Keats turns an old urn into a meditation on life and death in his *Ode on a Grecian Urn*; Whitman in his *Noiseless Patient Spider* turns a spider into a human soul surrounded by a vacant, vast expanse, yearning to be connected. What do all these poems have in common? Each finds transcendence in the ordinary.

THE SYMBOLISTS

Representative French Symbolist Poets and Poems

* Charles Baudelaire (1821–1867)—"Spleen"; "Harmonie du soir (Harmonies of Evening)"; "Correspondances (Correspondences)"

* Stephane Mallarmé (1842–1898)—"L'Apres-midi d'un faune (The Afternoon of a Faun)"; "Soupir (Sigh)"; "Salut (Salutation)"

* Paul Verlaine (1844–1896)—"Il pleure dans mon couer (It Rains in My Heart)"; "Chanson d'automne (Autumn Song)"; "Langueur (Langour)"

* Arthur Rimbaud (1854–1891)—"Le bateau ivre (The Drunken Boat)"; "Voyelles (Vowels)"

Symbolist-Influenced Poets Who Wrote in English

* Oscar Wilde (1854–1900) —"Chanson"; "Impression du Matin"; "Harmony"

* W. B. Yeats (1865–1939)—"The Lake Isle of Innisfree"; "Towards Break of Day"; "Broken Dreams"; "Leda and The Swan"; "Sailing to Byzantium"

* Arthur Symons (1865–1945)—"White Heliotrope"; "Colour Studies"; "Perfume"

* T. S. Eliot (1888–1965)—"The Love Song of J. Alfred Prufrock"; "Ash Wednesday"

Related Symbolist Prose

A Rebours (Against the Grain) by Joris-Karl Huysmans (1848–1907) and *The Picture of Dorian Gray* by Oscar Wilde (1854–1900)

A Quick Definition

The symbolists are often considered the link between the schools of romanticism and modernism. Full of the yearning for transcendence, which they inherited from the romantic poets, the symbolists took this yearning in a more decadent and sensual direction, which foreshadowed the kind of sexual frankness one often finds in modernist work. Many of their poems will seem obscure on the first few readings, and College Board test-makers are probably not going to use any of the French symbolists on the exam, but if you take the time to analyze the deep symbols and intuitive associations found in their work, you will be in a better place when you are asked to interpret a poem by Yeats or Eliot, whose work often does show up on the exam.

What to Look for in Symbolist Poetry

- Many symbolist poems deal with the crepuscular (dusk and dawn), and with the time between waking and sleep. Consider Wilde's "Impression du Matin." Dreams or dream states figure prominently in many symbolist works of art, as dream experiences afford human beings one of their best opportunities to explore the relationship between states.

- Synaesthesia, the using of one sense to describe another, proved to be a favorite mode of the symbolists. For example, Rimbaud attributes colors and sounds to the different vowels in his poem "Voyelles."

- The French symbolists proved particularly adept at using words with three or four simultaneous meanings, creating a resonance among groups of these words. For example, Mallarmé in "Salut" toasts younger poets gathered around a white tablecloth that can simultaneously be seen as a white sail for a boat and a white, blank page upon which these poets will eventually write. By carefully choosing his words, the speaker of this poem keeps all three meanings viable throughout this beautifully dense poem.

- As you can tell from the other items in this list, symbolists were drawn to the properties of music, and attempted to create some of the same effects in their poetry by concentrating on simultaneous effects (similar to harmony) and by choosing mellifluous words meant to inspire a kind of languor in the reader.

- Often associated with the "art for art's sake" movement that placed aesthetics and form above political relevance or reducible message, symbolist poetry finds its artistic counterparts in these kinds of paintings: Whistler's *Nocturne Blue and Gold—Old Battersea Bridge*, Turner's *Moonlight* and Monet's *Waterloo Bridge in Grey Weather*.

MODERNISM

Representative Modernist Poets and Poems

- Wallace Stevens (1879–1955)—"Thirteen Ways of Looking at a Blackbird"; "The Snowman"; "Peter Quince at the Clavier"; "Anecdote of the Jar"

- William Carlos Williams (1883–1963)—"Red Wheelbarrow"; "This is Just To Say"; "Danse Russe"; "Spring and All"; "The Great Figure"; "The Yachts"; "Desert Music"; "The Descent"

- H. D. (Hilda Doolittle) (1886–1961)—"Star Wheels in Purple"; "Helen"; "Heat"

- Marianne Moore (1887–1972)—"Poetry"; "Baseball and Writing"; "To a Snail"

- T. S. Eliot (1888–1965)—"Love Song of J. Alfred Prufrock"; "Ash Wednesday"

- e. e. cummings (1894–1962)—"anyone lived in a pretty how town"; "next to of course god america i"; "spring is like a perhaps hand"; "i sing of Olaf glad and big"

Related Modernist Prose

A Portrait of the Artist as a Young Man by James Joyce (1882–1941), *Mrs. Dalloway* by Virginia Woolf (1882–1941), *As I Lay Dying* by William Faulkner (1897–1962), and *The Awakening* by Kate Chopin (1851–1904)

A Quick Definition

Modernism is often characterized as a revolutionary force. In the field of science, Einstein was reassessing time, space, and our relationship to these concepts. In global politics, two calamitous world wars bracketed decades of intense technological advances in the mass killing of soldiers and civilians. In the field of visual arts, surrealism, futurism, abstraction, and cubism overthrew most accepted traditional ideas about pictorial representation. Not surprisingly, literature in the twentieth century also saw a thorough questioning of what had come before and a willingness to experiment with new forms, a goal shared with the symbolists, but with which the modernists were much more daring in their first movements.

What to Look for in Modernist Poetry

- Chock full of allusions, these poems reduce human experience to fragments. For example, e. e. cummings breaks language down into its component parts, using pieces of overheard conversation alongside more grandiose pronouncements. H. D. , in her 18-line poem entitled "Helen," assumes the reader has a working knowledge of the incident that prompts the Trojan War (chronicled in *The Iliad* by Homer) to make sense of why "All Greece hates / the still eyes in the white face."

- Some of these poems are influenced by cubism, and they try to see the world from as many points of view as possible at the same time. Wallace Stevens's "Thirteen Ways of Looking at a Blackbird" comes in thirteen sections, each of which refers explicitly or implicitly to a blackbird, and can be seen as a kind of analogue to Picasso's cubist presentation of a still life in *Guitar, Bottle, Bowl of Fruit and Glass on Table*.

- Romantic notions of the importance of individuality were overtaken by systematic representations of human consciousness in the emerging fields of psychology and sociology, so poems from this time are often concerned with how an individual relates to his environment (see Eliot's "The Love Song of J. Alfred Prufrock") or how the environment helps to create the individual (see Stevens's "The Snowman").

- Romantic yearning for freedom (the bloody excesses of the French Revolution are an extreme example) was usurped by proponents of political systems, such as socialism or fascism, that saw human beings not as individuals but as servants of the state (see the Russian Revolution and the rise of the Third Reich). Modernist poems sometimes efface individuality, choosing to focus on machines or other inanimate objects rather than nature or human beings. For example, William Carlos Williams's "The Yachts" contains brutal imagery: "Arms with hands grasping seek to clutch at the prows / Bodies thrown recklessly in the way are cut aside. / It is a sea of faces about them in agony, in despair / until the horror of the race dawns staggering the mind." But this use of imagery does not ever really feel personal; it feels more like a representation of mass death.

THE HARLEM RENAISSANCE

Representative Poets and Poems of the Harlem Renaissance

- Paul Laurence Dunbar (1872–1906)—"Frederick Douglass"; "Sympathy"; "We Wear the Mask"

- Claude McKay (1889–1948)—"If We Must Die"; "The White House"; "The Tropics of New York"

- Langston Hughes (1902–1967)—"I, Too, Sing America"; "The Negro Speaks of Rivers"; "Theme for English B"; "Montage of a Dream Deferred"

- Countee Cullen (1903-1946)—"Incident"; "For A Lady I Know"; "Yet Do I Marvel"

Related Prose from the Harlem Renaissance

Their Eyes Were Watching God by Zora Neale Hurston (1891–1960), *Passing* by Nella Larsen (1891–1964), *Black Boy* and *Native Son* by Richard Wright (1908–1960), and *Invisible Man* by Ralph Ellison (1913–1994)

A Quick Definition

Art associated with the Harlem Renaissance was mostly created in the first half of the twentieth century, after World War I, during the movement of African Americans to northern industrial cities (called the Great Migration). Many African Americans who settled in these cities lived, or were forced to live, in the same neighborhoods. Harlem, in New York City, was one of the most famous African American neighborhoods during this time. Jazz, poetry, painting, dance, electrified blues, and the study of folklore thrived in these neighborhoods and took on many of the same concerns as the modernists. In fact, one could think of Harlem Renaissance poetry, and Langston Hughes's poetry in particular, as a branch of modernism.

What to Look for in Harlem Renaissance Poetry

- Content is often directly related to African American concerns and issues of the time. Consider Dunbar's "Frederick Douglass," which elegizes the famous abolitionist in such a way as to draw attention to his continuing positive influence on the culture: "Oh, Douglass, thou hast passed beyond the shore, / But still thy voice is ringing o'er the gale!"

- Many Harlem Renaissance poems rely on repetitive structure similar to blues lyrics (see Dunbar's "Sympathy") or on fragmented structure similar to jazz improvisation (see Hughes's "Montage of a Dream Deferred").

- Several of these poets, especially Langston Hughes, consciously sought a new American idiom alongside other African American artists such as blues singer Bessie Smith. Other poets combined European forms like the sonnet with a content and a tone more related to African American concerns, such as McKay's "If We Must Die."

POSTMODERNISM

A Quick Definition

Academic controversy continues as to whether works labeled postmodern are merely a later version of the modernist tendencies developed in the twentieth century or whether they are actually part of a new and separate movement. Usually the most that academics can agree on regarding the postmodern is that the term is insufficient. Most postmodern works were created in the second half of the twentieth century and though they share some of the concerns and motivations of modernists, they often take these principles to a much different end. If Einstein's theory of relativity represents the modern era, Heisenberg's uncertainty principle is the emblem of the postmodern. The uncertainty principle holds, in reductive terms, that one cannot know both the speed and the location of an object simultaneously, which introduces a note of chance or chaos into scientific inquiry.

Even more so than other literary labels, postmodern is a label that is rejected by the majority of artists who are labeled as such. Instead, smaller contingents of writers exist, often in conflict with other postmodern groups. These smaller groups include the **Beats**, the **confessional** poets, **the Black Arts movement, the Black Mountain school,** and **the New York school of poets**. Each of these groups is dealt with separately below because each had such a different aesthetic program. A few statements can be applied to postmodern art in general, however, and will be discussed before going into the specific sub-movements.

What to Look for in Postmodern Poetry

- Parody, irony, and narrative instability often inform the tone.

- Allusions are just as likely to be made to popular culture as they are to classical learning.

- Strictly binary concepts (hot and cold; black and white) often collapse. Here, ideas that spread across a spectrum, rather than fit strictly into one box or the other, predominate.

- There is no real center. The Internet is a perfect example of a postmodern invention.

- The surface is often more interesting to postmodern artists than any ideas of depth. The following quote is attributed to Andy Warhol, a kind of patron saint of postmodernism and a notorious wig wearer: "Wear a wig and people notice the wig. Wear a silver wig and people notice the silver."

THE BEATS

Representative Beat Poets and Poems

- Lawrence Ferlinghetti (b. 1919)—"A Coney Island of the Mind"; "The Changing Light"; "Vast Confusion"; "Wild Dreams of a New Beginning"

- Allen Ginsberg (1926–1997)—"Howl"; "America"; "A Supermarket in California"; "Kaddish"

- Gregory Corso (1930–2001)—"Marriage"; "Bomb"; "The Mad Yak"

- Gary Snyder (b. 1930)—"Four Poems for Robin"; "For All"; "Hay for the Horses"

Related Beat Prose

Naked Lunch by William S. Burroughs (1914–1997) and *On The Road* by Jack Kerouac (1922–1969)

A Quick Definition

A post–World War II phenomenon, the Beats used different settings over the years to practice their brand of hallucinogenic, visionary, anti-establishment art: New York City (many of the original group were Columbia University students or dropouts), San Francisco, Tangiers, Prague, and Mexico City witnessed Beat events, as did many places in between.

Beat poets were quite good at mythologizing themselves, and they shared a sense of personal frankness with the confessional poets and a sense of interdisciplinary energy (especially in its overlap with music) with the New York school. Buddhism was important to many members (especially Gary Snyder), as were many of the tenets of William Blake's version of romanticism, such as the importance of the individual, the imagination freed from society's constraints, and the yearning for transcendence. In Ferlinghetti's "The Changing Light," a reader can feel the deep connection Beats often felt to nature, even as the speaker of this poem is describing a city scene. In Corso's "Marriage," the oppositional stance the Beats took toward the suburban bourgeoisie is in bold relief. Ginsberg's "America" shares much of the same satirical tone, but Ginsberg was also capable of writing angry, ranting, Whitman-esque masterpieces like "Howl" and a tender, meditative elegy for his mother in "Kaddish."

"First thought, best thought" describes the aesthetic ideal of the Beat poet. Moved by jazz improvisation and Buddhist ideas of impermanence, these poets considered themselves the chroniclers of their age. Politics directly informs many of their poems, either through specific references to members of the government or specific references to issues important to them, such as Gary Snyder's commitment to the environment.

CONFESSIONAL POETS

Representative Confessional Poets and Poems

- John Berryman (1914–1972)—"Dream Song 1"; "Dream Song 4"; "Dream Song 29"

- Robert Lowell (1917–1977)—"Skunk Hour"; "For the Union Dead"; "Memories of West Street and Lepke"; "Home After Three Months Away"

- Anne Sexton (1928–1967)—"Wanting to Die"; "The Truth the Dead Know"; "For My Lover", "Returning to his Wife"

- Sylvia Plath (1932–1963)—"Daddy"; "Lady Lazarus"; "Balloons"; "Ariel"

Related Confessional Prose
The Bell Jar by Sylvia Plath

A Quick Definition
As the name suggests, confessional poets took the personal pronouns (I, me, my) seriously and explored intimate content in their poetry. Love affairs, suicidal thoughts, fears of failure, ambivalent or downright violent opinions about family members, and other autobiographically sensitive material moved front and center in these poets' works. As Berryman wrote, using his alter ego "Henry" as a mask for his own feelings of distress in *Dream Song 1*, "I don't see how Henry, pried / open for all the world to see, survived." These poets "pried open" their innermost thoughts and opened them for all the world to see, even if it meant sharing one's troubled feelings about one's father, as Plath did in a poem full of Holocaust imagery entitled *Daddy*, writing "Daddy, I have had to kill you. / You died before I had time..."

In a cultural milieu much more discreet than that of the current era, these poets ripped the façade off of an outwardly comfortable suburban life to reveal the doubts and anxieties that kept the occupants awake at night behind white picket fences. Robert Lowell, for example, wrote in "Home After Three Months Away" how he felt when faced with the details of his life, such as the recent birth of his child: "I keep no rank nor station. / Cured, I am frizzled, stale and small." And Anne Sexton wrote with existential dread, "Since you ask, most days I cannot remember. / I walk in my clothing, unmarked by that voyage. / Then the almost unnameable lust returns." The "unnameable lust" is the speaker's desire for death, and she writes eloquently about it at a time when mental illness was much less understood or accommodated by law.

More than just poets who shared personal stories with their readers, these poets also invested a good deal of time and effort in their craft, constructing verse that paid careful attention to rewritten prosody.

NEW YORK SCHOOL OF POETS

Representative New York School Poets

- Barbara Guest (1920–2006)—"The Blue Stairs"; "Wild Gardens Overlooked by Night Lights"; "Sound and Structure"; "Echoes"

- Kenneth Koch (1925–2002)—"One Train May Hide Another"; "Talking to Petrizia"; "To Various Persons Talked to All at Once;" "Variations on a Theme by William Carlos Williams"

- Frank O'Hara (1926–1966)—"In Memory of My Feelings"; "The Day Lady Died"; "A Step Away From Them"; "Lines to a Depressed Friend"

- John Ashbery (b. 1927)—"The Painter"; "The Instruction Manual"; "Daffy Duck in Hollywood"; "The New Higher"

A Quick Definition
New York school poets saw themselves as fellow travelers of the abstract expressionist school of painters. Many of these poets wrote art criticism, and Frank O'Hara even rose to the rank of assistant curator for the Museum of Modern Art. Their aesthetic mode overlapped with Beat spontaneity and with confessional-poet frankness, but was much more ironic, and more interested in the surreal combination of high art and popular art allusions. Many of their poems, especially those called Lunch Poems by Frank O'Hara, seem to be catalogues of what one might see on a walk in midtown

Manhattan. The urban environment, of course, allows for many spontaneous intersections. A taxi goes by a construction site. A billboard advertising tourism to a natural paradise hovers over a traffic jam, providing ironic contrast.

These poets often see themselves as helping the reader see the world in new and different ways. For example, Barbara Guest in "The Blue Stairs" writes in an ekphrastic mode (or a mode based on putting visual art into words), "Now I shall tell you / why it is beautiful / Design: extraordinary / color: cobalt blue" and O'Hara writes in "The Day Lady Died," an elegy for Billie Holiday, "and I am sweating a lot by now and thinking of / leaning on the john door in the 5 SPOT / while she whispered a song along the keyboard / to Mal Waldron and everyone and I stopped breathing." Barbara Guest's speaker describes looking at a painting while O'Hara's speaker describes hearing a song at a jazz club, but both speakers are interested in inspiring us to look or listen again.

Surrealists wanted to jar their audience's senses by juxtaposing uncommon objects. John Ashbery mixes "Rumford's Baking Powder, a celluloid earring, Speedy Gonzales, the latest from Helen Topping Miller's fertile Escritoire" in his poem "Daffy Duck in Hollywood," and Kenneth Koch consciously mixes tones in his poem "To Various Persons Talked to All at Once," writing, "I suppose I wanted to impress you. / It's snowing. / The Revlon Man has come from across the sea. / This racket is annoying. / We didn't want the baby to come here because of the hawk. / What are you reading? / In what style would you like the humidity to explain?" These poets reveled in the combination of the serious and the silly, the profound and the absurd, the highly formal and the relentlessly casual.

BLACK ARTS MOVEMENT

Representative Black Arts Movement Poets and Poems

- Gwendolyn Brooks (1917–2000)—"The Bean-Eaters"; "We Real Cool"; "The Lovers of the Poor"; "The Mother"

- Amiri Baraka (also known as Leroi Jones) (b. 1934)—"Preface to a Twenty Volume Suicide Note"; "Black Art"; "Ka'Ba"; "In the Funk World"

- Sonia Sanchez (b. 1934)—"Ballad"; "Malcolm"; "I Have Walked a Long Time"; "For Sweet Honey in the Rock"

- Ntozake Shange (b. 1948)—"My Father is a Retired Magician"; "For Colored Girls Who Have Considered Suicide When the Rainbow is Enuf"

A Quick Definition

These poets were often associated with members of the Black Power movement who grew frustrated with the pace of the changes enacted by the civil rights movement of the 1950s and 1960s. These poems are often politically charged, even aggressive, challenges to the white establishment.

BLACK MOUNTAIN POETS

Representative Black Mountain Poets and Poems

- Charles Olson (1910–1970)—Excerpts from "The Maximus Poems"

- Denise Levertov (1923–1997)—"The Mutes"; "In California During the Gulf War"; "When We Look Up"

- Robert Creeley (1926–2005)—"Age"; "For Love"; "A Wicker Basket"; "America"

A Quick Definition

Besides teaching in the same place (Black Mountain College in Black Mountain, North Carolina) for some time and sharing an abiding interest in process over product, these poets seem quite different. Olson's poems spill across the page, while Creeley's lines compress into tight corners. Levertov often tackles political issues head-on, while Olson delved deeply into the archeology and history of Gloucester, Massachusetts.

OTHER IMPORTANT REPRESENTATIVE POETS AND POEMS

176 poems were listed above, and another 24 poems are listed below, for a total of 200 poems. The poets and poems listed below are important but do not fit easily into the structure of literary movements.

Emily Dickinson (1830–1886). Writing in near absolute isolation during the transcendental period, this astonishingly prolific and powerful poet does not easily fit into the transcendental rubric, and she shares many more attributes with the compressed wit and irony of the metaphysical poets. Poems: "Because I could not stop for death"; "I heard a fly buzz when I died"; "Tell all the truth but tell it slant"; "I measure every grief I meet."

Robert Frost (1874–1963). Frost was active during modernism's heyday, and concerned himself with more traditionally minded verse forms and a locally colored content that cloaked a profound philosophical vein. Poems: "Out, Out"; "Birches"; "The Death of the Hired Man"; "Mending Wall"; "Design"; "Stopping by Woods on a Snowy Evening."

W. H. Auden (1907–1973). Auden wrote the first half of his poems as an English citizen before World War II, the second half of his poems as an American citizen after World War II, and is one of the giants of twentieth-century literature. His is more similar to the modernists than any other school, but he really transcends labels. Poems: "As I Walked Out One Evening"; "In Memory of W. B. Yeats"; "The Unknown Citizen"; "Musée des Beaux Arts."

Elizabeth Bishop (1911–1979). Sometimes placed with the confessional poets because of her friendship with Robert Lowell, Bishop is more reticent than the confessional poets. Poems: "In the Waiting Room"; "Filling Station"; "At the Fishhouses"; "One Art"; "The Moose."

Adrienne Rich (b. 1929). An important feminist and political poet, Rich shares some background with the confessional poets, but she has taken the role of the poet in society so seriously that she has transcended the personal and become a kind of icon. Poems: "Diving into the Wreck"; "North American Time"; "Aunt Jennifer's Tigers"; "Miracle Ice Cream."

Seamus Heaney (b. 1939). Heaney uses rural imagery to take on issues of identity, from the postcolonial confusion of what it means to be Irish to the late-twentieth-century confusion of what it means to be a poet. Poems: "Digging"; "The Harvest Bow."

PART ◆ II

Cracking the System: The Multiple-Choice Section

Basic Principles of the Multiple-Choice Section

WHAT ARE THE BASIC PRINCIPLES OF CRACKING THE SYSTEM?

As with any multiple-choice test, there will come a time when the studying is over, and you are as prepared as you are ever going to be. You will be sitting at your desk with a sealed exam booklet and an answer sheet in front of you. The proctor, droning on at the front of the room, will finally finish reading the instructions and say, "You may break the seal and begin the test."

At that moment, what you know isn't going to change. Your head will be crammed with knowledge, and you might wish you knew even more, but your score will depend on getting what you know onto that answer sheet.

Imagine your exact double sitting at the next desk. In terms of English literature, your double knows exactly what you know. Will you and your double's scores be the same? *Not if you know how to take a standardized test and your double doesn't.* You will squeeze every possible drop of what you know onto that answer sheet. Your double will let half of his or her knowledge go unused and wasted. The scores will reflect the difference.

The multiple-choice section of the AP English Literature and Composition Exam is not different from any standardized test in that there are two critical concerns:

> 1. You must manage a limited amount of time well.
>
> 2. You must guess wisely and aggressively.

If you manage your time poorly, you will not get a chance to use your knowledge. Questions you could have easily answered will vanish into oblivion, taking their points with them.

Guessing wisely and aggressively calls for the ability (and courage) to use partial knowledge. When you fail to guess, you let whatever partial knowledge you have go to waste. For any question you leave blank, the test records a complete lack of knowledge, even if you actually did know some of the relevant information. If you withhold your knowledge, the test, in turn, withholds points. We're here to make sure that doesn't happen.

HAVE A PLAN

In order to do your best on the AP Literature Exam, you need a plan. A plan lets you stop worrying about whether you are going about things the "right way" and lets you concentrate on what's important: earning points. The plan we suggest isn't complicated. In fact, it's quite simple, but with such a plan, you'll know that you are going about things the right way.

THE PLAN

Here's an outline of what you should do on the multiple-choice section:

1. Note the Time and the Number of Passages

When the section begins, make a note of the time. Most proctors put the starting time up on the board, but don't count on it. Sometimes there's a clock in the room, and sometimes there isn't (or it's not working, or it's not in your line of vision). Take a watch, so you know precisely how many minutes you have left at any given time. You have 60 minutes to complete the Multiple-Choice section, which has four or five passages for you to read and answer questions about. That means you have an average of 12 to 15 minutes per passage. Keep track of your pace. If you take more than 15 minutes to read a passage and answer the questions, you may need to speed up slightly. But don't rush too much—there's no point in making careless mistakes on easier passages just to get to a tougher passage you won't do as well on. Just keep an eye on the time.

2. Pick a Passage to Do First

Some passages on this test are easier than other passages. Contrary to what some books claim, there is no order of difficulty on this test; easy passages might come earlier or later. You know what you're good at, whether it's twentieth-century prose or Renaissance poetry. Do that first! It's an instant confidence booster, and it might put you ahead of your pacing plan. Then, you have even more time for the passages that challenge you.

3. Pick a Passage to Do Last (or Skip)

This part of the plan is a key safety device for your time and your score. It's your way of assuring yourself that if you start running out of time on the last passage, you'll know that it's the one that would have given you the most trouble anyway (for many students, it's excessively wordy prose or complicated poetry). Put a big X at the top of the page to remind yourself which passage is going to be the last passage.

4. Work the Passage

Note our verb choice: *work*, not *read*. You'll see what we mean when we get to the next chapter.

5. Answer the Questions in the Order That You Choose, Using the Techniques You'll Learn in This Book

Just as all passages are not created equal, the questions also differ in level of difficulty. No order of difficulty exists here, either, so you may not want to do the questions in the order in which they're presented. Again, you'll see what we mean in Chapter 5.

TIME MANAGEMENT

A key factor on standardized tests is time management. The AP English Literature and Composition Exam is no exception. You've got to answer roughly 50 questions in just one hour, and that includes reading the passages. There's no time to waste. Most students have difficulty getting to all the questions in the allotted time.

The more questions you answer correctly, the better you'll do. The only way to answer questions is to get to them. At the same time, working too fast poses its own problems. Some students earn better scores by slowing down and answering fewer questions, but getting a higher percentage of them right. So what should you do?

We don't know you and your specific strengths and weaknesses as a reader and test taker, so in this section you're going to have to analyze yourself carefully and honestly. We're going to present some general guidelines that every student should follow. Then we're going to lay out the time management options available to you, and offer suggestions that will help you decide which of our methods you should employ. They all work; you just need to find the best fit for you.

DO IT YOUR WAY

Have you ever heard this conversation following a standardized test?

Student A (bummed): "I didn't even get to the last passage."

Student B (rubbing it in): "NO? That was the *easiest* one! It was a total breeze, a piece of cake, a cinch, a given…"

Okay, student B deserves a swift kick, but that isn't the point. You don't want to be student A, and there's no reason you should be.

If you can get to all the passages and answer all the questions with five minutes left over, great, but don't count on it. Plan ahead. There's no law that says you have to do the passages in order. Don't.

As we've already mentioned, as soon as the Multiple-Choice section begins, the first thing you should do is quickly look over the passages—this is definitely allowed. Decide which passage to do first, but much more important—decide which passage to do last.

The object is to find the hardest passage and put off doing it until the end. There are a couple of reasons for doing this. First, if you're going to run out of time, why not run out of time on the passage where you were going to miss a lot of questions anyway? Second, the hardest passage is undoubtedly going to take the most time. You don't want to get into a situation where you have to rush just to finish three out of four passages. This is such a simple technique. All you have to do is remember to use it.

WHICH PASSAGE IS THE HARDEST?

There's no way of knowing which passage really has the hardest questions, so don't try to figure that out. You want to avoid the passage that is written in the form you find most confusing. For most students that means older poetry. If you're good with poetry or see a prose passage that has six words you don't know in the first paragraph, then pass over the prose passage and go for the poetry. In general, shorter passages are easier than long ones, and more recent passages are easier than older ones.

Remember, the point is to save time, not waste it. The decision process should take no more than one minute. Look at the first couple of lines of each passage. Do they make sense? Do you feel comfortable? Yes? Great. But if you see a passage that makes you go, "Huh?" put a big X at the top of the page to remind yourself to do it last, then start on the passage you like best, pronto.

SKIP A PASSAGE

There are four or five passages, and you are given 60 minutes to complete the section. Breaking it down, you have 15 minutes per passage. If there were only three passages, you would have 20 minutes per passage.

Yes, we are suggesting that you consider skipping a passage and gaining five minutes on each of the passages that you do attempt.

Essentially, some students will skip a passage whether they want to or not—they won't have time for the last passage. The idea here is to prepare yourself for that case. If you know from previous standardized tests that you've taken, such as the PSAT, that you have trouble finishing the reading comprehension section, then you can be pretty sure that you'll have time troubles with the AP test. The AP test gives more time for multiple-choice reading comprehension than the SAT does, but the AP passages are longer and far tougher, and the questions are tougher, too. One solution is to skip a passage entirely—don't even think about getting to it. The trade-off is accuracy for questions. You're letting go of those last 15 questions (and remember, they might be the questions for the *first* passage if that's the passage you decided was toughest for you) in order to improve your accuracy on the questions that you do answer.

Suppose you are coming up on the third passage. You look at your watch and realize you have 20 minutes left in the section. Don't think, "Oh no, 20 minutes left and still two passages to go...I've got to fly through this one to get to the next." That isn't reality. If there are 20 minutes left that means that you averaged 20 minutes on each of the two passages that came before. You should forget about the last passage, the one you've already marked as the hardest one, and take the 20 minutes you need to do a good job on the third passage. You are bound to get more questions correct than if you tried to do both.

YOU CAN SKIP A PASSAGE AND STILL GET A GOOD SCORE

It's true. It is completely possible to get a final score of five without doing all the passages. Go back to page 9 to review the evidence. No, it isn't easy. It calls for excellent essays and accurate answers on the passages you do attempt. If you'd be satisfied with a final score of 4 (and you should be; it's an excellent score), and if you know that reading comprehension questions are tough for you, then you should definitely consider skipping a passage.

GUESS AGGRESSIVELY BY UNDERSTANDING YOUR RAW SCORE

It all comes down to points. More points mean a higher score. It's that simple. But, because of the marking system—one point for a correct answer, zero points for a blank, and a quarter point deduction for an incorrect answer—there are several ways of arriving at the same score.

As we mentioned earlier, the AP English Literature and Composition Exam will have 55 multiple-choice questions. We think it puts you in a solid position to get a final score of 4. If you can do even better, great. Thirty-five points is a good, high number of multiple-choice points to shoot for.

1. To get a score of 35, student A might answer all 55 questions and miss 16. That means she got 39 questions right, but lost four points because of the guessing penalty.

2. Student B might score 35 points by answering 35 questions correctly and leaving 20 blank.

3. Student C might mix and match a little a bit, leaving some questions blank but answering most of them. For example, he might answer 37 questions correctly, get 8 wrong and leave 10 blank. 37 minus 2 penalty points is 35.

WHICH WAY IS THE RIGHT WAY?

When most students look at the examples above they think, "Well, student A seems to have answered too many questions and might have scored better by leaving more blank. Student B was too chicken and should have answered more. Student C seems to have found a good balance."

It sounds like common sense, but it is completely wrong. Both student B and student C left too many blanks. Both could have done better. Student B obviously knew her stuff, because she got all of the questions she answered correct. Maybe she worked too slowly, or maybe she was too timid; either way, it's certain she could have earned more points. If she'd correctly answered half of the questions she left blank, she'd have picked up seven more points and been in the running for a final score of 5. Student C is closer to his best score but still hasn't achieved it. By answering questions he left blank, he could have squeezed another two or three points out of the test and made things much easier for himself when it came time to write the essays. Student A maxed out. She went after every question and took her lumps (small quarter points) in order to get the rewards—big, full points. If student A had approached the test like either of the other two students her score would have been lower.

Yes, all three students got the same score, but that's because students B and C did worse than they could have, while student A did her best.

At this point a lot of students say, "I don't know…I'm not convinced. I don't like the sound of that guessing penalty. Why should I just take a dumb guess at a question I don't know the answer to and get penalized? Why not admit I don't know the answer and leave the question blank? At least I'll avoid the penalty." If this sounds like your thoughts, please read the next section carefully, and believe it.

THE GUESSING PENALTY SHOULD BE CALLED
THE "GUESSING BONUS"

Most students are afraid of the guessing penalty. They think it's going to eat up their score. These students don't answer a question unless they're pretty sure they've got it right. If the question is hard they think, "I'll leave it blank and avoid the guessing penalty." What they end up avoiding is their best score. Think about it: You can't get points if you don't answer questions. A blank means you definitely won't get the point that's available. "Yes," you say, "but at least there's no penalty." No penalty!? Does that mean you can just leave the whole test blank and get a perfect score? The scoring doesn't work that way. Leave the whole test blank and you'll score a humiliating zero. Don't think of a blank as a no-penalty. Think of it as minus one point. We know ETS says a blank is zero, but that zero *could* be a plus one. Each question is worth one point. Leave a question blank and it's essentially an automatic subtraction of one because you're losing the opportunity to earn that point.

The term *guessing penalty* is just a head-game. *Blank* looks so neutral, so harmless. It isn't. *Guessing penalty* seems nasty—*penalty*—and it looks nasty because it's a negative fraction. Who likes negative fractions? The truth is, a wrong answer hurts your score because you don't get the point that's available. That dropped quarter of a point is nothing but a pathetic little kick in the shins following the big damage. The missed point is the big damage. Don't even think about the guessing penalty. Ignore it. You'll score higher.

Still don't believe us?

Okay, suppose you've got ten questions you aren't sure about. If you leave them all blank you get zero points. If you guess on all of them and get eight questions wrong and two questions right, you break even and get zero points. No harm done. Get just three questions right out of ten and you're picking up bonus guessing points—full points, not little fraction points. How badly do you have to do to actually get hurt by guessing? You'd have to miss at least nine out of ten questions before you'd even get penalized! The *guessing penalty* should be called the *guessing bonus*.

Guessing is the only way to take advantage of your partial knowledge. If you've spent any time on a question, if you have the slightest inkling of what the answer might be, guess! That inkling is knowledge; don't waste it. Sure, you'll lose a quarter of a point here and there. So what? You'll harvest enough whole points to more than make up the difference. You may not know enough to be comfortable with an answer, but that isn't the issue. You don't have to be comfortable. You have to guess! Do you know anything? Can you eliminate even one of the answer choices? If so, then guess.

SHOULD YOU LEAVE ANY BLANKS?

Completely blind guessing on questions you haven't even read is not a good idea. Yes, it could help your score, but it could also hurt it. The odds are that guessing randomly will do nothing. We say don't chance it. Don't guess blindly.

> If you've read the passage, the question, and the answer choices, then always answer the question.

There are no exceptions to this rule. There are times, however, when some students will want to leave a block of questions unread (and unanswered) for strategic time management reasons. We will go into that case fully in the time management part of this chapter.

GUESSING WISELY WITH POE

POE is an acronym for Process of Elimination. You are probably already acquainted with POE in its simplest form: Cross out the answers that you know are wrong. The Cracking the System approach to POE isn't really different, just more intense.

There are always two ways to answer a multiple-choice question correctly. The first is to have the answer in mind right from the moment you read the question. If you understand the passage and the question, you'll often see the right answer among the choices. Great. Far more often, however, you'll be slightly (or not-so-slightly) unsure. ETS is pretty good at spotting places in a text where students are likely to have trouble, and they tend to write questions about these spots. ETS is also pretty good at writing wrong answers that are quite appealing. Before you doubt yourself, however, make sure you have read the question carefully. It's possible to understand the passage but misread a question. The extra second or two you devote to reading the question may increase the number of questions you answer correctly. Still, no matter how strong a reader you are, some questions will cause you to have doubts about the answer. That's when you use The Princeton Review–style POE. What does that mean? It means: *Stop looking for the right answer—look for wrong answers and eliminate them.* Let's look at an example. Here's a part of a passage from *A Confederacy of Dunces* by John Kennedy Toole, followed by a typical question:

> A green hunting cap squeezed the top of the fleshy
> balloon of a head. The green earflaps, full of large ears
> *Line* and uncut hair and the fine bristles that grew in the ears
> *(5)* themselves, stuck out on either side like turn signals
> indicating two directions at once. Full, pursed lips
> protruded beneath the bushy black moustache and, at
> their corners, sank into little folds filled with disapproval
> and potato chip crumbs. In the shadow under the green
> *(10)* visor of the cap Ignatius J. Reilly's supercilious blue and
> yellow eyes looked down upon the other people waiting
> under the clock at the D. H. Holmes department store,
> studying the crowd of people for signs of bad taste in
> dress. Several of the outfits, Ignatius noticed, were new
> *(15)* enough and expensive enough to be properly considered
> offenses against taste and decency. Possession of any-
> thing new or expensive only reflected a person's lack of
> theology and geometry; it could even cast doubts upon
> one's soul.

1. Lines 5–8 of the passage best describe the author's portrayal of Ignatius J. Reilly as

   (A) a sympathetic portrait of an effete snob
   (B) a comically ironic treatment of a social misfit
   (C) a harshly condemnatory portrait of a bon vivant
   (D) an admiring portrait of a great hunter
   (E) a farcical treatment of an overly sensitive man

This is a typical AP English Lit question. It asks for an evaluation of a passage for comprehension. The majority of the questions take this form. In the example above you've been asked, essentially, "What's going on in lines 5–8?" The actual passage would have been longer (usually around 55 lines), and the rest of the passage would certainly help you understand this section by putting it in context, but nevertheless, there is enough here to answer the question.

If you don't immediately spot the right answer, use POE. Go to each choice and say, "Why is this wrong?"

WHY IS THIS WRONG? HALF BAD = ALL BAD

The key is to take each answer a word at a time. Don't fixate on what's right about the answer; if any part of the answer is wrong, then eliminate the answer. **Half bad equals all bad**. In fact, one-tenth bad equals all bad. Now let's look at the answer choices:

(A) You might say, "Sympathetic? Effete? He appears to be a snob, but I am not sure what effete means." He is not portrayed in a sympathetic tone because the author describes Ignatius as "looking down...on bad taste." If one part of the question is wrong, then the choice is wrong. Eliminate this answer.

(B) He does seem to be a "social misfit" because of his odd appearance and his observer status, and the description *is* comical in its exaggerative use of detail, so hold on to this answer.

(C) The author may provide a condemning portrait of this character, but "harshly" is too strong a word. Besides, he is not a "bon vivant," which is a person who lives the good life. Half bad equals all bad, so eliminate this one.

(D) The narration does provide information about a hunting cap, but there is no indication in lines 5–8 that he is a hunter. Do not be distracted by a detail that may appear in the passage but does not provide the information needed to answer the question.

(E) The passage does seem to be farcical, but in these lines you cannot be sure if he is "overly sensitive."

ELIMINATE THE OBVIOUS AND COME BACK

That leaves answers (B) and (E).

Ask yourself: is he "overly sensitive"? You might find yourself thinking, "No, it isn't sensitivity exactly. It is funny, but he seems to be annoyed, rather than sensitive." However, you are not clear whether he is a "social misfit," and you are not positive what the word "ironic" means. What do you do? Be fearless.

BE FEARLESS!

Pick (B). You couldn't find anything wrong with (B). It had some tough vocabulary. So what? Don't be afraid to pick answers you aren't sure are right. Sometimes that's necessary. Just make sure you don't pick answers that you think are probably wrong. We know that sounds obvious, but students do pick weak answers, and they know they're doing it. Why? Because one answer was kind-of-but-not-really-right, and the other was totally unfamiliar. The student thinks that the unfamiliar answer might be right but that then again it might be embarrassingly wrong. The student picks the kind-of-but-not-really answer and loses points, but thinks that's okay, because at least it wasn't the embarrassing answer. Relax! You can't embarrass yourself on this exam. The multiple-choice questions are scored by a machine. No one—not your AP teacher, not your classmates, not the AP essay graders—knows or cares which answer you pick. Be fearless. If POE leaves you with two or three answers you aren't sure about—*pick one.*

In the example above, choice (B) was correct. If you were solid on the definition of "ironic," then you probably got the answer without much trouble. (In which case, we hope you followed our discussion of POE anyway, because you *will* need to use it many times during the actual test.) The passage is ironic. It treats Ignatius's taste in dress as the basis for the irony. He comments on the outward appearance of others as if it indicates that they have no taste in clothing and, therefore, no decency. However, his ruffled and gaudy appearance seems anything but tasteful. It is this contrast between the author's description of Ignatius's appearance and Ignatius's attitude toward the shoppers that produces irony. Often irony takes the form of a subtle kind of humor when what is said is different from what is meant. The character in this description means what he is saying, but the author is actually trying to convey the opposite of what this character believes to be true. **Irony** is an important term, both for the test and for the study of literature in general. We give it a full treatment in the glossary at the back of this book. But this is just one example, and irony comes in dozens of colors and flavors.

POE SUMMARY

- When in doubt, look for wrong answers and eliminate.
- Eliminate the obviously wrong, then look more closely at what's left.
- Half bad = all bad.
- Don't leave a question you've worked on blank, ever.

A PREVIEW OF COMING ATTRACTIONS

There's one more time management technique that you absolutely have to know. It's called the "Art of the Seven-Minute Passage." We'd like to tell you about it now, but unfortunately the full technique won't make sense until we've outlined the general principles of reading prose passages and poetry passages, and shown you examples of the kinds of questions you'll see on the AP Literature Exam. You'll find our full explanation of the Art of the Seven-Minute Passage at the end of Chapter 6.

But it's such a good technique we think you should get a preview. If, after all is said and done, you forget some of the details of the full Art of the Seven-Minute Passage, or like the Art of the Seven-Minute Passage (Lite) that we discuss below better, use it. It's extremely close to the real thing, and a little easier to remember.

THE ART OF THE SEVEN-MINUTE PASSAGE (LITE)

For many, many students, there's enough time on the AP test to do three and one-half passages. That is, you get through three passages and start reading the fourth one, maybe answering a question or two before you hear: "Please put down your pencils and close your exam booklet."

"Hey, wait a minute, I'm not finished!"

Don't let this happen to you. *Bring a watch*. When you get to your last passage, check the time. If you're running out of time (seven minutes or less), you've got to take emergency measures. There are points there for the taking, but you don't have time to read the passage and answer the questions. What do you do?

Don't read the passage. Go directly to the questions. There are no points given for reading the passage. The Art of the Seven-Minute Passage is the art of choosing questions. The principle is very simple.

Answer the questions that take no reading, then the questions that take just a little reading, then what's left over until you run out of time.

It's easy. Take the following three questions:

> 1. What is the main point of the passage?
>
> 2. The phrase *cold fire* is an example of
>
> 3. In the context of the passage, the phrase *wang-a-dang-doodle* (line 123) probably means

If you had seven minutes to answer these questions, you'd skip question 1 entirely. You don't have time for it. However, you'd answer question 2 immediately. That question doesn't even need a passage: it just wants to see if you know that *cold fire* is an **oxymoron,** which is the literary term for a pair of opposites (see the glossary). After doing question 2 (and if you didn't know what an oxymoron was, you still would have done the question using POE and taken your best guess), you'd look around for more questions like it. You might find one or two more, and you'd answer them next. Then you'd start looking for questions like number 3. It sends you back to a specific place in the passage and asks for the meaning of a particular word or phrase. All you'd have to read is a sentence or two. Do it, and then find and answer any other questions of this type (the AP exam is full of these questions). After you've done all those, you'll find you have read enough of the passage to start working on general, big-picture questions like number 1, and at least be able to come up with a good guess.

That's the Art of the Seven-Minute Passage Lite. The full version in Chapter 6 gives more detail about what order to do the questions in. If this lite version is the one you remember or like better, great. Just remember to use it if you need to.

ONE FINAL TIME TOOL: CONCENTRATION

After you've decided which passage to do last and have started on the passage you've decided to do first, concentrate. Does that sound foolish and obvious? It really isn't. Reading fast is easy: just blaze your eyes over the page and pronounce yourself finished. Unfortunately, though, you'll have no idea what you've just looked at. The trick is to understand what you read, and the only way to do that is to concentrate. Buckle down and remember that this test is pretty tough. You've got to force yourself to stay with what you're reading. For the purposes of the AP Literature Exam, concentration means just one thing: Don't blank out.

What do we mean? We mean that there almost always comes a time in reading a difficult text when you hit a sentence you don't understand. At that point, most students go blank. They're not reading anymore. Instead, they're just running their eyes over what appear to be complicated hieroglyphics, waiting for the part that makes sense again. About three-quarters of a page later the student snaps out of it thinking, "What's this…? Hey, wait a minute, it looks like some kind of a test! Oh no…" Then the student jumps back to the killer sentence and tries once more, often blanking out yet again.

Blanking out is really easy to do. Everyone does it, especially when tired or stressed or bored (you may be all three when you take the exam). But you can't afford to do it on the AP test. You don't have time. There's only one cure. When a sentence starts to get away from you—stop. Close your eyes. Take a deep breath. Open your eyes. Usually, the sentence has reverted from hieroglyphics to English. Make a conscious effort to concentrate totally on what you're reading. Now try the sentence again, and if it still doesn't make sense, move on—not blanking out, not worrying about that tough sentence—but making a conscious, concentrated effort to keep reading.

SUMMARY OF THE BASIC PRINCIPLES OF CRACKING THE SYSTEM

HAVE A PLAN

1. Note the time and the number of passages.

2. Pick a passage to do first.

3. Pick a passage to do last.

4. Work the passage.

5. Answer *all* the questions on the passage, using our techniques.

TIME MANAGEMENT

- Guess aggressively.

- Pick a passage to do last based on what you consider your greatest weakness.

- Skip a passage and still get a good score.

- Learn the Art of the Seven-Minute Passage (Lite or Full) and use it.

POE

- Guess aggressively. If you work on a question, answer it, always.
- Use POE (Process of Elimination).
- The best way to use POE is to look closely at the wording of each answer choice for what is wrong, and eliminate.
- Turn *guessing penalty* into a *guessing bonus*.

Advanced Principles: Reading the Multiple-Choice Passages

READING THE PASSAGES IN THE MULTIPLE-CHOICE SECTION

Because of the time constraints, you'll want to make sure that you go about reading the passages in the most efficient way possible. You'll want to use a slightly different approach depending on whether the passage is prose or poetry, but there are a few things you should keep in mind regarding both types of passage.

- **You are reading in order to answer questions**, not for enjoyment or appreciation. The object is to answer questions. As you read, ask yourself, "Do I understand this well enough to answer a multiple-choice question about what it means?"

- **You can come back to the passage anytime you want, and you *should* go back to the passage in order to answer the questions.**

Both of these points address the same issue. The passages are on a test, but you don't do most of your reading on tests. Generally, when you study for an English test, you read the works your teacher assigned and then have to answer questions—true/false, short answer, multiple-choice, or essay—from memory. You study the passage accordingly, taking notes, drawing family trees, looking up words you don't know, making flash cards so you can remember if Sebastian was shipwrecked on Illyria's coast, devoured by street children, or living in a North African monastery. Regrettably, the techniques that work well in English class don't work so well for the AP Literature and Composition Exam.

The bad news is you probably won't have seen the work before. The test writers deliberately select works that aren't quite in the major canon. The writers are great writers, but if the passage is by Charles Dickens, the excerpt will be from *Bleak House* or *Our Mutual Friend*, not *Great Expectations* or *A Tale of Two Cities*, those perennial favorites of high school English teachers. If they choose a Matthew Arnold poem, it won't be "Dover Beach. "

The good news is it is unlikely that anyone else taking the test has seen the work before, so you are starting with same level of knowledge as the vast majority of other test takers.

The best news is it's an open-book test. So, you don't have to read the passage in the same way you study for an English test. The test isn't next month, or next week, or even tomorrow. It's now. You don't have to remember anything about the passage. You just need to know the general idea and how it's structured, so that you can go back to it and find what you need to answer the questions the test writers are asking.

READING PROSE PASSAGES

The right way to read prose passages in the multiple-choice section is simple. It's the way you should read whenever your purpose is to assimilate information efficiently. (It is not a way to read for pleasure.) On the AP Literature Exam make a point of reading this way:

0. Preview the Questions

This is step zero because it's *optional*. People are divided on its efficacy because it is helpful to some students, worthless to others. For some students, a quick reading of the questions provides *context*. For others, it's a total waste of time. When you're practicing on passages, try it each way and see what works best for you. Then, stick to that strategy. What you'll want to do is read each question, and only the question. Don't read the answer choices. Don't try to memorize the questions. Just get a sense of what they're asking you about—questions about literary devices or a certain character, for example. This can provide clues that will make your reading more active.

1. Skim the Passage

Skimming should take no more than a minute. Don't confuse skimming with "fake reading" or just looking at the passage. Read the first sentences of paragraphs or stanzas carefully, and then glance over the rest to see if it's about what you thought. Read the last sentence of the passage or line of the poem. You don't know enough to answer any questions, but you probably do know who or what it's about.

Most people don't skim because it's uncomfortable, especially in a test situation where every impulse says, "I've got to get this." Let the skimming be slightly uncomfortable; that means you're doing it right. Skimming, also called pre-reading, aids efficient comprehension, which is exactly what you want on the AP Exam.

2. Read the Passage

The second step, the step you've been waiting for, is reading—plain old-fashioned reading. Just read, without fixating on details, without getting stuck or going blank. When you hit a sentence you don't understand in a book, you don't panic, do you? You don't assume: "I might as well throw this book away...without that sentence it's just a useless collection of incomplete alphabetical symbols." When you read normally, you read for the main idea. You read to understand what's going on. When you hit a tricky sentence, you figure that you'll be able to make sense of it from what comes later, or that one missing piece of the puzzle isn't going to keep you from getting the outline of the overall picture. This is exactly how you want to read an AP English Literature Exam passage.

GET THE MAIN IDEA

Get the main idea of the passage. One way to have a clear understanding of the main idea of the passage is to visualize what you are reading. If you think of the passage as a short movie clip, you may be able to get the bulk of the points you need.

WHAT IS THE MAIN IDEA?

For the AP English Literature Exam, main idea means the general point. It is the ten-words-or-fewer summary of the passage. The main idea is the gist, or the big picture. For example, suppose there's a passage about all the different ways a man is stingy, how he cheats his best friend out of an inheritance, and scrimps on food around the house so badly that his kids go to bed crying from hunger every night. The passage goes on for 50 or 60 lines describing this guy. The main idea is that this guy is an evil, greedy miser. If the passage gives a reason for the miser's obsession with money, you might include that in your mental picture of the main idea: This guy is an evil, greedy miser because he grew up poor. No doubt the passage tells you exactly how he grew up and where (in an orphanage, let's say), and exactly what kind of leftover beans he eats (lima) and exactly how many cold leftover lima beans he serves to his starving kids each night (three apiece), but those are details, not the big picture. Use the details to build up to the big picture.

THE MAGIC TOPIC SENTENCE HAS VANISHED

We don't want you to think the main idea can be found in some magic "topic sentence." The writers on the AP test are sophisticated; they often don't use any obvious clues like topic sentences. On poetry passages, looking for topic sentences is a complete waste of time.

SUMMARY — HOW DO YOU READ AN AP MULTIPLE-CHOICE PROSE PASSAGE?

- Preview the questions (optional)
- Skim
- Read for the main idea

READING POETRY PASSAGES

Ideally, you read a poem several times, ponder, scratch your head, and read some more. Then again, ideally, you have your favorite poem by your favorite poet, and all afternoon—not 15 minutes with some poem you couldn't care less about and 15 multiple-choice questions staring you in the face.

It's a test, so you've got to read the poem efficiently. Well, the key to the process is keeping your mind open, especially the first time through the poem.

It might help to be clear about the difference between a narrative and the kind of poetry you'll see on the AP test. A narrative unfolds and builds on itself. Although one's understanding of what came earlier in the narrative is deepened and changed by later developments, by and large the work makes sense as it flows; it is meant to be understood "on the run."

Verse is different. Yes, the way it unfolds is important, but one often doesn't even grasp that unfolding until the second or third (or ninetieth) read. A poem is like a sculpture; it is meant to be wandered around, looked at from all sides, and finally, taken in as a whole. You wouldn't try to understand a sculpture until you'd seen the whole thing. In the same way, think of your first reading of a poem as a walk around an interesting sculpture. You aren't trying to interpret. You are just trying to look at the whole thing. Once you've seen it, and taken in its dimensions, then you can go back and puzzle it out.

What we've just said applies to poetry in general. But how can you apply that to the AP exam? Here's the answer: *When you approach a poem on the AP exam, always read it at least twice before you go to the questions.*

THE FIRST READ

The first read is to get all the words in your head. Go from top to bottom. Don't stop at individual lines to figure them out, not even a little. If everything makes sense, great. If it doesn't, no problem. The main thing you want is a basic sense of what's going on. The main thing to avoid is getting a fixed impression of the poem before you've even finished it.

THE SECOND READ

The second read should be phrase by phrase. Focus on understanding what you read in the simplest way possible. This is when you should look for the main idea.

Don't worry about symbols. Don't worry about deeper meanings. The questions will direct you toward those aspects of the poem. You will need to go back and read parts of the poem, perhaps the entire poem, several more times, but only as is necessary to answer individual questions. To prepare yourself for the questions, all you need is a general sense of what the poem says, and to get that understanding you need only the literal sense of the lines. We can't emphasize this point enough: *Keep it simple.*

PANIC AND OBSESSION

If you find that after two reads you don't have the poem's main idea, don't panic. Chances are, at least half the people in the room with you are completely baffled by the same poem. Don't skip the passage. Move on to the questions. The questions will often help you understand the poem, or the vocabulary terms used in the questions will be familiar, which will help you use POE to crack a series of questions on a poem. But whatever you do, don't obsess over a difficult poem. Don't read and reread and reread as though you could pummel the poem into submission and force it to give up its meaning. This obsessive reaction won't work. You'll just use up time and further frustrate yourself. If a poem gives you tons of trouble, chances are it's giving everyone trouble. Go to the questions.

THE PROBLEM WITH POETRY

Poetry, especially good poetry, makes conscious use of all language's resources. By pushing at the limits of language, poetry typically creates a heightened awareness of language in the reader. When a poet successfully speaks to a reader, the poem seems intensely meaningful, suggestive of new ideas and connections, and yet surprisingly exact. Given the situation within which you are reading this poem, you may not have the time or mindset to allow for an intensely meaningful experience. When you read a complex poem under time constraints, the heightened sense of language may send you down a maze of false alleys, and myriad ambiguities lead you so far from the home-base of meaning that you end up feeling lost. Poets use difficult vocabulary, odd figures of speech, and unusual combinations of words in strange orders; they play with time and stretch the connections we ordinarily expect to see between ideas. All these things, essential to poetry, can also make things difficult. It's easy to get lost, and it's often a struggle to get anything from a poem, let alone find it beautiful or enjoyable. Finally, many poems are deliberately open to a number of valid interpretations.

NO PROBLEM AT ALL

The kinds of poems you're likely to see on the AP English Literature Exam will use complex, challenging language, but underneath it all will be a spine of good old-fashioned, straightforward meaning. As you read through the poem, take a close look at the diction, or individual words, that the poet uses in the first two lines of the poem. The poet's word choice will often give you a clue to the tone of the poem, which is important in trying to figure out what attitude the poet has about the subject. For instance, if the poet uses the word *morose* instead of the word *sad*, you will know that subject of the poem is depressed and not merely disappointed. By looking at the diction of the poet, you may have a better handle on the approach the poet is taking toward the subject of the poem.

Don't forget to pay attention to the title of the poem if they've included it. By quickly glancing at the diction, the last few lines, and the title of the poem, you are on your way to having a fairly good foundation for understanding the poem. The more you practice these techniques, the better you will become at recognizing tone, theme, and purpose.

THE PROS READ POETRY FOR PROSE

The secret to understanding AP poetry passages quickly and fully is to simply ignore the "poetry parts." Ignore the rhythm, ignore the music of the language, and above all, ignore the form. That means

- Ignore line breaks.

- Read in sentences, not in lines. Emphasize punctuation.

- Ignore rhyme and rhyme scheme.

- Be prepared for "long" thoughts—ideas that develop over several lines.

When approaching poetry, many students tend to do the opposite of what we suggest here: They emphasize lines and line breaks and totally ignore sentence punctuation. If you don't get slammed on the AP test for doing that, you're lucky.

True, sometimes there's no problem: When lines break at natural pauses and when each line has a packet of meaning complete in itself (these are termed *end-stopped* lines) the poem becomes easier to read.

Easier Poetry

Look at these lines from Thomas Gray's "Elegy Written in a Country Churchyard":

> Now fades the glimmering landscape on the sight,
> And all the air a solemn stillness holds,
> Save where the beetle wheels his droning flight,
> And drowsy tinklings lull the distant folds.

Read this passage aloud and you can't help but stop on the line endings, even if there were no commas. The lines build, one upon the next, shaping a picture as they combine to form a mildly complex sentence. The ease with which these lines can be read stems from the fact that each line contains only complete thoughts; there are no loose ends trailing from line to line. This is "nice" poetry; that is, it's nice to you. Each line ends on a natural pause that lets you gather your thoughts. Each line holds something like a complete thought with very little run-over into the next line. Although the stanza is written in one sentence, it easily could have been written in four separate sentences:

> The landscape fades.
> The air is still.
> The beetle wheels and drones.
> The tinklings [of bells worn by livestock] lull the folds.*
> *Folds are enclosures where sheep graze, or the flocks of
> sheep themselves.

This paraphrase is lousy poetry, but it gets the main idea across. If the poetry you see on the AP test reads like the example above, great. But if you think every poem should be like that stanza, if you try to make every poem read like that one, you're headed for trouble. The poetry on the AP test is likely to be more challenging.

Challenging Poetry

Consider the next selection. It's the first 13 lines of "My Last Duchess" by Robert Browning. This is the kind of poetry you can expect to find on the AP test, but it is unlikely that you would see a poem that is this well known.

The poem is a monologue, spoken by a nobleman, the Duke of Ferrara, to a representative of the Count of Tyrol. Ferrara seeks to take the wealthy count's daughter for his bride and is in the midst of discussing the arrangement with the count's representative. When Ferrara speaks of his "last duchess," he refers to his first wife, who has quite recently died, at the age of 17, under mysterious circumstances. The implication is that Ferrara has had his first wife murdered, an implication the poem brings home with understated menace.

You won't be given this kind of information on the test, but with practice, you should be able to figure out many of the aspects of the poem by yourself. For example, the first two lines of the poem (which is printed below in sections) give a careful reader some important information. The speaker of the poem is a duke, as he is talking about his "last duchess." He is standing in front of a painting of this woman, who is no longer alive. All of this information, if assimilated readily and with an eye toward tone and the big picture, will help you answer questions, even if the questions don't ask specifically who the speaker is or if the duchess is alive.

My Last Duchess

FERRARA

That's my last duchess painted on the wall,
Looking as if she were alive. I call
That piece a wonder, now: Frà Pandolf's hands
Line Worked busily a day, and there she stands.
(5) Will't please you sit and look at her? I said
"Frà Pandolf" by design, for never read
Strangers like you that pictured countenance,
The depth and passion of its earnest glance,
But to myself they turned (since none puts by
(10) The curtain I have drawn for you, but I)
And seemed as they would ask me, if they durst,
how such a glance came there; so, not the first
Are you to turn and ask thus…

Now this isn't particularly difficult poetry, but legions of students have trouble making heads or tails of it. The first few lines present little difficulty: The Duke points to the painting, remarks on its lifelike quality, mentions the artist (Frà Pandolf), and invites his listener to sit and contemplate the portrait for a moment. Although lines 3–4, "Frà Pandolf's hands/ Worked busily a day" are distinctly unmodern speech and might give some folks a moment's pause, most of us get through the opening without too much difficulty. Even if you don't know that "Frà" is used as a title of address to an Italian monk (and who does?), you can still figure out the big picture of this poem.

Then comes the remainder of the passage, beginning from line 5, "I said/ 'Frà Pandolf' by design, for never read" and the trouble begins. Now, the truth is that what is written there is easy enough that if you can break the habit of placing too much emphasis on line breaks, you can read it as prose. Browning has deliberately written his verse so that the lines break against the flow of the punctuation. If you expect little parcels of complete meaning at every break, you'll end up lost. Let's consider the troubling part written as prose:

"I said 'Frà Pandolf' by design, for never read strangers like you that pictured countenance, the depth and passion of its earnest glance, but to myself they turned (since none puts by the curtain I have drawn for you, but I) and seemed as they would ask me, if they durst, how such a glance came there."

This is just one long sentence, broken by parenthetical asides, in which the duke says, "I said 'Frà Pandolf'" on purpose because strangers never see that portrait (or its expression of depth and passion) without turning to me (because nobody sees the portrait unless I'm here to pull aside the curtain) and looking at me as though they want to ask, if they dare, 'How did that expression get there?'"

Read the poem as prose and you'll see it isn't so hard. If you have trouble doing this, try putting brackets around each sentence.

Now, if you're really alert, you'll notice that the Duke still hasn't exactly explained why he mentioned Frà Pandolf on purpose. He eventually does (in his sideways fashion), but if you read poetry without being ready for long thoughts that develop over several lines, you're going to read "I said, 'Frà Pandolf' by design, for never…" and expect the explanation—pronto. When it doesn't come you think you're lost, and once you think you're lost, you are. How is "that pictured countenance" an explanation of why he said, "Frà Pandolf?" It isn't, and it never will be, but you can spend hours trying to come up with reasons why it is.

Don't get the wrong impression. Browning isn't easy reading. But you'll find that if you follow our suggestions for reading poetry, Browning, and poets like him, aren't nearly as difficult as they seem to be. Ignore line breaks and instead pay close attention to punctuation and sentence structure. Be ready for "long" thoughts that develop over several lines or even stanzas. You'll still find the poems on the AP test challenging for a variety of reasons: because of their vocabulary, because of their compression of a great deal of information into just a few lines, and because of their often complicated and unusual sentence structure. If you read poetry the way we suggest, however, you'll find that you can make sense of those difficulties by using the context of what you do understand.

Taken together, these pieces of advice boil down to one simple concept: Before you read a poem as poetry, read it as prose.

Here's Browning's "My Last Duchess" in complete form. Read it according to our advice and see what you can get from it. (Many discussions of this famous poem exist online, and you can read a few in order to compare what you've figured out with what others have said about it.)

FERRARA

That's my last duchess painted on the wall,
Looking as if she were alive. I call
That piece a wonder, now: Frà Pandolf's hands
Line Worked busily a day, and there she stands.
(5) Will't please you sit and look at her? I said
"Frà Pandolf" by design, for never read
Strangers like you that pictured countenance,
The depth and passion of its earnest glance,
But to myself they turned (since none puts by
(10) The curtain I have drawn for you, but I)
And seemed as they would ask me, if they durst,
how such a glance came there; so, not the first
Are you to turn and ask thus. Sir, 'twas not
Her husband's presence only, called that spot
(15) Of joy into the Duchess' cheek: perhaps
Frà Pandolf chanced to say, "Her mantle laps
"Over my lady's wrist too much," or "Paint
"Must never hope to reproduce the faint
"Half-flush that dies along her throat": such stuff
(20) Was courtesy, she thought, and cause enough
For calling up that spot of joy. She had
A heart—how shall I say?—too soon made glad,
Too easily impressed; she liked whate'er
She looked on, and her looks went everywhere.
(25) Sir, 'twas all one! My favor at her breast,
The dropping of the daylight in the West,
The bough of cherries some officious fool
Broke in the orchard for her, the white mule
She rode with round the terrace—all and each
(30) Would draw from her alike the approving speech,
Or blush, at least. She thanked men—good! but thanked
Somehow—I know not how—as if she ranked
My gift of a nine-hundred-years-old name
With anybody's gift. Who'd stoop to blame
(35) This sort of trifling? Even had you skill

In speech—which I have not—to make your will
Quite clear to such an one, and say, "Just this
"Or that in you disgusts me; here you miss,
"Or there exceed the mark"—and if she let
(40) Herself be lessoned so, nor plainly set
Her wits to yours, forsooth, and made excuse,
—E'en then would be some stooping; and I choose
Never to stoop. Oh sir, she smiled, no doubt,
Whene'er I passed her; but who passed without
(45) Much the same smile? This grew; I gave commands;
Then all smiles stopped together. There she stands
As if alive. Will't please you rise? We'll meet
The company below, then. I repeat,
The Count your master's known munificence
(50) Is ample warrant that no just pretense
Of mine for dowry will be disallowed;
Though his fair daughter's self, as I avowed
At starting, is my object. Nay, we'll go
Together down, sir. Notice Neptune, though,
(55) Taming a sea-horse, thought a rarity,
Which Claus of Innsbrück cast in bronze for me!

SUMMARY

BASICS OF READING PASSAGES

- You are reading in order to answer the questions—that's the whole point.
- Reading for a test is different from normal reading. You have limited time, and you have to approach the passages in a way that takes that into account.
- You can reread the passage anytime you want, and you should go back to the passage in order to answer the questions.

READING PROSE PASSAGES

- Preview the questions if it helps you.
- First, skim the passage.
- Skimming should never take more than a minute.
- Read for the main idea.

READING POETRY PASSAGES

- Preview the questions if it helps you.

- On the AP test, read a poem twice before you answer the questions.

- The first read is to get all the words in your head.
    The main thing you want is a basic sense of what's going on.
    Try not to get a fixed impression of the poem before you've even finished it.

- The second read should be phrase by phrase. Focus on understanding what you read in the simplest way possible. Don't worry about symbols. Don't worry about deeper meanings. Try to visualize what you read as you follow the narration of the poem.

- You will need to go back and read parts of the poem, perhaps the entire poem, several more times, but only as necessary for your work on individual questions.

POETRY INTO PROSE

- Find the spine—the prose meaning—of the poem.
    Ignore line breaks.
    Emphasize punctuation. Read in sentences, not in lines.
    Be prepared for "long" thoughts: ideas that develop over several lines.

- Before you read a poem as poetry, read it as prose.

5

Cracking the System: Multiple-Choice Questions

THE QUESTIONS

Once you've finished reading a passage, you need to answer the questions. If you've paid attention thus far, you already know you're going to answer all the questions, taking your best guess when you aren't completely sure of yourself. You're fearless, remember? You should also know by now that we think you should approach the test efficiently, making the best possible use of your time in order to get the best possible score.

In order to answer the questions efficiently, you need to be able to recognize three types of questions.

- General comprehension questions
- Detail questions
- Factual knowledge questions

You can easily distinguish among these three broad categories.

GENERAL COMPREHENSION QUESTIONS

General comprehension questions are those that ask about the overall passage. These are the questions that don't send you back to any specific place in the passage.

Here are some examples of general comprehension questions:

> The passage is primarily concerned with…?

> Which one of the following choices best describes the tone of the passage?

> Which one of the following choices best describes the narrator's relationship to her mother?

> To whom does the speaker of the poem address his speech?

> It is evident in the passage that the author feels his hometown is…

> Which of the following best describes the speaker's changing attitude toward the object being described over the course of the first, the second, and the third stanzas, respectively?

DETAIL QUESTIONS

Detail questions almost always send you back to specific places in the passage. They tell you where to look and ask about what is going on in that specific segment of the passage.

Here are some examples of detail questions:

> What significant change occurs in the speaker's attitude toward her mother in lines 5–9?

> How do the final words of the third paragraph, "but then, I should have known better than to trust him," alter the remainder of the passage?

> What does the author mean by "formalist" (line 19)?

> Which of the following is the best paraphrase for the sentence that begins at line 9?

FACTUAL KNOWLEDGE QUESTIONS

Factual knowledge questions ask you about the English language and its grammar and the basic terminology of criticism and poetry. Factual knowledge questions sometimes (but very rarely) ask for a widely known cultural fact related to the passage.

Here are some examples of factual knowledge questions:

> The author's use of irony has what effect on the poem?

> How does the author's use of symbolism contribute to the mystical tone of the passage?

> What parallel structure helps to emphasize the attitude of the speaker?

> In the context of the following lines (1–5), the phrase "This loaf's big" is used as a metaphor for the...

> When in the third stanza the playwright character says, "I believe my tragedy is worthy of performance at the Globe, " he is referring to...

The last question is an example of a question that tests your knowledge of a cultural fact. You can be sure that the right answer mentions that many of Shakespeare's plays were premiered at the Globe Theatre, and because of this the Globe Theatre is indelibly associated with Shakespeare's name. This is the sort of cultural fact that ETS expects literate high school students to know. Questions about cultural facts are one type of question that is impossible to study for, and there are very few of this question type on the test, anyway; one or two at most, and often none.

HOW MUCH GRAMMAR DO YOU NEED TO KNOW FOR THE AP TEST?

There are usually three or four questions on basic grammar. That's one grammar question or fewer per passage, so grammar is not a big deal on the Multiple-Choice section. The samples we provide in Chapters 6 and 7 should give you a good idea of what the grammar questions are like. Because there are so few grammar questions, we don't recommend you spend a lot of time studying grammar. You'd be far better off working on writing timed essays or reading some difficult poetry.

MASTER SENTENCE I

Here's a great simple sentence to memorize for basic grammatical relations:

> *Sam threw the orange to Irene.*

It isn't poetry, but this sentence clearly shows the basic grammatical relationships you need to concern yourself with on the AP test.

- *Sam* is the subject.

- *The orange* is the direct object.

- *Irene* is the indirect object.

Notice that in this sentence, the direct object is in fact an object (an orange). The orange is thrown to Irene, the indirect object. In other words, the indirect object receives the direct object. The concept is pretty simple.

MASTER SENTENCE II

There are two more sentence elements you should understand: the phrase and the clause. Here's a model sentence that should help you keep clear on their definitions.

Feeling generous, Sam threw the orange to Irene, who tried to catch it.

The heart of the sentence is still *Sam threw the orange to Irene*. Subject, verb, direct object, and indirect object all remain the same. But we've added a phrase to the beginning of the sentence, and a dependent (also called *subordinate*) clause to the end. Both phrases and dependent clauses function as modifiers. *Feeling generous*, a phrase, modifies *Sam*; and *who tried to catch it*, a clause, modifies *Irene*.

The difference between clauses and phrases is simple:

A **clause** has both a subject and a verb.

A **phrase** does not have both a subject and a verb.

Because a clause has both a subject and verb, a clause is always close to being a sentence of its own. The dependent clause, *who tried to catch it*, could be turned into a complete sentence by replacing *who* with *Irene* or *she*.

The hallmark of a phrase is its lack of a subject or verb (or both). Phrases obviously cannot stand alone. *Feeling generous* needs the addition of both a subject, *Sam*, and a verb, *was*, in order to become the sentence *Sam was feeling generous*.

Our model sentence contains another clause besides the dependent clause we've already mentioned. The other clause is *Sam threw the orange to Irene*. Because it has both a subject and a verb, it must be a clause. Notice that it doesn't need any changes in order to stand alone as a complete sentence: that makes it an *independent* clause.

GLOSSARY OF BASIC PARTS OF SPEECH

You also need to know the basic parts of speech. The last time you studied this was probably sometime in sixth grade. We're not trying to be insulting, but we've provided a review just in case you're rusty:

Noun: A person, place, thing, or idea (or an abstraction—for example, *strength* and *determination* are nouns)

Verb: An action word or a word that expresses a state of being

Adjective: A word that modifies, describes, or limits a noun or pronoun.

Adverb: A word that modifies, describes, or limits a verb, an adjective, or another adverb. (In the phrase *the profoundly nasty little poodle*, *nasty* and *little* are adjectives, but *profoundly* is an adverb, as it modifies the adjective *nasty*.)

Preposition: A word that shows the relationship between a noun or pronoun and some other word in the sentence. A preposition should not be the last word in a sentence in formal writing. A preposition is the first word of a prepositional phrase. The phrase will begin with a preposition and end with a noun or pronoun. (Take, for instance, the phrase *in the lake*. *In* is the preposition and *lake* is the noun that ends the phrase.)

Pronoun: A word that replaces a noun. Words such as *he, she, it, they, them, who,* or *that* can replace a noun. The noun to which a pronoun refers is called the *antecedent*. You find the antecedent by looking back from the pronoun to the part of the passage immediately preceding the pronoun and looking at the nouns that are in those sentences. One of those nouns, either because it is the closest to the pronoun or because it makes the most sense in context, is the noun to which the pronoun refers.

Gerund: A word that serves two functions. It acts like a noun and it acts like a verb. Look at the following sentence. *Swimming across the lake is fun. Swimming* is the gerund.

Participle: A word that serves two functions. It acts like an adjective and it acts like a verb. Look how *swimming* is used in the following sentence. *The girl, swimming across the lake, reminds me of my sister.* In this case the word *swimming* is describing the girl and, therefore, is a participle.

Infinitive: A phrase that begins with the word *to* and is followed by a verb form. *To swim* is an infinitive. In the following sentence, *to swim* is the infinitive: *To swim across the lake is fun.* Infinitives function as verbs, but they can also function as nouns, adjectives, or adverbs.

AND NOW THE BAD NEWS

You probably think that you're sure to answer all the grammar questions on the test correctly, because this stuff is a piece of cake.

Actually the *grammar* part is easy, but the *questions* aren't.

The reason we don't think you should bother studying much grammar for the AP test (unless the stuff you read above is totally new to you) is that ETS uses grammar as an indirect way to test reading comprehension. The grammar is seldom the hard part. ETS likes to ask grammar questions about tangled up sentences. If you didn't quite get what you were reading the first time, you'll have trouble answering these questions despite knowing darn well what nouns, modifiers, and clauses are.

DO IT YOUR WAY, OR ORDERING THE QUESTIONS

You can do the questions in any order you like, but that doesn't mean you should jump around and do them in any old order. After you finish reading a passage, but before you begin answering the questions, ask yourself, "Do I feel confident about this passage? Would I be able to explain this to a friend? Could I explain its main idea?"

The answer to this question determines the order in which you should tackle the test questions.

- If you feel confident about your comprehension of the passage, complete the questions in the order ETS gives them to you. Don't worry about the order of the questions; you're in good shape.

- If you don't feel confident about the main idea, do the detail questions first.

The reasoning behind this ordering method is simple. The main idea is the crucial thing to get from a reading passage, either prose or poetry. When you've got the main idea nailed down, you aren't likely to miss more than a few questions on the passage. Knowing the main idea will help you to answer all the other general questions and many of the specific questions as well.

When you don't feel confident about the main idea (usually this means the passage is pretty confusing), you want to start with the specific questions because they tell you exactly where to go and also give you something on which to focus.

As you reread the lines toward which the specific questions point you, you should become more and more familiar with the passage. Often, after doing a specific question or two, the meaning of the passage "clicks" for you, and you will get what's going on. Don't answer the general questions until you have a firm sense of the main idea. If, after answering all the specific questions, you still don't really know what the point of the passage is, give the general questions your best shot and move on.

CONSISTENCY OF ANSWERS #1

The main idea should be your guiding rule for most of the questions on any passage. We call this principle *Consistency of Answers*. As you work on a passage, you will find that the right answer on several of the questions has to do with the main idea. The rule is, **when in doubt, pick an answer that agrees with the main idea.**

CONSISTENCY OF ANSWERS #2

Pick answers that agree with each other. You'll also find that correct answers tend to be consistent. It's a simple idea that comes in very handy. For example, if you're sure the correct answer to question number 9 is choice (B), and choice (B) says that Mr. Buffalo is extremely hairy, you can be sure that question 10's Mr. Buffalo isn't bald. Correct answers agree with each other.

The best way to understand how to use this very effective technique is to see it at work. You'll see plenty of examples in the following chapters; we'll discuss this technique in detail when we work on actual questions.

SUMMARY

- Recognize three basic categories of questions.
    1. General Comprehension
    2. Detail
    3. Factual Knowledge

- Don't sweat grammar for the AP English Literature Exam. It isn't worth enough points to cause perspiration.

- Do it your way.
    If you know the main idea, do the questions in order.
    If you're uncomfortable with the main idea, answer detail and factual questions first.

- Use Consistency of Answers.
    When in doubt, pick an answer that agrees with the main idea.
    Pick answers that agree with each other.

6

Answering Prose Passage Questions

HOW TO USE OUR SAMPLE PASSAGES AND QUESTIONS

There's no limit to the different kinds of questions that ETS can (and does) write for the AP English Literature Exam. As a result, we can't show you every type of question that may show up on the test. We can come pretty close, though. ETS has a bunch of questions it uses and reuses on hundreds of tests. The best way to study these questions is by practicing on examples. To understand and use the example questions, you need a passage.

In this chapter and the next, we provide passages with sample questions. Chapter 6 has a prose passage. Chapter 7 has a poetry passage. Read the passages carefully using our reading techniques, and then look over the questions.

There's no need to do the questions immediately because we're going to take you through them one step at time, discussing the best approaches and specific techniques to use in answering them. Of course, if you want to see how you do on them before referring to our instructions, go right ahead.

After you've looked over the passages, read each question, try to answer it, and then follow our explanations. The correct answer to each question is given in the explanation, but don't just skim through the explanation looking for the answer to see if you chose correctly. Read all of each explanation, regardless of whether you got the question right. Our explanations will point out details you overlooked and discuss how you might have approached the question differently.

SAMPLE PROSE PASSAGE AND QUESTIONS

Edgar Allan Poe's "The Duc De L'Omelette"

Keats fell by a criticism. But who ever died of inept poetry? Ignoble souls!—De L'Omelette perished of an ortolan*[1]. The story then, in brief:

Line
That night the Duke was to sup alone. In the
5 privacy of his bureau he reclined languidly on that ottoman for which he sacrificed his loyalty in outbidding his king—the notorious ottoman of Cadet.

He buries his face in the pillow. The clock strikes! Unable to restrain his feelings, his Grace swallows an
10 olive. At this moment the door gently opens to the sound of soft music, and lo! the most delicate of birds is before the most enamored of men! But what inexpressible dismay now overshadows the countenance of the Duke? *"Horreur! Dog! Protestant! —the*
15 *bird! Ah Good God! This modest bird you've quite unclothed and served without paper!"* It is superfluous to say more:—the Duke expired in a paroxysm of disgust….

"Ha! ha! ha!" said his Grace on the third day after
20 his decease.

"He! he! he!" replied the Devil faintly, drawing himself up with an air of hauteur.

"Why surely you are not serious," retorted De L'Omelette. "I have sinned—that's true—but, my
25 good sir, consider!—you have no actual intention of putting such—such—barbarous threats into execution."

"No what?" said his Majesty—"come, sir, strip!"

"Strip, indeed! very pretty i' faith! no, sir, I shall
30 not strip. Who are you, pray, that I, Duke De L'Omelette, Prince de Foie-Gras, just come of age, author of the 'Mazurkiad,' and member of the Acad-

*An ortolan is a small dovelike bird considered a supreme delicacy by nineteenth century gourmets. (Story adapted from Edgar Allan Poe's "The Duc De L'Omelette")

emy, should divest myself at your bidding of the
sweetest pantaloons ever made by Bourdon, the
35 daintiest dressing gown ever put together by
Rombert—take say nothing of undressing my hair—
not to mention the trouble I should have in drawing
off my gloves?"

"Who am I?—ah, true! I am Baal-Zebub, Prince of
40 the Fly. I took thee, just now, from a rosewood coffin
inlaid with ivory. Thou wast curiously scented, and
labeled as per invoice. Belial sent thee—my Inspector
of Cemeteries. The pantaloons, which thou sayest
were made by Bourdon, are an excellent pair of linen
45 drawers, and thy dressing gown is a shroud of no
scanty dimensions."

"Sir!" replied the Duke, "I am not to be insulted
with impunity!—Sir! you shall hear from me! In the
meantime au revoir!"—and the Duke was bowing
50 himself out of the Satanic presence, when he was
interrupted and brought back by a gentleman in
waiting. Hereupon his Grace rubbed his eyes,
yawned, shrugged his shoulders, reflected. Having
become satisfied of his identity, he took a bird's-eye
55 view of his whereabouts.

The apartment was superb. Even De L'Omelette
pronounced it "quite well done." It was not its length
nor its breadth—but its height—ah, that was appalling!—there was no ceiling—certainly none—but a
60 dense whirling mass of fiery-colored clouds. His
Grace's brain reeled as he glanced upward. From
above, hung a chain of an unknown blood-red
metal—its upper end lost. From its nether extremity
swung a large cresset. The Duke knew it to be a ruby;
65 but from it there poured a light so intense, so still, so
terrible. Persia never worshipped such, no great
Sultan ever dreamed of such when, drugged with
opium, he has tottered to a bed of poppies, his back to
the flowers, and his face to the God Apollo. The Duke
70 muttered a slight oath, decidedly approbatory.

The corners of the room were rounded into niches,
and these were filled statues of gigantic proportions.
But the paintings! The paintings! O luxury! O love!—
who gazing on those forbidden beauties shall have
75 eyes for others.

The Duke's heart is fainting within him. He is not,
however, as you suppose, dizzy with magnificence,
nor drunk with the ecstatic breath of the innumerable
censers. (It's true that he thinks of these things to no
80 small degree—but!) The Duke De L'Omelette is
terror-stricken; for, through the lurid vista which a
single uncurtained window is affording, lo! gleams
the most ghastly of all fires!

The poor Duke! He could not help imagining that
the glorious, the voluptuous, the never-dying melo-
dies which pervaded that hall, as they passed filtered
and transmuted through the alchemy of the en-
chanted window-panes, were the wailings and the
howlings of the hopeless and the damned! And there,
too!—there!—upon the ottoman!—who could he
be?—he, the Deity—who sat as if carved in marble,
and who smiled, with his pale countenance, bitterly?

A Frenchman never faints outright. Besides, his
Grace hated a scene—De L'Omelette is himself again.
Hadn't he read somewhere? wasn't it said "that the
devil can't refuse a card game?"

But the chances—the chances! True—desperate; but
scarcely more desperate than the Duke. Besides
wasn't he the slyest player in the craftiest card-club in
Paris?—the legendary "21 club."

"Should I lose," said his Grace "I will lose twice—
that is I shall be doubly damned—should I win, I
return to my ortolan—let the cards be prepared."

His Grace was all care, all attention, his Majesty all
confidence. His Grace thought of the game. His
majesty did not think; he shuffled. The Duke cut.

The cards are dealt. The trump is turned—it is—it
is—the king! No—it was the queen. His Majesty
cursed her masculine habiliments. De L'Omelette
placed his hand upon his heart.

They play. The Duke counts. The hand is out. His
majesty counts heavily, smiles and is taking wine. The
Duke palms a card.

"It's your deal," said his Majesty, cutting. His Grace
bowed, dealt, and arose from the table—turning the
King.

His Majesty looked chagrined.

Had Alexander not been Alexander, he would have
been Diogenes; and the Duke assured his antagonist
in taking his leave, "Were one not already the Duke
De L'Omelette one could have no objection to being
the Devil."

1. The primary purpose of the passage is to portray

   (A) the characteristics of an exaggerated type
        through the figure of L'Omelette
   (B) a reassuringly humorous vision of hell through
        a narrative in which the Devil himself is
        bested
   (C) the evil consequences of excessive pride
   (D) the developing relationship between
        L'Omelette and the Devil
   (E) the pivotal change that occurs in L'Omelette
        through his encounter with the Devil

2. Which of the following best describes the Duke De
   L'Omelette?

   (A) He is a typical eighteenth-century nobleman.
   (B) He is a caricature of a snob.
   (C) He is a man more wicked than the Devil.
   (D) He is a man with perfect aesthetic judgment.
   (E) He is a man transformed by his encounter with
        a power greater than his own.

3. In context, lines 29–38 serve to reinforce the
   reader's impression of the Duke's

   (A) quick temper
   (B) exquisite taste
   (C) sense of self-importance
   (D) accomplishments and social position
   (E) misunderstanding of his situation

4. The author's portrayal of the Duke De L'Omelette
   is best described as

   (A) a sympathetic portrait of a man with overly
        delicate sensibilities
   (B) a comically ironic treatment of an effete snob
   (C) a harshly condemnatory portrait of a bon
        vivant
   (D) an admiring portrait of a great artist
   (E) a farcical treatment of the very rich

5. Which of the following descriptions is an example
   of the narrator's irony?

   (A) "Unable to restrain his feelings, his Grace
        swallows an olive." (lines 9–10)
   (B) "I took thee, just now, from a rosewood coffin
        inlaid with ivory." (lines 40–41)
   (C) "The Duke knew it to be a ruby; but from it
        there poured a light so intense, so still, so
        terrible." (lines 64–66)
   (D) "And there, too!—there!—upon the ottoman!—
        who could he be?—he, the Deity—who sat
        as if carved in marble, and who smiled, with
        his pale countenance, bitterly?" (lines 89–92)
   (E) "His Grace was all care, all attention, his
        Majesty all confidence." (lines 104–105)

6. In lines 58–59, the word "appalling" suggests the Duke

(A) has found the room's decorum unacceptable
(B) has approbation for clouds
(C) suffers from insomnia
(D) finds the apartment extraordinary
(E) suffers from a paroxysm

7. Which of the following best implies the contextual meaning of the phrase "sacrificed his loyalty" (line 6) within the context of the story?

(A) The Duke has fallen into disfavor with the King by outbidding him.
(B) The Duke has betrayed his country.
(C) The Duke has allowed his desire for the ottoman to override his deference to the King.
(D) The Duke recognizes no one as more powerful than himself.
(E) The Duke values the ottoman more greatly than his prestige.

8. In which of the following lines is the narrator most clearly articulating the Duke's thoughts?

(A) "Ignoble souls!" (line 2)
(B) "It is superfluous to say more:—" (lines 16–17)
(C) "Having become satisfied of his identity, he took a bird's-eye view of his whereabouts." (lines 53–55)
(D) "But the chances—the chances! True—desperate;" (line 97)
(E) "They play." (line 111)

9. Which of the following lines implies a speaker other than the narrator?

(A) "But who ever died of inept poetry?" (lines 1–2)
(B) "That night the Duke was to sup alone." (line 4)
(C) "The apartment was superb." (line 56)
(D) "His majesty did not think, he shuffled." (lines 105–106)
(E) "Had Alexander not been Alexander, he would have been Diogenes." (lines 118–119)

10. Which of the following best describes the situation in lines 19–22 and the events that came immediately *before* it?

(A) The Duke has just noticed the Devil and laughs at him. The Devil returns the laugh, but quietly because he feels insulted.

(B) The Duke has just heard the Devil explain the tortures that lie in store for him. He believes the Devil is joking and laughs. The Devil mocks his laughter, implying that it is no joke.

(C) The Duke and the Devil have been talking, but the exact topic has purposefully been left vague.

(D) The Duke has just heard the Devil's plans for him and laughs defiantly at the Devil. The Devil puns on the Duke's use of the word "Ha!" by saying "He!" By doing so, the devil indicates "He," that is the Duke, will be punished for his sins.

(E) The Duke, believing he speaks with a lowly servant, laughs at the threats the Devil has made. The Devil plays along, laughing with the Duke in order to draw out the Duke's eventual humiliation.

11. Which of the following reinforces the effect of the passage most strongly?

(A) Light-hearted situations narrated with deep seriousness

(B) Humorous irony in the introduction, contrasted with serious reflection in the conclusion

(C) Calculated objectivity offset by occasional interjections of subjective emotion

(D) Underlying contempt partially concealed by objectivity

(E) First-person outbursts of effusive emotion in an otherwise third-person narration

12. The narrator's attitude toward the Duke can be best described as

(A) complete objectivity
(B) ambiguous pity
(C) slight distaste
(D) bemused confusion
(E) satiric glee

13. The passage contains

      I. abrupt shifts in tense
     II. an abrupt shift in place
    III. abrupt shifts in emotional state

(A) I only
(B) I and II only
(C) I and III only
(D) II and III only
(E) I, II, and III

14. The phrase, "as if carved in marble" (line 91), is an example of

(A) an apostrophe
(B) irony
(C) lyricism
(D) a metaphor
(E) a simile

15. Grammatically, the phrase, "Were one not already the Duke De L'Omelette" (lines 120–121), establishes the

(A) simple past tense
(B) past imperfect tense
(C) present conditional tense
(D) subjunctive mood
(E) simple present tense

About Poe's "The Duc De L'Omelette"

This passage was adapted from a short story called "The Duc De L'Omelette." You'll sometimes see adapted passages on the AP English Literature Exam. All it means is the passage was edited to make it appropriate for all high school students and to meet the test's length requirements. The actual Poe story uses a great deal of French, but keeping the French parts would give students who had studied French an unfair advantage.

The passage uses the kind of language and stylistic devices you'll see on prose passages on the AP English Literature Exam, but all the same it is a difficult one; they aren't all this weird. If it seemed long, don't panic—it is about one-third longer than the usual AP passage. (We wanted to use a long passage in this example to give you plenty to work with and to provide abundant fodder for our sample questions. Keep in mind that with a total of 55 questions, some passages on the test will have fewer than 15 questions.) If you see a passage of this length on the test, there will then be a shorter passage to compensate.

ANSWERS AND EXPLANATIONS TO THE QUESTIONS

We give detailed explanations to the 15 questions that followed the passage. Fifteen is the number of questions you should expect to see on a passage of this length. The passages and questions on our practice test are designed to imitate a real AP test. Here, we've chosen the questions with an eye toward teaching you our techniques, but even so, the mix of the types of questions is fairly representative of the questions you'll see on an AP passage.

We've broken the questions down into small groups in order to illustrate specific types of questions you're likely to see. Earlier we used the categories of general, detail, and fact. Now we'll break the questions down according to the subject matter. We don't want you to memorize the names of these types or spend a lot of time practicing identifying these types. There are no points for doing that. If you do remember them, great, but all we want is for you to become familiar with the most common types of questions on the test and to see how the same techniques, applied in slightly different ways, work on question after question.

GENERAL QUESTIONS

The first question is a general question. As you no doubt remember from Chapter 5, general questions ask about the whole passage, not some detail of the passage.

The question sets will often (but not always) start out with general questions. We've placed the questions on this passage in the order that lets us best explain them to you. Remember that when you actually take the test, you want to do the questions in the order given (if you felt comfortable with your comprehension of the passage). If you felt pretty lost, then you should put any general questions off until last, in the hope that working with the specific questions will give you more confidence about your comprehension of the passage and its main idea.

PRIMARY PURPOSE

The classic general question is the primary purpose question:

    1. The primary purpose of the passage is to portray

      (A) the characteristics of an exaggerated type
           through the figure of L'Omelette
      (B) a reassuringly humorous vision of hell through
           a narrative in which the Devil himself is
           bested
      (C) the evil consequences of excessive pride
      (D) the developing relationship between
           L'Omelette and the Devil
      (E) the pivotal change that occurs in L'Omelette
           through his encounter with the Devil

Here's How to Crack It

Understand the question by understanding the answer choices. What does "primary purpose" mean?

When you see a primary purpose question, it means you must look for an answer that covers the broad outline of the story. This advice goes for all general questions; it is what makes them general. Remember that you are looking for a choice that accurately describes some facet of the entire passage.

Now use the answer choices themselves to focus on exactly what primary purpose the test writers are looking for.

The question itself indicates that the primary purpose of the passage is to portray something. What is it portraying? Use POE. (After all, the passage was written by Edgar Allan Process of Elimination.)

Take choice (A). Does the whole passage deal with an exaggerated type? Well, the Duke is an exaggeration of something: This is a guy who takes time to approve of the decor in hell. (A) seems to be a reasonable summation of the whole passage. Leave it. Now take each of the remaining choices in turn.

Now to choice (B). The whole passage is not all about a "reassuringly humorous vision of hell." Each paragraph does not point out how harmless hell is. The humorous part is the Duke's taking it all more or less in stride. Eliminate (B).

Answer choice (C) talks about "the evil consequences of excessive pride." The passage is all about the Duke's excessive pride, but what are the consequences? There are none. The end of the story finds the Duke returning to his ill-prepared ortolan, which is right where he started, so you have to wonder if it's going to kill him all over again. Remember, *half bad equals all bad*. Eliminate (C).

And while you're at it, eliminate (D), unless you think that the whole passage is about the relationship between L'Omelette and the Devil. It isn't. The Devil doesn't have much personality in the story at all. He serves as a foil for the Duke, little else.

Eliminate (E) because the Duke doesn't change at all. When the point of a passage is to show a dramatic change, you'll know it. The whole passage will build to that change.

You're left with (A), the correct answer.

What phrase have we kept repeating? "The whole passage." General questions call for you to consider the whole passage, not one small piece of it.

Another thing we did was focus on key phrases in the answer choices. "What consequences?" we asked when we looked at choice (C). We didn't get taken in by the phrase "excessive pride." Learning how to focus on an answer choice is a skill that comes with practice. As you follow our explanations, your skill will improve. In fact, after that discussion, the next question should be a breeze.

OVERALL CHARACTER

AP passages tend to be focused on one thing. Here the focus is on the Duke. A passage might focus on the description of an event or a place, but the most common focus is on a character.

> 2. Which of the following best describes the Duke De L'Omelette?
>
>   (A) He is a typical eighteenth-century nobleman.
>   (B) He is a caricature of a snob.
>   (C) He is a man more wicked than the Devil.
>   (D) He is a man with perfect aesthetic judgment.
>   (E) He is a man transformed by his encounter with a power greater than his own.

Here's How to Crack It

The correct answer is (B), and finding it probably didn't cause you much trouble. About the only problem might have been the term *caricature*, which means "exaggerated portrait." It is a term you should know (it's in our glossary). Do you notice any similarities between the correct answer to question 1 and the correct answer here? You should. One speaks of an exaggerated portrayal of a type, and one speaks of a caricature of a snob. These are almost the same answer. The only difference is that the second question spells out what "type" is being caricatured: the snob. This is an example of Consistency of Answers. Both answers are consistent with the main idea, and naturally when answers are consistent with the main idea, they are consistent with each other. In this case the answers are extremely similar. When in doubt, make your answers agree with each other. If you thought the Duke was an exaggerated portrayal in question 1, why would he suddenly become a "typical eighteenth-century nobleman" in question 2? That would be inconsistent, so eliminate choice (A). The Duke is either exaggerated or he's typical, but he can't be both. Choice (C) is for students who read into things too much. The Duke wins the card game at the end. Does that mean he's more wicked than the Devil? No. Choice (D) is too strong. "Perfect?" De L'Omelette thinks his tastes are perfect, but does the story suggest that his tastes are perfect? No, only that they are extremely, almost comically, particular. Choice (E) isn't supported by the passage. You'd think the Duke would be transformed by his encounter with the Devil, but he isn't. At the end of the story you should have gotten the feeling that L'Omelette is going to go right back to his old ways.

Consistency of Answers doesn't just apply to general questions. It is just as helpful with detail questions.

DETAIL QUESTIONS

Detail questions (a.k.a. specific questions) make up the majority of questions on the Multiple-Choice section of the test. These are questions (or answer choices) that direct you to a specific place in the passage and ask about your comprehension of the details.

LINE-REFERENCE QUESTIONS

Most of the time (but not always), the detail questions give you a line number or a range of lines with which to work. We call these questions line-reference questions. For line-reference questions there are just two things you need to keep in mind:

- Go back to the passage and reread the lines in question. Also, read at least one full sentence before the line reference and one full sentence after the line reference. Keep in mind that a word or phrase you are being asked to define may not have the meaning you would infer from the wording of the question. It is important that you refer to the word in the context of the line.

- Keep the main idea in mind, and use Consistency of Answers whenever possible.

Try This One

3. In context, lines 29–38 serve to reinforce the reader's impression of the Duke's

    (A) quick temper
    (B) exquisite taste
    (C) sense of self-importance
    (D) accomplishments and social position
    (E) misunderstanding of his situation

Here's How to Crack It

This question calls for you to go back and read a fairly large range of lines—a whole paragraph. Go back and read it. Because the several lines referred to in this question make up a more or less self-contained paragraph, reading a full sentence before and after the reference doesn't make a big difference in getting the question right, but it doesn't hurt, either, and takes just an extra two or three seconds. Make it a habit to read a little above and below the lines referred to; it'll be worth a couple of points in the long run.

Essentially, the lines in question discuss the Duke's outrage at the Devil's command to disrobe.

If you misunderstand the question, you have a good chance of getting the answer wrong. The passage shows aspects of all the answer choices. The Duke does (A)—show a quick temper, does (B)—mention his tastes (by the way, the Duke's tastes are not so much exquisite as they are ostentatious), does (D)—mention his accomplishments and does (E)—misunderstand his situation. But the correct answer is (C).

Everything seems right, so what gives? The solution lies in understanding the question and how the question relates to the main idea. The question asks: What does the passage serve to reinforce?

Nearly everything in this very compact story serves to reinforce the central impression of the story—the Duke's outrageous sense of self-importance. He isn't merely a snob; he's completely besotted with his own fabulous self. The Duke thinks he's the apex of human intellectual and social development. In fact, choices (A), (B), (D), and (E) are all facets of the Duke's vanity. His anger is angered vanity. His tastes are flawless; they must be, thinks the Duke, because they're his. When the Duke mentions his work, the "Mazurkiad," you can almost see him puff up with the greatness of it all. Even his misunderstanding is an aspect of his vanity. The Duke doesn't quite comprehend his surroundings because he can't imagine being in a position to take orders from anyone. All these things revolve like planets around the Duke's sense that he's the center of the universe.

If you had a solid grasp on the central theme of the story, the Duke's self-love, you might have found this question easy. Choices (A), (B), (D), and (E) are details. (C) is the main thing. If you had trouble, all you had to do to get this question correct was muse, "Hmm, they all look possible, but which one is most consistent with the main idea?" Well, a snob thinks he's better than everyone; he thinks he's very important. Choice (C), sense of self-importance, is most in agreement with that.

Question 3 is an example of using the technique we call Consistency of Answers. Here's another:

4. The author's portrayal of the Duke De L'Omelette is best described as

   (A) a sympathetic portrait of a man with overly delicate sensibilities
   (B) a comically ironic treatment of an effete snob
   (C) a harshly condemnatory portrait of a bon vivant
   (D) an admiring portrait of a great artist
   (E) a farcical treatment of the very rich

Here's How to Crack It

Take each answer a word at a time, and remember, half bad equals all bad. If any part of the answer is wrong, don't hesitate to eliminate it. Yes, it's true that the portrait is of a man with delicate sensibilities (A), but is it sympathetic? Hardly. Get rid of it. You might not understand "effete" in choice (B), so hold on to it. "Harshly condemnatory" in choice (C), however, should look wrong. The Duke is harshly condemnatory of the servant who brings in his meal, but the passage itself does not disapprove of either of them. Half bad equals all bad, so eliminate it. Now look at choice (D): John Keats was a great artist, but the Duke? From these 12 lines you sure can't say that, so cross this one off too. On to choice (E). "Farcical?" Perhaps. But is this passage about the "very rich"? No, it's about the Duke De L'Omelette. Half bad equals all bad, so you're left with (B), even if you're not quite sure what it means. But here's a pop quiz: What technique tells you the answer must be (B)?

If you said Consistency of Answers, you're right.

Now, we aren't saying every single question uses Consistency of Answers. It should be one of the first things you think about when you approach a question, but there are definitely questions that focus on a detail in such a way that Consistency of Answers doesn't come into play. Here's an example:

5. Which of the following descriptions is an example
   of the narrator's irony?

   (A) "Unable to restrain his feelings, his Grace
       swallows an olive." (lines 9–10)
   (B) "I took thee, just now, from a rosewood coffin
       inlaid with ivory." (lines 40–41)
   (C) "The Duke knew it to be a ruby; but from it
       there poured a light so intense, so still, so
       terrible." (lines 64–66)
   (D) "And there, too!—there!—upon the ottoman!—
       who could he be?—he, the Deity—who sat
       as if carved in marble, and who smiled, with
       his pale countenance, bitterly?" (lines 89–92)
   (E) "His Grace was all care, all attention, his
       Majesty all confidence." (lines 104–105)

Here's How to Crack It

Notice that in this question the line references come in the answer choices. That's not uncommon. Properly speaking, this isn't a specific question or a general question or a literary-term question. The answer choices send you back to the passage to find a specific example of something that occurs throughout the whole passage: irony, which is a literary term. So this question is a mixed breed. But, you don't get points for putting questions in categories anyway; the important thing is to get the question right, efficiently.

The way to get this question right is to know what irony is. You can count on only a very few specific things showing up on the AP test. One of them is irony. Learn to recognize its many forms. We discuss irony in our glossary of literary terms for the AP English Literature and Composition Exam. (Yep, we're going to say that every time we mention irony.)

The correct answer is (A). You should have noticed the entire tone of the piece is somewhat ironic. Most of the passage is written with a deliberate undercurrent of meaning that changes the effect of the literal meaning of the lines. This, above all, is the hallmark of irony; there's more than meets the eye. But let's get back to choice (A). Why is it ironic? Let's take the statement "Unable to restrain his feelings, his Grace swallows an olive." At face value, the Duke's feelings became so strong, he had to swallow an olive. Now, in no way can swallowing an olive be the outcome of unrestrained feelings unless one has pretty unusual feelings, which is precisely the point. The Duke's anticipation of dinner having reached a fevered pitch, he buries his face in a pillow. The clock bangs out the long-awaited hour and unable to restrain himself, the Duke swallows an olive. One thing this shows is how fanatically seriously the Duke takes his meals. At the same time, the juxtaposition (to *juxtapose* means to place things side by side) of the Duke's unrestrained feelings and his act of swallowing an olive show something else: the Duke's biggest feelings are actually puny; the Duke's crescendo of passion is capped by swallowing an olive. That's the ironic part. The author in effect says, "In the Duke's opinion this is something big, but we can all see that it's rather small." When the literal meaning of a word or phrase implies its opposite, you're dealing with irony.

Hey, didn't we say that the whole piece was ironic? If that's true, what makes the other choices wrong? Well, okay, the whole piece *is* ironic. In effect, the passage tells us that the Duke thinks he's absolutely first-rate, but we can see that he's really quite laughable. However, for this question you must consider the answer choices in isolation. None of them, by itself, carries that double meaning which is so crucial to irony. (B) is a description of a coffin. (C) describes the ruby that illuminates the Devil's chamber in hell. (D) describes the moment the Duke realizes, at last, that the creature he's dealing with is truly the Devil himself. (E) simply describes the Duke's and the Devil's attitude as they begin the card game.

Okay, enough about irony, on to the next kind of question.

SINGLE PHRASE OR WORD QUESTIONS

AP questions will often ask you to look at a single word or phrase:

6. In lines 58–59, the word "appalling" suggests the
   Duke

   (A) has found the room's decorum unacceptable
   (B) has approbation for clouds
   (C) suffers from insomnia
   (D) finds the apartment extraordinary
   (E) suffers from a paroxysm

Here's How to Crack It

Yes, on the AP English Literature and Composition Exam a strong vocabulary helps a lot. If you did not know the meaning of *decorum* in choice (A), *approbation* in choice (B), *insomnia* in choice (C), and *paroxysm* in choice (E), you may have been at a loss. You could eliminate (A) because you know that the Duke found the apartment "superb," and you could have guessed that the referenced line has nothing to do with the Duke's inability to sleep (that he suffers from insomnia). Then you would be left with (B), (D), and (E).

Keep in mind that you are only to answer the question being asked of you, i.e., you are asked to examine the contextual meaning of one word. You can safely eliminate choice (E) from the list because in the sentence that contains the word "appalling," a reference to the Duke's suffering or discomfort is not implied. Even if you don't know what *paroxysm* means (a convulsion), you can use POE to get rid of this answer choice. Now look carefully at choice (B). In lines 58–59, "appalling" refers to the room, not the clouds. So you can eliminate this choice too, even if you don't know that *approbation* is approval. You're left with the correct answer, (D).

Questions 5 and 6 are two questions in a row that don't use Consistency of Answers. The streak's over. Here's a question that asks about a single phrase, but even so you can use Consistency of Answers to assist your POE.

7. Which of the following best implies the
   contextual meaning of the phrase "sacrificed his
   loyalty" (line 6) within the context of the story?

   (A) The Duke has fallen into disfavor with the King
        by outbidding him.
   (B) The Duke has betrayed his country.
   (C) The Duke has allowed his desire for the
        ottoman to override his deference to
        the King.
   (D) The Duke recognizes no one as more powerful
        than himself.
   (E) The Duke values the ottoman more greatly
        than his prestige.

Here's How to Crack It

When approaching this question, you should first go back and read around the citation. Because the citation is a fragment of a sentence, you should read at least a full sentence before and after the reference. (If you want to read more, by all means, do. The full sentence before and after is just a guideline. If it takes you a little more reading to get your bearings in the passage, that's fine.)

Now, use POE to get rid of what is obviously wrong. If you stay focused with what the phrase in question means it shouldn't be too hard to eliminate a few answers. Does "sacrificed his loyalty" mean the Duke has betrayed his country? That should sound a little too intense: We're talking about buying a couch here (an ottoman is a kind of couch). Eliminate choice (B). Does the Duke recognize no one as more powerful than himself? That may or may not be true, but how could you get that meaning from "sacrificed his loyalty?" Of course, if you try really hard you can talk yourself into anything. Don't talk yourself into answers. This is Process of Elimination. Eliminate (D).

Can you eliminate four answers? The best way is to ask yourself which answer choice is most in keeping with the Duke's character. Do you think the Duke cares about his prestige more than his couch? Of course he does. He would never sacrifice his prestige. L'Omelette thinks of appearances above all else. Eliminate choice (E). What about (A)? It is certainly reasonable that the Duke fell into disfavor with the King for outbidding him. But is this what "sacrificed his loyalty" means? No. And if you have any doubts, ask yourself what that interpretation has to do with the rest of the passage. Is the rest of the passage about the Duke's loss of favor with the King? No. That leaves (C), the correct answer. It is perfectly in keeping with the other answers and the rest of the passage: The Duke shows little deference to the Devil; why would he defer to the King?

The next two questions ask for your comprehension of a detail, but the questions center less around the meaning of the words than about what they indicate about the narrator.

QUESTION-COMPREHENSION QUESTIONS

Some questions are straightforward, some are vague, and a few are downright tricky. You need to pay close attention to the wording of questions, and when you see an unusual phrase, it's a good idea to ask yourself why the phrase is worded that way. On many questions, just understanding what the question is asking is half the battle.

8. In which of the following lines is the narrator most clearly articulating the Duke's thoughts?

 (A) "Ignoble souls!" (line 2)
 (B) "It is superfluous to say more:—" (lines 16–17)
 (C) "Having become satisfied of his identity, he took a bird's-eye view of his whereabouts." (lines 53–55)
 (D) "But the chances—the chances! True—desperate." (line 97)
 (E) "They play." (line 111)

Here's How to Crack It

This question has little to do with the main idea. Your first task is to understand the question. What is meant by "articulating the Duke's thoughts"? Well, try to put it in your own words. The question could be rewritten as: "When is the narrator speaking for the Duke?" There's nothing wrong with putting a question in your own words so as to understand it better. In fact it's a good idea, as long as you're careful and don't just drop off the parts of a question that confuse you. Reading the questions accurately is just as important as reading the passages. The passage isn't worth any points; the questions are.

Use POE. Eliminate what you can right away. When is the narrator clearly speaking as himself? Choices (B), (C), and (E) all seem like examples of straightforward narration, so eliminate them. That leaves just (A) and (D). In choice (A), the narrator responds to a question. He exclaims in a very Duke-like way, but the Duke hasn't even been introduced yet. How could the reader know it was the Duke speaking? The reader couldn't. All that's left is (D), the correct answer. In (D), the narrator steps into the Duke's mind for a moment to record his thoughts, and then just as quickly steps out with the words "but no more desperate than the Duke."

Question 9 picks up where question 8 left off; it is a similar, but more difficult variation on the same theme:

9. Which of the following lines implies a speaker other than the narrator?

   (A) "But who ever died of inept poetry?" (lines 1–2)
   (B) "That night the Duke was to sup alone." (line 4)
   (C) "The apartment was superb." (line 56)
   (D) "His majesty did not think, he shuffled." (lines 105–106)
   (E) "Had Alexander not been Alexander, he would have been Diogenes." (lines 118–119)

Here's How to Crack It

Read questions carefully. The difference between question 8 and question 9 is that question 8 asks which answer choice shows the Duke's speech (or thoughts), whereas question 9 wants to know which implies a speaker other than the narrator. Question 9 is tougher. If your approach to question 9 got stuck somewhere back on question 8 and you were still looking for the narrator to speak the Duke's thoughts (or perhaps the Devil's), you might have easily gotten this question wrong.

As always, use POE. Clearly, choices (B), (C), (D), and (E) are spoken by the narrator. What about (A)? Well, (A) is spoken by the narrator as well, but it *implies* another speaker, someone who asks the question, "Who ever died of poor poetry?" The narrator, speaking as himself, responds to that question: "Ignoble souls!" If the structure of this interchange wasn't clear to you, here's an explanation: "Who ever died of poor poetry?" is a rhetorical question (a question to which the answer is obvious—of course, most people would say, no one has ever been killed by a bad poem). That's where the narrator jumps in and says, "Oh ho, you think the answer to that question is so very obvious but that's because your souls have no finer qualities; it may seem unbelievable to you but some very delicate spirits have died of immaterial things like bad poetry. L'Omelette, for example, died of a badly prepared meal." All that (and a little more) is contained in the first paragraph of the passage. This paragraph is a good example of how gifted writers make every word count.

Ready for one more detail question? It's a good example of how weird things can get on the AP test. It asks about the meaning of a piece of the passage that isn't there.

10. Which of the following best describes the situation in lines 19–22 and the events that came immediately *before* it?

    (A) The Duke has just noticed the Devil and laughs at him. The Devil returns the laugh, but quietly because he feels insulted.

    (B) The Duke has just heard the Devil explain the tortures that lie in store for him. He believes the Devil is joking and laughs. The Devil mocks his laughter, implying that it is no joke.

    (C) The Duke and the Devil have been talking, but the exact topic has purposefully been left vague.

    (D) The Duke has heard the Devil's plans for him and laughs defiantly at the Devil. The Devil puns on the Duke's use of the word "Ha!" by saying "He!" By doing so, the devil indicates "He," that is the Duke, will be punished for his sins.

    (E) The Duke, believing he speaks with a lowly servant, laughs at the threats the Devil has made. The Devil laughs in order to play along with the Duke and draw out the Duke's eventual humiliation.

Here's How to Crack It

Expect the unexpected at least once or twice on the test. Question 10 is not an easy question. Use POE. Remember to read at least one sentence before and one sentence after the citation. The key to this question is making sense of the line immediately following the line reference: "'Why surely you're not serious,' retorted De L'Omelette." Which interpretations make that line a non sequitur? (A *non sequitur* is a statement that doesn't follow from what came before. For example, Q: What time is it? A: Yes.) You see, somehow, the Duke understands that the Devil is serious. It's just that he still can't believe it. That's why he asks this question. If the Devil were merely acting offended (or making some bizarre pun using the word *he*) then the Duke would have no reason to respond as he does. If you apply this thought, you'll see that you can eliminate (A), (C), (D), and (E). And that leaves (B), the correct answer. The Devil's mocking laughter lets the Duke know that, yes, the Devil is serious. Notice that this answer is the simplest explanation.

Staying simple doesn't just apply to poetry. Many students get into trouble when reading the answer choices. They think about the wrong answers so much they get led into outer space. This comes from looking at every answer choice as though it could be correct. Four out of the five answer choices are wrong. At least one answer choice is usually wildly wrong. If something looks nuts, don't spend five minutes trying to figure it out. If it looks nuts, it is.

STYLE, STRUCTURE, AND TONE QUESTIONS

Style, structure, and tone questions are related.

Style questions will test your understanding of the kinds of sentences that the passage contains. Are they simple or complex? Do they contain modifying clauses? Do the sentences interpret or do they describe? Are they loose or periodic (see the glossary)?

Structure questions ask about how the passage is put together. Does it begin with a general statement and then support that statement with examples? Does it describe an isolated incident and make a generalization from it? Does it begin humorously but end seriously? Is there a sudden shift in emphasis in the middle?

Tone questions ask for your understanding of the underlying emotion of the passage, about how the passage feels. Is the narrator angry? Does the narration seem to describe the scene as a camera would record it, without judgment, or does the narration seem to describe with passion, the emotions of the characters? By far the most critical aspect of tone is the choice of words the author uses, and what the author conveys, but unless you are sensitive to structure and style you can easily identify the tone incorrectly. Diction, structure, and style in part produce the tone.

Here's a question that relies on your understanding of all three elements:

> 11. Which of the following reinforces the effect of the passage most strongly?
>
>   (A) Light-hearted situations narrated with deep seriousness
>   (B) Humorous irony in the introduction, contrasted with serious reflection in the conclusion
>   (C) Calculated objectivity offset by occasional interjections of subjective emotion
>   (D) Underlying contempt partially concealed by objectivity.
>   (E) First-person outbursts of effusive emotion in an otherwise third-person narration

Here's How to Crack It

Again, from the question alone you can't know exactly what the question asks. That's fine. Look over the answer choices. You can see that they refer to the tone, style, and structure of the passage. ETS likes to throw these mixtures at you. The way to work on this kind of question is to break the answer choices into bite-size parts, then check the passage to see if you can find an example of that part. For example, are there light-hearted situations (A)? Well, going to hell isn't exactly light-hearted. (So the choice is already wrong, but let's keep going.) Are the situations narrated with deep seriousness? No, not exactly. Narrated with a straight face perhaps, but not deeply serious. The idea is to break the choices into pieces you can use. Remember, half bad equals all bad.

The correct answer is (E). As always, use POE and look at the whole passage. Make your initial eliminations. Choice (A) is wrong because the situations are not so much light-hearted as absurd, and the narrator is not deeply serious, but nearly as bizarre and out of control as the Duke. Choice (B) isn't worth a second look unless you really think cheating the Devil at cards is deadly serious. Choice (D) should be unappealing as well. What "contempt"? What "objectivity"? Eliminate it.

This leaves (E) and (C). Take each answer choice and go back to the passage. Do you see any "calculated objectivity?" Not really; almost every sentence is loaded with one of the Duke's preposterous emotions. Almost everything comes to us through a filter of the Duke's impressions, especially in the longer sentences. It isn't accurate to call the subjective (first-person element) "occasional." That is enough to eliminate (C), leaving you with just one remaining choice, (E). For safety's sake you should now examine it. "Outbursts of effusive emotion"? Well, there are all those exclamation points all over the place. As a matter of fact, half the time the author seems to be shouting. The story is told in the third person, yet much of the time the Duke's persona, his voice, or the attitude behind his voice seems to be speaking. (E) is correct.

If any of the terms we've used in this explanation—*first person*, *third person*, *subjectivity*—gave you trouble, you should refer to their definitions in the glossary.

Attitude questions are just like tone questions; they ask about the underlying emotional content of the passage:

12. The narrator's attitude toward the Duke can be best described as

    (A) complete objectivity
    (B) ambiguous pity
    (C) slight distaste
    (D) bemused confusion
    (E) satiric glee

Here's How to Crack It

The correct answer is (E). POE, as usual, helps a great deal. On tone questions, ETS often has a couple of answers that you can dismiss without a second glance. There's no way you could call the passage an example of (A), complete objectivity; it's much too weird. Doesn't the whole passage feel high-strung, as though old Edgar A. Poe had a few too many cups of coffee on top of whatever else he was drinking that day? That feeling never goes with objectivity. Choice (B), pity, is just off the wall. Choice (C) might have been appealing because it didn't sound too extreme. In general, mild is better than extreme on tone questions, but unfortunately, "slight distaste" is wrong; there's no evidence that the narrator feels a slight distaste for the Duke. Remember, you wanted to pick what the *narrator* feels. You might have felt slight distaste, but the question didn't ask how you felt. Speaking of how you felt, choice (D) is a type of answer ETS has been known to use occasionally. Students, especially when they're struggling, are drawn to answers that suggest their own mental state. It's amazing, but students really do pick words like *confused*, *depressed*, *anxious*, and *fearful* on tests when it doesn't make sense to do so. The answer feels right, not because it's correct but because it's how the student feels taking a test. There's no evidence in the story that the narrator is confused or doesn't understand the Duke; in fact, he seems to understand the Duke a little too perfectly.

This brings up (E), the correct answer. "Glee" may seem a bit strong, but it fits. The narrator tells the story with energy, enthusiasm, and a completely unabashed use of exclamation points—that's a tip-off right there. Good writers, and you'll see nothing but very good writers on the AP test, don't overuse exclamation points. (The great Irish novelist James Joyce called them, derisively, "shriek marks.") Poe doesn't overuse them here, but it could easily seem like it. Poe uses exclamation points because, if for the Duke a badly prepared bird is upsetting enough to kill him, the Duke's life must be filled with exclamation points. This is one of the elements (and there are many) which make the passage satiric. *Satire* is an important concept for the AP test. When a passage pokes fun at an exaggeratedly foolish type (in this case, the type of arrogant man who considers himself supreme in all things), you can be sure it's satire (yes, we do cover the concept in the glossary). The gleefulness stems from the evident enjoyment Poe takes in describing the Duke's peculiar foolishness. Of course Poe has the Duke win in the end, which makes sense because Poe himself had a lot of the Duke in him.

I, II, III QUESTIONS

Question 13 tests whether you've noticed certain structural and stylistic devices in the passage. The question uses a form you're sure to see on the test; it's one of ETS's favorites.

13. The passage contains

    I. abrupt shifts in tense
    II. an abrupt shift in place
    III. abrupt shifts in emotional state

    (A) I only
    (B) I and II only
    (C) I and III only
    (D) II and III only
    (E) I, II, and III

Here's How to Crack It

If you've taken an ETS test before, you've seen I, II, III questions. Most students see them and groan. Somehow they look like more work. It's as if three questions are worth one measly point. The truth is you should think of them as questions with just three answer choices. Take each point one at a time, and look to the passage to see if what you want is there. If you know where to look, this question is a snap.

Let's start with point II. (Why point II? It's the easiest of the three to see, and why not? You don't have to examine the I, II, III points in order.) When the Duke dies "in a paroxysm of disgust" (lines 17–18) there is an abrupt change of place—to hell. So eliminate any answer that doesn't contain II—choices (A) and (C).

Now to point I. Did you also notice that there is an abrupt change of tense at that same line about "a paroxysm of disgust"? The change from the Duke's bedroom to hell is so striking that many students overlook the fact that the tense of the story changes. The second paragraph is in the present tense. It changes when the narrator says, "it *is* superfluous to say more—the Duke expir*ed* in a paroxysm of disgust." That's the simple past and the simple present in one sentence; your English teacher would hang you for it! (And the tense changes back to the present for one paragraph at the end when L'Omelette and the Devil play cards. It's easy to overlook.) Okay, so that means you can eliminate anything that doesn't contain point I—choice (D). You're already down to just two answer choices—(B) and (E).

All that's left is point III. Abrupt shifts in emotional state. You probably knew they happened. It felt like they happened, but where exactly? Was it really abrupt? Hey, don't overthink and worry yourself to death. There are abrupt shifts in emotional state. In the middle of the story the Duke goes from admiring the Devil's decor to being stricken with terror when he realizes that he is in fact dealing with Satan, to getting control of himself again and challenging the Devil to cards, all in the space of about 20 lines. That qualifies as abrupt. Points, I, II, and III, are all examples contained in the passage, so they must be in the answer choice. The correct answer is (E).

LITERARY TERM QUESTIONS

14. The phrase, "as if carved in marble" (line 91), is an example of

    (A) an apostrophe
    (B) irony
    (C) lyricism
    (D) a metaphor
    (E) a simile

Here's How to Crack It

This is an absolutely straightforward literary terms question. You are sure to see a few questions like it on the test you take. Of course you should use POE, but the best solution for literary term questions is to know the terms. That's why we've included our glossary of terms. Second, as we mentioned earlier, there are just a few things you can be sure will make an appearance somewhere on the test. Among those things are the terms *simile* and *metaphor*.

The correct answer here is (E). The phrase is a simile. A comparison that uses *like* or *as* is a simile. Even if these terms don't show up on your test as the right answers to a question (and chances are that's exactly how they will show up), at the very least they'll show up as answers you'll be able to eliminate. If you aren't aware that the phrase in question is a simile, eliminate what you can and take your best guess. Believe it or not, all the terms in the question are defined in our glossary.

Okay, one more question.

GRAMMAR QUESTIONS

15. Grammatically, the phrase, "Were one not already
    the Duke De L'Omelette" (lines 120–121),
    establishes the

    (A) simple past tense
    (B) past imperfect tense
    (C) present conditional tense
    (D) subjunctive mood
    (E) simple present tense

The correct answer is (D). When a sentence begins with *were*, it's subjunctive, count on it. What's a *mood*? Well, to those who make it their business to know (language scholars, mostly), *mood* refers to what a verb form indicates besides time. In the sentence "Go away!" *go* isn't just in the present tense. It expresses command. Thus, it is in the imperative mood. In "Jack laughs," *laughs* indicates a state of being. It is in the indicative mood. *Indicative*, *imperative*, and *subjunctive* are the principle moods of English. The use of the subjunctive and its forms have faded from our language, which is why starting a sentence with the word *were* might sound a little strange. It is grammatically correct English, however.

Unless you intend to teach Latin, or go to graduate school in linguistics, mood isn't a term you'll need to know precisely; for your purposes on the test, and probably for the rest of your life, you can think of a mood as not exactly a verb tense, but close.

There may be a few grammar questions on the AP test you take. Use POE and take your best shot. In general, studying specific points in English grammar for the sake of a few points on the Multiple-Choice section is not worth the time. Studying grammar for other reasons is by no means a waste of time. A working command of English grammar is essential for effective writing. We'll have more to say about grammar in the next chapter, when we deal with a sample poetry passage and questions.

If you're rusty on your grammatical terms, Chapter 5 contains definitions with examples of the basic terms you need to know, such as *direct object*, *indirect object*, *phrase*, and *clause*.

A FEW LAST WORDS (ALMOST)

If you worked through the passage as we instructed, you just learned a great deal about how to take the multiple-choice questions on the AP English Literature and Composition Exam. It probably took close to five times longer here than working on a real passage would, but that's to be expected—you're learning. This does bring up an important point though: time. We've taken you through the passage and familiarized you with some typical questions so that when you're on your own you can work efficiently and accurately, answering all the questions in about 15 minutes.

But what if it doesn't work that way? Let's say you had reasoned that this passage was the hardest on the test and decided to do it last. By the time you got to it, you had only seven minutes left. Seven minutes to do that passage! You would use up most of that time just reading it. Should you give up?—No! This is where all the study you've put into the questions can really pay off. Check out the Art of the Seven-Minute Passage. Enjoy!

THE ART OF THE SEVEN-MINUTE PASSAGE

When you hit the last passage on the test, check your time. If you have seven minutes or fewer left, you have to change your strategy. You don't have enough time to do the passage the normal way. It's time for emergency measures. What is the worst thing to do in an emergency? Panic. Don't. You'll want to, but don't. The best defense against panic is preparation. Know exactly what you're going to do. Here it is:

- Don't read the passage. Not even a little. Just *don't* do it.

- Go straight to the questions.

- Answer the questions in the following order:

    1. **Answer any literary term or grammar questions.** You barely need the passage at all for these questions. If you know the point at issue you'll just snap up a point. Otherwise apply as much POE as you can and guess.
    2. **Go to any question that asks for the meaning of a single word or phrase.** These questions always include a line reference. Go to the passage and read a sentence before and after the reference. Answer the question.
    3. **Go to any other question that gives you a line reference in the question.** (Not line-reference answer choices, but questions.) Read the reference and answer the question.
    4. **Go to any question on tone or attitude.** By this time, you've read quite a bit of the passage just by answering questions. You've read enough to be able to make a good guess about where the author's coming from.
    5. **Go to any questions that have line references in the answer choices.** Answer them all.
    6. **Do whatever is left over**—character questions, primary purpose questions, weird questions, etc. If you need to, read some of the passage to get them. Go ahead and read. Keep working until the proctor tells you to put down your pencil.
    7. **Put down your pencil.** Take a deep breath. You did great.

That's the Art of the Seven-Minute Passage. It works in six, five, four, three, two, or one minute too; with less time, you don't get as far down the list, that's all.

What If I Have Seven Minutes and Three Seconds Left?

Seven minutes or fewer is a good rough guideline for when to use the Don't Read the Passage technique. Your pace on multiple-choice passages should be about 15 minutes a passage. If you have an awkward amount of time left for the last passage—that is, somewhere between seven and fifteen minutes—you'll have to decide which approach to use. You have two choices. The first is to just read and work faster, to step on the gas big-time. The other choice is to go straight to the questions, that is, to use the Art of the Seven-Minute Passage technique. It's your call. Seven minutes and three seconds (or 30 seconds etc.), go straight to the questions. With ten minutes left you should probably try to read the passage fast but then do the questions in the seven-minute order. At, say, 14 minutes, you should just work normally, but keep in mind that you don't have any time to waste worrying about those silly things students worry about, like whether you've guessed too many (C)'s, or what the occult meaning of the pattern of dots you've made is.

SUMMARY

- When a question seems unclear, the answer choices can help you make sense of it.

- On every general question, you are looking for a choice that accurately describes some facet of the entire passage.

- Learn to focus on key phrases in the answer choices in order to eliminate using the half bad equals all bad technique.

- Use Consistency of Answers.

- For line-reference questions:
  - Keep the main idea in mind, and use Consistency of Answers whenever possible.
  - Go back to the passage and reread the lines in question, as well as one full sentence before and after the line reference.

- Pay close attention to the wording of questions. Put questions in your own words if that makes things easier for you. Be careful not to just ignore confusing parts, though.

- Expect a weird question or two. ETS likes to get creative on the AP English Literature and Composition Exam. We can't prepare you for everything, just almost everything.

- Don't be bummed out by I, II, III questions. POE works wonderfully on them.

- This is a public service announcement: Our glossary of terms has many valuable definitions and will get you some points.

- Grammar questions aren't worth studying for unless you're really weak on the basic terms.

THE ART OF THE SEVEN-MINUTE PASSAGE

- When you get to the last passage, check your time.

- If you have seven minutes or fewer left use the Seven Minute Passage technique.
  - Don't read the passage.
  - Answer the questions going from the questions that require no knowledge of the passage to those that require a complete knowledge.

- If you're left with between seven and 15 minutes for the last passage, it's your call.

The Poetry Passage and Questions

INTRODUCTION

Answering multiple-choice questions about poetry passages involves many of the same principles as does answering questions about prose. There are some differences, however.

First, the poetry passages tend to contain more questions that rely on knowledge than the prose passages do. You will certainly see a question or two on the literary devices (personification, metaphor, etc.) in the poem. You might see a question about the way a line scans, or what the rhyme scheme is called, but these are nothing to worry about: Recent tests have not included a single question on scansion or the names of classical poetic forms. ETS does, however, like to use poetry for its questions about grammar because poets use the kind of tangled syntax that makes for challenging grammar questions.

Second, the poetry you'll see on the AP test tends to make for harder reading than the prose passages do. ETS has a style of poetry it likes to select for the AP test. In order to write questions properly, ETS is limited in the kind of material it can use. As a result, you won't see poems that stretch language and meaning to its limits or poems that are open to such a variety of interpretations that asking meaningful multiple-choice questions about them is too difficult. Nor will you see beautiful and elegant but direct and simple poems: ETS wouldn't have anything to write questions about. ETS likes poems of 30 to 70 lines that use difficult language to make a precise point. The poem below and the questions that follow should give you a good idea of what to expect on the test. This is an excellent place to practice what you've learned in previous chapters. Use all the techniques we've taught you:

- Read the poem as prose.

- Focus on the main idea.

- When answering the questions, use POE and Consistency of Answers.

- Be sure to read before and after line references.

SAMPLE POETRY PASSAGE AND QUESTIONS
ANDREW MARVELL'S "ON A DROP OF DEW"

Read the following poem carefully and choose answers to the questions that follow.

> See how the orient[1] dew,
> Shed from the bosom of the morn
>   Into the blowing[2] roses,
>
> *Line* Yet careless of its mansion new,
> (5) For the clear region where 'twas born
>   Round in itself incloses:
>   And in its little globe's extent,
> Frames as it can its native element.
>   How it the purple flow'r does slight,
> (10)   Scarce touching where it lies,
> But gazing back upon the skies,
>   Shines with a mournful light,
>   Like its own tear,
> Because so long divided from the sphere.
> (15)   Restless it rolls and unsecure,
>   Trembling lest it grow impure,
> Till the warm sun pity its pain,
> And to the skies exhale it back again.
>   So the soul, that drop, that ray
> (20) Of the clear fountain of eternal day,
> Could it within the human flow'r be seen,
>   Remembering still its former height,
>   Shuns the sweet leaves and blossoms
> green,
> (25)   And recollecting its own light,
> Does, in its pure and circling thoughts, express
> The greater heaven in an heaven less.

[1] pearly, sparkling
[2] blooming

In how coy[3] a figure wound,
Every way it turns away:
(30)   So the world excluding round,
yet receiving in the day,
Dark beneath, but bright above,
Here disdaining, there in love.
How loose and easy hence to go,
(35)   How girt and ready to ascend,
Moving but on a point below,
It all about does upwards bend.
Such did the manna's sacred dew distill,
White and entire, though congealed and chill,
(40) Congealed on earth: but does, dissolving, run
Into the glories of th' almighty sun.

[3] modest

1. The overall content of the poem can best be described by which statement?

   (A) The characteristics of a drop of dew are related to those of the human soul.
   (B) The life cycle of a drop of dew is contemplated.
   (C) The human soul is shown to be a drop of dew.
   (D) The physical characteristics of a drop of dew are analyzed.
   (E) The poet offers a mystical vision of a drop of dew as a spiritual entity that has all the qualities of the human soul.

2. The poem contains

   I. A biblical allusion
   II. An extended metaphor
   III. An evocation of spiritual longing

   (A) I only
   (B) II only
   (C) III only
   (D) I and II only
   (E) I, II, and III

3. In context, "careless of its mansion new" (line 4) most nearly means

   (A) the dew drop does not understand the value of its beautiful surroundings

   (B) the dew drop does not assist the flower in any way

   (C) the dew drop is unconcerned with its beautiful surroundings

   (D) the human soul does not value the body

   (E) the human soul does not take part in the care of the body

4. The speaker's metaphor for the human body is

   (A) "the orient dew" (line 1)

   (B) "the sphere" (line 14)

   (C) "the clear fountain" (line 20)

   (D) "the sweet leaves and blossoms green" (lines 23–24)

   (E) "th' almighty sun" (line 41)

5. Which of the following is the antecedent of "its" in "Does, in its pure and circling thoughts, express" (line 26)?

   (A) "soul" (line 19)

   (B) "day" (line 20)

   (C) "flow'r" (line 21)

   (D) "height" (line 22)

   (E) "leaves" (line 23)

6. All of the following aspects of the dew drop are emphasized in the poem EXCEPT

   (A) its disregard for the physical world

   (B) its desire to regain the heavens

   (C) its purity

   (D) its will to live

   (E) its roundness

7. Lines 9–14 suggest the drop of dew is

   (A) frightened of death

   (B) full of unhappy longing

   (C) envious of the rose's vitality

   (D) part of a larger body of water in the sky

   (E) uncertain of the future

8. Lines 19–27 make explicit

   (A) the analogy between the drop of dew and the soul

   (B) the actual differences between the drop of dew and the soul

   (C) the true nature of the drop of dew

   (D) the soul's need for the body

   (E) the soul's thoughts

9. Each of the following pairs of phrases refers to the same action, object, or concept EXCEPT

(A) "mansion new" (line 4)…"purple flow'r" (line 9)
(B) "globe's extent" (line 7)…"the sphere" (line 14)
(C) "that drop" (line 19)…"that ray" (line 19)
(D) "exhale" (line 18)…"dissolving" (line 40)
(E) "Every way it turns away" (line 29)…"It all about does upwards bend" (line 37)

10. Which of the following best paraphrases the meaning in context of "So the world excluding round,/ yet receiving in the day" (lines 30–31)?

(A) Although the dew drop evaporates in the sun, it arrives anew each day.
(B) The world evaporates the drop of dew when it receives the light of the sun.
(C) The dew drop is impervious to everything but time.
(D) Although the dew drop and the soul shut out the material world, they let in the light of heaven.
(E) The only thing that matters to the dew drop is light.

11. In line 41 the sun is symbolic of

(A) fire
(B) rebirth
(C) the soul
(D) God
(E) time

12. Which of the following sets of adjectives is best suited to describing the poem's tone?

(A) mysterious, moody, and spiritual
(B) pious, proper, and academic
(C) intricate, delicate, and worshipful
(D) witty, clever, and ironic
(E) straightforward, impassioned, and sincere

13. In the final four lines of the poem the poet suggest that

(A) the dew drop will ultimately be destroyed by the sun
(B) the cycle of life and death is continual
(C) the dew drop will return to earth in the form of "manna"
(D) souls as pure as a drop of dew will ascend to heaven
(E) death brings spiritual unity with God

14. Which of the following adjectives is least important to the poem's theme?

   (A) "blowing" (line 3)
   (B) "clear" (line 20)
   (C) "pure" (line 26)
   (D) "bright" (line 32)
   (E) "loose" (line 34)

ABOUT ANDREW MARVELL'S "ON A DROP OF DEW"

This poem is a challenging one, but absolutely typical of what you will find on the AP test. Marvell (1621–1678) was one of the metaphysical poets (check your overview of literary movements), and the previous poem is an excellent example of this school of poetry's verse. The metaphysical poets were a loosely connected group of seventeenth-century poets who fashioned a type of elaborately clever, often witty verse that has a decidedly intellectual twist to it. The metaphysical poets are noted for taking a comparison—for example, "a drop of dew is like the soul"—and developing it over dozens of lines. Lots of metaphysical poetry appears on the Multiple-Choice section; this is not because metaphysical poetry is necessarily great, but because unlike most poetry, it lends itself well to multiple-choice questions. So, reading any of the metaphysicals' poetry is great practice for the AP test. Others of the metaphysical school include John Donne, George Herbert, Thomas Carew, Abraham Cowley, and Richard Crashaw.

ANSWERS AND EXPLANATIONS TO THE QUESTIONS

1. The overall content of the poem can best be described by which statement?

   (A) The characteristics of a drop of dew are related to those of the human soul.
   (B) The life cycle of a drop of dew is contemplated.
   (C) The human soul is shown to be a drop of dew.
   (D) The physical characteristics of a drop of dew are analyzed.
   (E) The poet offers a mystical vision of a drop of dew as a spiritual entity that has all the qualities of the human soul.

Here's How to Crack It

This is a main-idea question. Remember, you could have left it alone and come back to it if you hadn't found the main idea yet. Chances are you didn't have too much trouble. If you had any trouble eliminating choices, it was probably with choice (C). Does the poet really show that the human soul is a drop of dew? No. Marvell uses a drop of dew to speak about the human soul, but he isn't suggesting that a person's inner spirit is actually composed of condensed water. In fact, in the poem the drop of dew isn't so much a water droplet as it is a receptacle for light. This point becomes important in later questions. If choice (D) threw you, then you weren't paying attention to the word *physical*. You should have asked yourself, "Wait a minute, this dew drop trembles with fear at the thought of becoming impure: Can I call that a physical analysis?" Marvell's drop of dew is a being with a personality and desires; all of these things are studied, not just its physical characteristics. The correct answer is (A).

2. The poem contains

    I. A biblical allusion
    II. An extended metaphor
    III. An evocation of spiritual longing

(A) I only
(B) II only
(C) III only
(D) I and II only
(E) I, II, and III

Here's How to Crack It

Question 2 is one of the notorious I, II, III questions. Remember to use POE and work from the easiest point to the hardest. You should see that item II is found in the passage: The dew drop is an extended metaphor for the human soul. An extended metaphor is also known as a **conceit**, and they appear frequently in metaphysical poems. You can eliminate choices (A) and (C); they don't include item II.

Item III might send you back to the poem, where lines 11–13 ("But gazing back upon the skies,/ Shines with a mournful light,/ Like its own tear") should convince you that item III is a keeper. Eliminate choices (B) and (D). You're finished.

Only (E) is left. If you're curious about item I, the biblical allusion is the word *manna*, which refers to a kind of bread that came to the starving Israelites from out of heaven. If you had any doubts about item I (or item III) you might have reasoned that both points are consistent with the main idea and should be kept. The correct answer is (E).

3. In context, "careless of its mansion new" (line 4) most nearly means

(A) the dew drop does not understand the value of its beautiful surroundings
(B) the dew drop does not assist the flower in any way
(C) the dew drop is unconcerned with its beautiful surroundings
(D) the human soul does not value the body
(E) the human soul does not take part in the care of the body

Here's How to Crack It

Question 3 is a straightforward line-reference question. After reading around the line reference, you can easily eliminate choices (D) and (E). The line in question discusses only the dew drop upon a rose petal. It does not refer to the human soul. Of the remaining choices, (A) and (B) both imply that in context, "careless" means that the dew drop does not take care of the rose, which is simply a misreading. Chances are you didn't have much trouble on this question. The correct answer is (C).

4. The speaker's metaphor for the human body is

(A) "the orient dew" (line 1)
(B) "the sphere" (line 14)
(C) "the clear fountain" (line 20)
(D) "the sweet leaves and blossoms green" (lines 23–24)
(E) "th' almighty sun" (line 41)

Here's How to Crack It

To answer this question you must either trace Marvell's involved metaphor, noting that in lines 19–21 he describes the soul as being housed within the "human flow'r," or, use POE. All four correct answers refer to either a spiritual entity (the dew) or its source (the sphere, fountain, and sun) and so can be eliminated. The correct answer is (D).

> 5. Which of the following is the antecedent of "its" in
>   "Does, in its pure and circling thoughts, express"
>   (line 26)?
>
>   (A) "soul" (line 19)
>   (B) "day" (line 20)
>   (C) "flow'r" (line 21)
>   (D) "height" (line 22)
>   (E) "leaves" (line 23)

Here's How to Crack It

Question 5 is a typical grammar question. It hinges on your knowing the term **antecedent**. That term, and other grammatical terms you need for the test, can be found in the glossary. By asking for the antecedent, the question is simply asking what the word *its* stands for in the given phrase. Analyzed grammatically, the only correct usage (and ETS will only ask about correct usage) is the soul. You might also have reasoned, "For which of the choices would it make sense to have 'pure and circling thoughts'?" Only choice (A) makes sense. The correct answer is (A).

> 6. All of the following aspects of the dew drop are
>   emphasized in the poem EXCEPT
>
>   (A) its disregard for the physical world
>   (B) its desire to regain the heavens
>   (C) its purity
>   (D) its will to live
>   (E) its roundness

Here's How to Crack It

Question 6 is an EXCEPT question. An excellent way to proceed is to disregard the EXCEPT; cross EXCEPT out. This strategy works on NOT and LEAST questions as well.

Eliminate any choice that fits the remaining question: All of the following aspects of the drop of dew are emphasized in the poem.

To do this you *must* refer back to the passage. Remember: Never work from memory! "Careless of its mansion new" lets you eliminate (A). "Like its own tear/ Because so long divided from the sphere" takes care of (B). "Trembling lest it grows impure" lets you eliminate (C). The dew drop's roundness is emphasized in several places; choice (E) was easy to eliminate. This leaves only choice (D). The correct answer is (D).

> 7. Lines 9–14 suggest the drop of dew is
>
>   (A) frightened of death
>   (B) full of unhappy longing
>   (C) envious of the rose's vitality
>   (D) part of a larger body of water in the sky
>   (E) uncertain of the future

Here's How to Crack It

Question 7 is a line-reference question that tests your comprehension of a set of lines. It shouldn't have posed too many difficulties. If you had trouble with this question you should practice reading poetry for comprehension. You can eliminate choices (C) and (E) easily: They have nothing to do with the poem. The other choices can almost be justified from the poem, but *almost* means *wrong*. Choice (A) could be eliminated because of the word *frightened*. The drop of dew is perhaps frightened of earthly life (remember, it "trembles" at the thought of becoming "impure"), but as a metaphor for the soul, it is not afraid of death. Certainly no such statement can be found in the poem. Choice (D) is incorrect because Marvell treats the dew drop not only as water, but as a container of light and as a metaphor for the soul. For Marvell the drop comes from the sky, not a body of water in the sky. The correct answer is (B).

8. Lines 19–27 make explicit

　　(A) the analogy between the drop of dew and the
　　　　　soul
　　(B) the actual differences between the drop of dew
　　　　　and the soul
　　(C) the true nature of the drop of dew
　　(D) the soul's need for the body
　　(E) the soul's thoughts

Here's How to Crack It

The key here is to understand the question. When something is made explicit, it is stated or spelled out. *Explicit* is the opposite of *implicit*. Your task is to see what lines 19–27 show clearly. Using POE, you should eliminate choice (C) immediately; it only talks about the drop of dew; the lines in question refer primarily to the human soul. Choice (E) is a trap answer. The lines in question do refer to the soul's thoughts, but they do not spell them out; the thoughts are not made explicit. Choice (D) is similarly wrong: The drop of dew's "true nature" is not the subject of these lines; only the likeness of the drop of dew and the soul is. Choice (B) talks about differences between the soul and the drop of dew. This answer choice is the exact opposite of the lines' intent. They discuss the similarities of the drop and the soul. In fact, they make the analogy between the drop of dew and the soul explicit—hence (A) is the correct answer.

9. Each of the following pairs of phrases refers to the
　　same action, object, or concept EXCEPT

　　(A) "mansion new" (line 4)…"purple flow'r" (line 9)
　　(B) "globe's extent" (line 7)…"the sphere"
　　　　　(line 14)
　　(C) "that drop" (line 19)…"that ray" (line 19)
　　(D) "exhale" (line 18)…"dissolving" (line 40)
　　(E) "Every way it turns away" (line 29)…"It all
　　　　　about does upward bend" (line 37)

Here's How to Crack It

This is another EXCEPT question. They're common on the AP English Literature Exam. Cross out EXCEPT and eliminate answers that satisfy the remaining statement: Each of the following pairs of phrases refers to the same action, object, or concept. Use POE. In (A), "mansion new" and "purple flow'r" both refer to the rose the drop of dew perches on. Eliminate it. In (C), "that drop" and "that ray" seem to refer to different things, but both in fact refer to the soul—so eliminate (C). In (D), "exhale" and "dissolving" both refer to the process by which the drop of dew vanishes (evaporation, if you want to be scientific about it). In (B), "globe's extent" and "sphere" seem to both refer to the dew drop, but in fact, the sphere refers to the skies above—the "heavenly sphere." Thus, (B) is the correct answer.

Nit-picking? Maybe, but this question is an excellent example of the kind of careful reading you'll be called upon to do on the actual test.

10. Which of the following best paraphrases the meaning in context of "So the world excluding round,/ yet receiving in the day" (lines 30–31)?

(A) Although the dew drop evaporates in the sun, it arrives anew each day.
(B) The world evaporates the drop of dew when it receives the light of the sun.
(C) The dew drop is impervious to everything but time.
(D) Although the dew drop and the soul shut out the material world, they let in the light of heaven.
(E) The only thing that matters to the dew drop is light.

Here's How to Crack It

This kind of comprehension question is probably the most common type of question on the AP test. ETS gives you a line and asks, "So, what does it mean?" As always, read around the line and then use POE. Paraphrase "the world excluding round" as "the drop that turns away from the world" and you can eliminate (A), (B), and (E). None of those choices include that idea. Choice (C) mentions that the drop of dew is impervious. That isn't a good paraphrase of "world excluding round," and you can eliminate it with confidence by reasoning that *time* is not mentioned in the lines in question at all. That leaves only the correct answer, (D).

11. In line 42, the sun is symbolic of

(A) fire
(B) rebirth
(C) the soul
(D) God
(E) time

Here's How to Crack It

Get used to the range of difficulty on the AP test. Some of the questions are subtle, and challenge even the most experienced readers; others—like question 11—are a piece of cake. Don't freak and think you must have missed something when a question seems easy: just collect the point. Don't miss the easy questions by over-thinking. And don't worry about missing the hardest questions: If those are all you miss, you're on your way to a score of five.

On this question, we hope you saw that the sun symbolized God. The word *almighty* should have been a big clue. Additionally, metaphysical poets are often concerned with spiritual issues. If you've used your overview of literary movements to prepare for this exam, the answer may be even more obvious. The correct answer is (D).

12. Which of the following sets of adjectives is best suited to describe the poem's tone?

    (A) mysterious, moody, and spiritual
    (B) pious, proper, and academic
    (C) intricate, delicate, and worshipful
    (D) witty, clever, and ironic
    (E) straightforward, impassioned, and sincere

Here's How to Crack It

This is a tone question. On tone questions, always use POE. On this question, remember half bad equals all bad. Every answer choice has something right in it, but only the correct answer choice has *nothing* wrong in it. In (A), yes, the poem's tone is spiritual, but is it mysterious and moody? Not really. Eliminate it. (B) *Pious*, *proper*, and *academic* sounds school-marmish. That isn't right. Eliminate it. In (D), well, it's true the poem is witty and clever, but is it also ironic? Metaphysical poets typically are ironic—that is, hidden messages and contradictions often lurk below the surface of a metaphysical poem's text, but "On a Drop of Dew" is an exception. Marvell says what he means, cleverly, but not ironically. Choice (E) should just sound wrong. "On a Drop of Dew" is an intensely crafted work, but it is not impassioned nor straightforward. That leaves (C), which sums things up fairly well: intricate, delicate, and worshipful. The correct answer is (C).

13. In the final four lines of the poem, the poet suggests that

    (A) the dew drop will ultimately be destroyed by the sun
    (B) the cycle of life and death is continual
    (C) the drop of dew will return to earth in the form of "manna"
    (D) souls as pure as a drop of dew will ascend to heaven
    (E) death brings spiritual unity with God

Here's How to Crack It

If you answered question 11 correctly, this one shouldn't be much tougher. If you understand that the sun symbolizes God, then you should also understand that the dew's dissolving into the sun is a metaphor for the soul's ascent to heaven. The incorrect answer choices all add extraneous points or misconstrue the emphasis of this essentially simple idea. Choice (A) suggests that the dew would be destroyed. That misses the point. The dew's evaporation is not a destruction, but a reunion with the divine. Choice (B) is extraneous: The cycle of life is not a thematic point of the poem. Choice (C) tries to trap you by confusing the manna with the dew drop. The poem suggests that the dew drop is like manna in that both are distilled from the spiritual realm. The poem does not suggest that the dew will somehow become manna. Choice (D) should have been easy to eliminate: Nowhere does the poem talk about whether or not souls are as pure as a drop of dew. The correct answer is (E).

14. Which of the following adjectives is LEAST important to the poem's theme?

   (A) "blowing" (line 3)
   (B) "clear" (line 20)
   (C) "pure" (line 26)
   (D) "bright" (line 32)
   (E) "loose" (line 34)

Here's How to Crack It

ETS is fond of asking questions about theme, despite the fact that pinning down the theme of many poems is problematic. When ETS asks about the theme, don't try to come up with an exact definition of the theme. Just think about the main point, the important stuff. Again, POE is the way to work. Cross out LEAST and work with the remaining question, eliminating choices that are important to the theme. An important aspect of the poem is the metaphor of the dew drop and the soul. A good way to start would be to eliminate those choices which describe any aspect of that relationship. In this way you could eliminate (B), (C), and (D), because all are qualities of the dew drop that relate to qualities of the soul. A moment of study should tell you that (E) is also important. The dew drop is "loose," or ready to ascend; it grips this world only lightly. That is a thematic point. And (A)? Well, *blowing* means blooming. Is it important that the rose is in bloom? Does Marvell return to the fact of the rose being in bloom later in the poem? Does blooming somehow relate to the soul? No. (A) is least thematically important, and thus, (A) is the correct answer.

BONUS GRAMMAR QUESTIONS

Try these for strenuous, but excellent, practice. They're harder than real AP questions, but not by much. The following is an excerpt from Percy Bysshe Shelley's "Alastor; or, The Spirit of Solitude."

> Nature's most secret steps
> He like her shadow has pursued, wher'er
> The red volcano overcanopies
> Its fields of snow and pinnacles of ice
>
> *Line*
> (5) With burning smoke, or where bitumen lakes
> On black bare pointed islets ever beat
> With sluggish surge, or where the secret caves
> Rugged and dark, winding among the springs
>
> Of fire and poison, inaccessible
> (10) To avarice or pride, their starry domes
> Of diamond and of gold expand above
> Numberless and immeasurable halls,
>
> Frequent with crystal column, and clear shrines
> Of pearl, and thrones radiant with chrysolite.

1. The word "inaccessible" (line 9) modifies which of
   the following words?

   (A) "lakes" (line 5)
   (B) "caves" (line 7)
   (C) "springs" (line 8)
   (D) "poison" (line 9)
   (E) "avarice" (line 10)

You should recognize that *inaccessible* is an adjective (the ending *-ible* gives it away). That observation means that you need to decide what noun or pronoun it modifies. Unfortunately, all of the choices are nouns. If you look carefully, you will see that *or* in (line 6) introduces an independent clause. Because of the use of commas, the participial phrase *winding among the springs* modifies *caves*. *Of fire and poison* is a prepositional phrase modifying *springs*. *To avarice or pride* is another prepositional phrase that limits *inaccessible*. The correct answer then is (B), *caves*. Tough, isn't it?

Try this poem by Emily Dickinson.

> There's a certain Slant of light,
> Winter Afternoons—
> That oppresses, like the Heft
> Of Cathedral Tunes—
>
> *Line*
> (5) Heavenly Hurt, it gives us—
> We can find no scar,
> But internal difference,
> Where the meanings, are—
>
> None may teach it—Any—
> (10) 'Tis the Seal Despair—
> An imperial affliction
> Sent us of the Air—
>
> When it comes, the Landscape listens—
> Shadows—hold their breath—
> (15) When it goes, 'tis like the Distance
> On the look of Death—

2. In line 5, "it" refers to

   (A) "Cathedral Tunes" (line 4)
   (B) "heavenly love" (line 5)
   (C) "Slant of light" (line 1)
   (D) "look of Death" (line 15)
   (E) "imperial affliction" (line 11)

Asking what a pronoun refers to is an ETS favorite. Do you see that this isn't so much a question of grammatical analysis as it is of comprehension? The correct answer is (C). The *slant of light* is the antecedent.

SUMMARY

- Don't worry about scansion (you know: iambic pentameter, dactyls, spondees, etc.). You probably won't see even one question on it.

- Remember
  - Read the poem as prose.
  - Focus on the main idea.
  - When answering the questions, use POE and Consistency of Answers.
  - Be sure to read around line references.

- Metaphysical poetry is excellent practice for the kind of poetry you'll see on the AP test. John Donne, Andrew Marvell, George Herbert, Thomas Carew, Abraham Cowley, and Richard Crashaw are all poets whose work provides excellent AP practice. Also, the poetry of Emily Dickinson and Robert Frost is rich in intricate grammatical structures.

- On EXCEPT, NOT, and LEAST questions, cross out the negative word and eliminate any choice that fits the remaining question.

- Remember that grammar questions on the AP Literature exam are usually disguised comprehension questions—that is, the grammar part of the question isn't terribly difficult, but comprehending the sentence well enough to answer the question is.

PART ◆ III

Cracking the System: The Essays

Basic Principles of the Essay Section

FORMAT AND CONTENT OF THE ESSAY SECTION

The format of the Essay section on the AP English Literature and Composition Exam has been consistent for decades. Here's what to expect:

- You will be asked to write essays on three subjects:
  1. A passage of prose
  2. A passage of poetry or a comparison of two thematically related poems
  3. An open essay: an essay on a given topic, supported by your own reading

- You'll be given all the paper you need (including scratch paper), and you'll be instructed to write in pen. Bring a blue or black pen.

- You'll have two hours to complete this section.

WHAT WILL YOU BE WRITING ABOUT?

When ETS considers the mix of literary periods and styles on the test, they include the essay section in that mix. If you see two passages on eighteenth-century poetry in the multiple-choice section, you won't see any eighteenth-century poetry in the essay section. ETS also tries to give male and female authors (roughly) equal representation, and aims to include at least one author who identifies as African American, Native American, Latino, or Asian.

PACING

On each individual essay, you can take as much or as little time as you like, so long as you don't go over the two-hour limit for all three essays. Each essay is worth the same number of points, so it's a good idea to pace yourself and allot 40 minutes for each, give or take a few minutes. If you spend an hour and a half on your first essay, you're not going to finish the other two. Remember to bring a watch so that you don't lose track of time.

THE IMPORTANCE OF THE ESSAY SECTION TO YOUR SCORE

The essay section of the AP English Literature and Composition Exam counts for 55 percent of your total score. It is only slightly more important than the multiple-choice section of the test. It's obvious, but let's say it anyway: Both sections are important to your score.

Which section *feels* more important is another issue. For most students, the essay section feels like the whole test. The multiple-choice section seems like a bunch of hoops you have to jump through before getting to the part that matters—the essays. Students tend to look at the essay section with a combination of awe, fear, and excitement, thinking, "They're going to grade my writing—gulp!" Well, yes, some total stranger is going to read your words and give you a score from zero to nine. It can certainly seem scary. However, we're going to take the anxiety out of this process and replace it with knowledge and confidence.

Here's the interesting part: The essays are more important. Huh? Didn't we just say the two sections are essentially equal? It's true that the multiple-choice and essay sections are nearly equal in respect to determining your score. In respect to your score *improvement*, however, there is a world of difference between the two sections.

WHEN IT COMES TO IMPROVING YOUR SCORE, THE ESSAYS ARE KING

If you're the kind of student who gets A's in class and then bombs on standardized tests, using our multiple-choice techniques will make a huge difference. If you are already a natural test-taker, that's great—our techniques won't help that much because you're doing 90 percent of what we say without even knowing it. You probably fall somewhere in between (the vast majority of students do) and so using our techniques for the multiple-choice section squeezes out a half-dozen or so points and ensures that you get your best possible score. Why settle for anything less? But when you work on improving your score (and your skills), the essays are different.

THESE ESSAYS ARE DIFFERENT

Essay points add up fast. If we can show you a way to improve your essays by just one point—*bam*—that means three extra essay points just like that, one for each essay. And there are only 27 total essay points available. One more point on each essay works out to better than a 10 percent improvement on your essay score. If you can improve your essays just two notches, from, say, a five to a seven, you're in a whole new scoring bracket. Study this section and you will improve at least one point, and probably more.

THESE ESSAYS ARE DIFFERENT (DIDN'T WE JUST SAY THAT?)

Think about this: Unlike familiar old multiple-choice, the essays are completely new. You've never done anything like them before, so you may as well learn to do them in a way that will get you the most points. "What!?" you're thinking, "It's the multiple-choice that's weird; I write essays *all the time* in school."

Sorry, but you're mistaken. You write essays, true—but not AP essays.

YOUR TEACHER KNOWS YOU

You write essays for teachers who know you and (we hope) care about you. They know what your writing looked like at the beginning of the semester, they know whether you do your homework, they know whether you spend most of class daydreaming, they know you occasionally make brilliant comments in class, they know your real passion is for track or violin or painting or science or maybe even writing. They even know that there's a kid a few rows over with a hopeless crush on you and they wonder why you haven't noticed yet. (Why *haven't* you noticed?)

When your teachers see your name at the top of the page they already know a thousand things about you, and they all go into their reading of your writing and into the grades you get. The AP Reader, on the other hand, doesn't know you at all.

YOU KNOW YOUR TEACHER

Second, and just as important, you don't know anything about the Reader of your AP essays. Who is she or he? In school, you know your teacher. You know what she wants to hear. You may know that she detests misspellings, or that she loves it when you use humor, or that she gives extra credit for artistic originality. Or you may know that she's utterly mad, wears the same cat-hair-covered, neon-purple scarfy shawl thing every day, and that she channels Geoffrey Chaucer in her spare time. The AP essays are written to a featureless face: Is it a kind face? Mean? Crazy? You'll never know. When was the last time you wrote an essay to a total stranger for a grade?

READ IT—WRITE IT—GO!

Finally, AP essays are written under intense time pressure, without a lesson: "Hey kid, here's a passage—read it—write about it—go!" That's totally unnatural. Your teachers have undoubtedly spent a lot of time telling you that "good writing is rewriting." Perhaps they've insisted that for assignments you turn in a first draft and then revise that draft. Good. Your teachers are 100 percent correct in doing so. Writing well takes patience and care. One of the joys of writing is getting into its slowed down, reflective pace. In short, the "ready, set, write" attitude of ETS is the opposite of the right way to approach writing and is, we hope, diametrically opposed to the way you've been trained to write.

Unless your AP English teacher is drilling you with this style of essay, the closest thing to writing for the AP test you might have experienced is an in-class essay test, but even in that case the differences are significant. For example, in-class essay tests usually come after you've spent at least several classes on the subject at hand and know what your teacher expects you to have learned. Second, on in-class essay tests, the teacher wants to see what you know, not just how well you write. On the AP test you'll be writing cold, on a passage you read for the first time just two minutes before, with no time to revise and rework the way good writers always do, and you'll be graded on your writing as well as on what you say. Remember, both comprehension and originality are important.

It's ironic (there's that word again), but the very best practice for the AP test comes from the panicked-slacker method of homework preparation. What's that? Oh, you know (we know you know): writing a paper—fast—on a book you haven't really read, in the study hall before class. The AP essays call for a kind of speed-writing in which you have to come up with an idea and get it down right, all on the first try.

HORRIBLE? YES, BUT MAKE THE MOST OF IT

It's an awful way to have to write, but at least everyone else is working under the same conditions. In fact, if you know how to make the most out of these bizarre conditions, if you understand that you're doing something you haven't done before and work in the best way possible given the demands of the test, your essay will shine in comparison to the others. This chapter is about giving you the tools to do just that. In order to use those tools, you need to understand how the essays are scored, because really, a high score is all you're after. We aren't going to try to teach you how to write well. We are going to teach you how to write a high-scoring AP essay.

ALL ABOUT AP ESSAY SCORING

THE ZERO TO NINE SCALE

Each of your essays will be graded according to a nine point scale. Zero is the worst score you can get, and nine is the best. Students' scores are *not* spread out evenly over that range; the number of nines does not equal the number of fives. In fact, the numbers aren't even close. This chart provides a rough breakdown of how scores on the prose and poetry essays are distributed. (On the open essay, the curve is a little flatter and the average score a little lower, for reasons we'll discuss later.)

Score	Approximate Percentage of Students Receiving Score
9	1%
8	5%
7	10%
6	20%
5	23%
4	22%
3	15%
2	3%
1	1%
0	less than 1%
–	less than 1%

As you can see, about 65 percent of all essays are scored in the middle range: four, five, and six. The extreme scores taper away quickly. ETS doesn't tell its essay Readers to bunch up the scores this way, and they don't fudge the scores around later in order to produce this tidy bell curve. It works out this way because of the nature of student writing and the nature of essay scoring in general.

"HOLISTIC" SCORING

The essays are scored "holistically." What this means is that the Reader goes through your essay and gets an overall impression. That impression is translated into a single number, zero to nine, which is your essay's score. There is no checklist of points, such as two points for style, two points for grammar, one point for vocabulary, and one point for writing about, say, the metaphor in paragraph one. Nothing like that.

Instead, about a week before the actual grading session, ETS goes through several essays to get a feel for the students' writing. Next, the ETS staff combs through the student writing looking for the perfect representative nine essay, the perfect five, the perfect three, etc. These representative essays are the "sample essays." The Readers are given the samples and are trained for a day, during which they read student essays, compare them with the samples, and discuss the grades they would assign. The next day, the Readers start giving out the real grades. An ETS consultant checks graded essays at random to make sure the scoring is consistent. ETS tries hard to keep things standard and fair. Each Reader only grades one type of essay. But there's no way around the facts: The Readers are individual people making subjective judgments.

THE READER WANTS AN ESSAY THAT'S EASY TO SCORE

Readers are dedicated high school, college, and university instructors who take a week out of their year to come to one site to grade essays. Of course, they are compensated for their time, but at times the grading can become monotonous. You need to make sure that your essay stands out from the hundreds of essays that each Reader scores.

Your job is to write an essay that's obviously better than average. You have to let the Reader feel confident about giving you at least a seven. Four out of five essays are average or worse. Slogging through these mediocre essays, the Reader gives a score and turns to the next essay hoping for that outstanding paper. The Reader *wants* to be persuaded and to read an essay that possesses stylistic flair. Usually, the essays are generic and have no distinctive style to them. Often the essays are plot summaries that barely address the question. In many cases, the question is rewritten and the essay does not explore the topic adequately or with skill. Readers want to reward the writers for what they do well, but the topic must be addressed. If an essay starts out dull and poorly written but makes one completely original point right at the very end, the writer can be rewarded. Sometimes, however, there are too many grammar and spelling errors that distract the Reader, and the one important statement that the writer makes is lost among the myriad errors on the paper. If you merely summarize the plot of the passage or do not adequately address the question, the Reader may have to decide on a score of four or five. You want to make it as easy as possible for the scorer to think your essay is good. Before we get to the basic tips for making it easy for the Reader to give you a high score, let's look at a scoring guide AP Readers use.

A TYPICAL SCORING GUIDE

Every Reader gets a scoring guide for the essay he or she is grading. The scoring guides for AP essays are always very similar. We've taken a few scoring guides and combined them, taking out the details that are particular to a passage or a poem, such as the author's name and the names of characters and places in the story or poem. Notice as you look over the scoring guide how little specific guidance ETS actually provides; the Readers are given a lot of leeway.

Eight to Nine
These are well-organized and well-written essays that clearly analyze the work and how the author dramatizes the situation. These essays use apt, specific references to the passage in order to discuss the author's use of elements such as diction, imagery, pace, and point of view. While not flawless, these papers demonstrate an understanding of the text and of the techniques of composition. These writers express their ideas skillfully and clearly.

Six to Seven

The content of these papers resembles that of higher scoring essays, but is less precise and less aptly supported. These essays deal with literary elements such as diction, imagery, and pace, but are less effective than the upper-range essays. Essays scored at seven will generally exhibit fewer mechanical errors and draw from the passage more incisively than those scored at six.

Five

These essays are superficial. Although not seriously in error about the content and literary technique of the passage, they miss the complexity of the piece and offer only a perfunctory analysis of how the subject has been dramatized. The treatment of elements such as diction and imagery is overly generalized or mechanical. The writing adequately conveys the writer's thoughts, but the essays themselves are commonplace, poorly conceived, poorly organized, and simplistic.

Three to Four

These essays reflect an incomplete understanding of the passage and do not completely respond to the question. The discussion is unclear or simply misses the point. The treatment of literary elements is scanty or unconvincing, with little support drawn from the passage. Typically, these essays reveal a marked weakness in a writer's ability to handle the mechanics of written English.

One to Two

These essays contain the errors found in essays receiving a score of three to four, but to an even more pronounced degree. One- to two-point scoring essays either completely misunderstand the passage or fail to address the question. Typically, these essays are incoherent, too short, or both. The writing demonstrates no control of written English, either grammatically or organizationally.

Zero

This is a response that fails to address the question. There may only be a reference to the task.

Blank

This indicates that the response is completely off topic or that a response has not been made.

ANALYSIS OF THE SCORING GUIDE

Look carefully over this guide. What do you see? There are two major points we want stamped into your mind.

First, the high-scoring essays are clear. They aren't perfect, they aren't moving and profound, they're just clear. Practically every point made in the eight to nine description is just another way of saying *clear*. Well-organized means *clearly organized*. *Apt examples drawn from the passages* is another way of saying the writer has used *clear* examples. Clarity is the goal.

Second, notice the jump that happens at the five score. Notice how the whole tone of the guide changes. Suddenly the guide isn't talking about the fine points of answering the question; it's talking about the life-choking drabness of it all. You can imagine the Reader perusing such an essay and thinking, "Another one that's just like the last twenty essays." Five score essays are just a trap—a trap that is easy to fall into if you aren't ready for the AP essays. Many five-point essays are written by good students, many of them A students, and half of those students *think they wrote a pretty good essay*. But they didn't; they just wrote a generic essay. These are the kinds of adjectives that show up in the five category of AP scoring guides: *mechanical, perfunctory, pedestrian, commonplace, adequate*. In other words, the same dull essay most students write (or try to write until they get totally lost, leading to an even lower score). After grading her fifty-fifth essay, the Reader writes down the score and turns to the next essay, praying, "Please, not another boring one."

If you understand what you read and can write in grammatical English, a five is your absolute low-end score. You will almost certainly do better than that with our help.

BRILLIANT STUDENTS — DULL ESSAYS

A student who can write an essay that scores a five can write an essay that scores a seven or better. And remember, any student who understand what he or she reads and can write a grammatically sound essay that is semi-legible can get a five. The reason we think that we can improve your essay score so much is that you probably already have what it takes to write a successful essay. If you can write a proper English sentence, if you can write a mediocre, dull, I-hate-writing-this-but-I've-got-to-do-it-anyway kind of essay, then you can write a high-scoring essay. You just need a new approach. In the scoring guide, ETS comes right out and says that there's nothing terribly wrong with the essays that receive scores of five, they're just vague, generalized, mechanical, and dull. Essays like that come out of an incredibly common approach, which is why scores of five are so common.

Let's look at the way *not* to write an AP essay.

THE FIVE-SCORING ESSAY FORMULA

Almost every five-scoring essay is written by a student who doesn't know how to craft a real essay idea based on the question and thinks that the "essay formula" can somehow save him. Here's the thought process that invariably leads to a middle score: "Let's see…they want me to write about the language…well, what *else* would I write about? The whole *thing* is language. This is crazy. And 'how the author dramatized the story'—well, with *language* of course—great, that's about one sentence worth of essay. What am I going to say? I don't know what they want! Oh God. I can't sit here forever; *I've got to write something*. I know! I'll restate the question as a statement and then come up with three examples: one for diction, one for imagery, and one for point of view. Then I'll summarize it all for a conclusion. *That's the essay formula, right?* Okay, here goes."

PANIC + NO IDEA OF WHAT IS WANTED = THE FIVE-SCORING ESSAY

This student is perfectly intelligent. The "formula" isn't crazy; in fact, it's taught all over the place. Restate the question as a statement. Support the statement with three examples from the passage. Summarize it for a conclusion.

It sounds good, but when a student tries to use it he'll realize he still doesn't have one interesting thing to say. From beginning to end he'll feel lost, and writing the essay will feel like one big, meaningless exercise. He'll struggle and pick out bits of the passage that catch his eye and try to discuss them. He won't be exactly sure why they catch his eye, but he'll make up something. The discussion will be vague, over generalized, and mechanical. (That's the description of five-scoring essays in the AP scoring guide, remember.) The five-scoring essay has to be vague, because if it were precise the student would reveal that he has no precise understanding of what he's supposed to be writing about. The formula turns the essay into garbage. Worst of all, boring garbage.

The formula, however, is actually a heroic effort on the student's part, because writing this way is painful and hard. It takes a huge amount of brain power to come up with new and vague ways to say general things about something or other—just what, you aren't quite sure—without looking like a loser. When you're writing this way, a five is a success.

HOW TO MAKE IT EASY FOR THE READER TO GIVE YOU A HIGH SCORE

The most important part of your essay is the content. Your goal is to write meaty, content-filled essays that just blow the Reader away. But the Reader has to get to that content. There are just a few vital things you must do to let your excellence come shining through with full impact. These basics have to do with the surface of your writing. That might seem cheap, but it's not. If the surface of your essay is clean and clear, the Reader can see through to the depths.

NEATNESS COUNTS

Studies have shown that neatly written essays earn higher scores on holistically graded tests. It's not fair, but it's a fact of life. Do everything in your power to make your essays readable. Write slowly. Write large. Write dark. Your writing doesn't have to be pretty, but it must be legible.

Take pains to be as neat as you possibly can. When a neatly written essay shows up, the wave of relief, of *love*, flooding the Reader is difficult to describe. A clearly written essay makes the Reader think, "Ah, now I can do my job!" A messy essay annoys the Reader. The Readers will try hard not to let poor handwriting affect the score, but if your essay is messy and difficult to read, they'll lose patience quickly.

If your cursive script isn't great, and you've been writing essays on a computer for years, seriously consider printing or writing in italics, which is a sort of hybrid of cursive and printing. Trust us here. You may think this advice is ridiculous and that your handwriting shouldn't matter. The fact is, it does. As persecuted as you feel writing these essays, the Reader feels twice as persecuted reading them. Script is harder to read than print. If it weren't, this book would be written in a nice cursive typeface. If your normal handwriting looks like that on a wedding invitation, or you're president of the Calligraphy Club at school, then you can use cursive. Otherwise, practice your handwriting.

INDENT

Your Reader's first impressions are crucial. Think about that character at the job interview with gum in his hair. If his battle isn't already lost, it's definitely an uphill fight the rest of the way. The overall look of your essay is a first impression. It's the smile on your face as you walk in the door. Your essay should look neat, organized, and clear. Make your paragraphs obvious. Indent twice as far as you normally would. When in doubt, make a paragraph. Ever look at a book, flip it open, and see nothing but one long paragraph? Your next thought is usually, "Oh please, don't make me have to read this!" That's exactly what the Reader thinks when she sees an essay without paragraphs. Make sure the Reader can see the paragraphs right away. Neat presentation, clear handwriting, paragraphs just screaming out, "I'm so organized, it's scary!" will have the Reader thinking, "Now here's a high-scoring student" before she's even read a word.

WRITE PERFECTLY...FOR THE FIRST PARAGRAPH

Your second first impression (that's an *oxymoron*...see the glossary) is the first paragraph of the essay. Take triple care with your first paragraph. If you're unsure about the spelling of a word, don't use it. If you're unsure how to punctuate the sentence, rewrite it in a way that makes you feel confident. Don't make any mistakes in the first paragraph. Don't fret as much about the rest of the essay; the Readers expect mistakes. But paragraph one has got to be strong. If you try to write the whole essay perfectly you'll write so slowly, or fill up your brain with so much worry, that you'll probably run out of time.

All you need is a few sentences to convince the Reader that you can write a good sentence when you want to. The glow of a good beginning carries over the whole essay. Mistakes later on look like minor errors not even worth bothering with. After all, the Reader's already seen that you can write. Mistakes at the very beginning look like just the opposite—they look like telling signs of inability and a weak grasp of fundamental English mechanics. Take extra care at the beginning of your essay, then relax and just write (*neatly*).

SHOW OFF YOUR LITERARY VOCABULARY

Readers do not give great grades to students who merely parrot the prompt. A good way to show that you understand what the question is asking is by paraphrasing the prompt in your response. If the prompt asks about diction, knowing that diction means "word choice" is great. Articulating how the author uses a particular form of diction is even better. Be sure that you know the meaning of the major terms ETS asks about (remember that glossary at the back of this book), and have some good synonyms at hand so you can display varied word choice. For poetry, the big five are *diction*, *imagery*, *metaphor*, *rhyme*, and *form*. For prose, substitute *point of view* and *characterization* for *rhyme* and *form*. Using the word "speaker" to refer to the poetry narrator and "narrator" when dealing with prose are conventions worth employing because they will show that you are comfortable with the modes of writing that the Readers will recognize from teaching students about literature.

USE SNAPPY VERBS AND TASTY NOUNS

Juice up your writing. Try to write with some pizazz. Don't let the test environment, the tension, or the anxiety caused by writing for a stranger take over your brain. Take risks: You may fall flat every so often, but the Reader will appreciate your effort and reward it. When you've gotten our essay techniques down, you'll understand that 90 percent of dull student writing on AP essays comes from confusion about what to write, which leads to inhibition. Don't be inhibited. Jazz it up a little. Show some flair—not 37 pieces of flair—but stylistic flair.

If you write like someone who enjoys writing, the Readers will be impressed. For example, a student might write, "When Judy first sees Roger going down the street, she thinks he seems interesting." That's probably true, but what a bore! There are a thousand ways to liven up that sentence. It all depends on your personality and what is really happening in the story. How about, "When Judy first glimpses Roger dashing through the shadows of Sullivan Street, her heart flutters; she's already in love, she just doesn't know it yet." Or, "When Judy spots Roger flying down the sidewalk with the Sullivan Street gang nipping at his heels, she's dumbstruck by the wild vitality of his whirling limbs and blazing eyes." Cheesy? Over the top? Who cares? Nobody expects you to write like Marcel Proust. Actually, the Readers expect you to write like someone who's suffering through a tedious, nerve-wracking exercise, because that's exactly how most of the essays are written.

We aren't saying you have to write tangled, complex sentences; in fact, you should try to avoid them. Great, long, looping sentences usually just wander off into error and confusion. All you need to do is pay attention to your word choice. When you find yourself using a generic verb like *look*, *see*, *says*, *walk*, *go*, *take*, or *give*, or a generic noun like *street*, *house*, *car*, or *man*, ask yourself if there isn't a more precise, more colorful word you can use. Why write *house* when you're referring to a *mansion*, or *car* when you're really writing about a *jalopy*? Just a little bit of this goes a long way. It shows you're not scared, and it might even look like you're having fun, which is very good.

Obviously, it's possible to go overboard in this area, and if the Reader gets the impression you're just being silly, it won't help your score. But a dash of glitter is much better than none at all. By the way, big, important-sounding phrases are not your ticket to a high score. They're an obvious sign that you're full of it. So please don't try to write this kind of gibberish: "When Judy initially perceived Roger's rapid ambulatory movement along the pedestrian walkway bordering the automotive thoroughfare, she experienced tachycardia."

THE QUESTIONS

Each passage will be preceded by instructions to "Read the passage below carefully and then write a well-organized essay about...." These instructions may also contain some additional material orienting you to the passage, telling you things like who wrote it, the novel it was drawn from, and any other special information ETS feels you need to know in order to understand the passage. Be sure to give the instructions a complete look, in case there's any useful information there.

Answer the Question

If you write a great essay that the Reader doesn't think addresses the question, you'll get a lousy score. All three essays will be directed essays; ETS will tell you what they want—that's the theory, anyway. In reality, the questions can be infuriatingly vague. At the same time, not answering the question is the ultimate sin. Understanding and answering the question are crucial to writing a high-scoring essay.

Ordering the Section

Just as with the reading passages in the Multiple-Choice section of the test, you should put the essays in the order that works best for you. Which one looks easiest and most appealing to you? Do it first. Get your writing juices flowing. You definitely want to write all three essays, so don't get lost in your writing and run out of time. If you do happen to run out of time, however, you want it to be on the hardest essay; think of ordering the essays as a safety measure.

But *don't run out of time*. You have 40 minutes per essay.

SUMMARY

GENERAL ESSAY INFORMATION

- There are three essays. One essay on a prose passage, one essay on one or two poetry passages, and one essay on a work that you select (the open essay).

- You have two hours to complete all three essays. Time yourself. Spend 40 minutes on each essay.

- The essays are a great place to improve your score.

ESSAY SCORING

- Each essay is scored by a Reader who grades only that particular type of essay.

- Each essay is given a score from zero to nine.

- The essays are scored "holistically." There is no checklist of available points.

- The Reader wants to read an essay that's easy to score.

- When in doubt, the Reader will push your score toward the middle range of scores.

- High-scoring essays are interesting, clear essays. Middle-scoring essays are generic and boring. Low-scoring essays are plain old bad.

PRESENTATION

- Do everything in your power to make your essays readable.

- Write carefully in large, dark handwriting. Your writing doesn't have to be pretty, but it must be clear.

- Make your paragraph indentations easy to spot.

- When in doubt, create a new paragraph.

- Your first paragraph should be grammatically perfect. Your Reader will make a very quick judgment about your ability to write. Once the Reader has decided you can write a sentence, he'll cut you some slack later on (as long as you write neatly).

- Have a solid literary vocabulary. You'll express yourself with greater clarity.

- Use snappy verbs and tasty nouns. It will impress the Reader and make her think you're comfortable, confident, and smart. Don't stress too much about overdoing the jazzy language, but don't go bananas.

- Don't confuse snappy verbs and tasty nouns with ten-dollar vocabulary words. Use the best word you can think of, not the longest.

- Understand the question. (Don't worry, there's much more on this subject in the next chapter.)

- If you write a great essay that doesn't address the question, you'll get a lousy score.

- Order the section. Do the essay you like best first, and save the worst one for last.

- Keep track of time—try to complete each essay in about 40 minutes.

The Idea Machine: Starting Your Essays with a High Score

FROM IDEA TO EXECUTION

We're going to take you through our AP English writing process. The process has been specifically designed for AP essays. The hardest part of writing essays under time pressure is coming up with something to say quickly. In this chapter we'll show you how to get the ideas that let you have something to write about in the first place. We aren't going to teach you how to write; you've already spent years learning to write. However, AP essays are unlike anything you've had to write before. You probably haven't spent years learning how to write AP essays.

About 90 percent of this chapter is about how to get an overall idea of your essay and create a great first paragraph. If you can get off to a good start, you're more than halfway to a great score.

THE APPROACH

Just as with the multiple-choice section, you want to have a common sense, step-by-step approach to the essay section (and know how to use it). Here it is:

- Bring a watch and note the time. Remember, 40 minutes per essay.
- Pick the essay (prose, poetry, open) you want to write.
- Identify the key words in the essay prompt.
- Skim the passage.
- Work the passage, making notes and identifying quotations you will want to use.
- Use the Idea Machine (explained below) to plan your first paragraph.
- Support and develop the points you made in your first paragraph in your body paragraphs.
- Get a solid conclusion on the page. Your conclusion can be as important as your introduction.
- Repeat the process with the other essays.

Don't Write an Outline

You don't have time to write an outline. Outlines are for organizing longer, more complex pieces of writing, like research papers—pieces of writing that you have the time to revise and plan. We know you've probably had outlining drummed into you by your teachers. Other books on the AP test recommend making an outline. These people don't understand AP test taking! Short essays, like the ones you'll write for the AP test, don't call for an outline. You don't even have time to rewrite. Our method shows you how to come up with a solid beginning from which you can build so that you can just write the rest of the essay without an outline.

The Idea Machine

We've developed a method of approaching AP essays that we call the "Idea Machine." Hey, don't get us wrong, the *real* idea machine is in your skull. The point here is to focus your brain, your imagination, and your analytical skills in a way that's productive for the AP test. This approach won't let you down. Use it and your essays will shine.

The Idea Machine is a series of questions that direct your reading to the material needed to write an essay. Take these questions, apply their answers to the essay question, and in the end you'll find you've written the kind of essay the Readers want to see.

The Idea Machine

1. What is the meaning of the work?

    a. What is the literal, face-value meaning of the work?
    b. What feeling (or feelings) does the work evoke?

2. How does the author get that meaning across?

    a. What are the important images in the work and what do those images suggest?
    b. What specific words or short phrases produce the strongest feelings?
    c. What elements are in opposition?

That may not look like much, but when we put all the pieces together in this chapter and the next you'll see just how powerful a tool we're giving you.

THE CLASSIC ESSAY QUESTION

Whether you are working on a prose or poetry passage, there is a classic essay question that you will be asked to address. Here it is in its most basic form:

> Read the following work carefully. Then, write a well-organized essay in which you discuss the manner in which the author conveys ideas and meaning. Discuss the techniques the author uses to make this passage effective. Avoid summary.

The Hidden Question Is the First Question

Okay, so what does ETS want from you on that classic essay question? At first glance, they seem to want you to write an essay that discusses the methods the author uses or how the author conveys his meaning. That is partly true, but the answers to those questions come later. If you start from there you will find yourself confused and lost.

The classic essay question actually breaks down into three questions. The first two should look familiar because they're part of the Idea Machine. The three questions are:

1. What does the poem or passage mean?

2. How did the author get you to see that?

3. How do the answers to question 1 and 2 direct your knowledge to adequately answer the question?

The first question is hidden, but totally important. It's the foundation on which you build the rest of your essay. Your (high-scoring) essay answers those three questions in that order. The question ETS poses will ask only question 2 directly. (They feel question 1 is implied.)

If the first question is "What does the passage or poem mean?" Well…what does that mean? What is *meaning*?

The Meaning of *Meaning*

For the AP essays, the meaning of a work of prose or poetry is the most basic, flat, literal sense of what is said plus the emotions and passions behind that sense.

The passages and poems they ask you to write about on the AP English Literature and Composition Exam will present some event or situation in the same way a newspaper article presents an event or a situation. But AP essay passages will, of course, do more than that. They will make the event or situation "come alive" by bringing in human emotions and passions in such a way that those emotions and passions are as important as the facts.

Let's consider a well-known story:

ATHENS DAILY NEWS
Scandal in Thebes!

The Athens Daily News reports: Murder solved! Popular King Oedipus of Thebes has been revealed as both the son and murderer of the late King Laius. Photos and full coverage of this bizarre incident begin on page 3.

Think of how much will be lost by the newspaper version. Will they really let us know the degree of Oedipus' suffering, his sense of terrible, yet undeserved guilt? Of course not, but those emotions are parts of what the story means, and are the most important part of your essay.

When we say the first question is, "What does the poem or passage mean?" We want you to answer two simple things:

1. What is the basic literal sense of things (the newspaper version)?
2. What emotions are involved both for the characters in the story and for you, the reader?

The combination of these questions is the *meaning*.

Avoid Summary

You must absolutely avoid talking about the newspaper version only. Doing that amounts to a summary. The ETS Readers do not want to read a summary of the passage. Discuss the way emotions are involved in the story and focus on the feelings the language produces, and you'll be discussing meaning in the right way. Always identify point of view, tone, and figurative language usage. Discussing these literary elements will, at a minimum, ensure that you are moving beyond a summary.

THE MODIFIED CLASSIC ESSAY QUESTION

Your AP exam may well have the classic question on it almost word for word, but probably not. What you will likely see is a modified classic essay question. There is an endless number of modifications that ETS can throw at you. For example, the question might ask you to discuss "the narrator's attitude toward the nature of war," "the speaker's attitude toward society," or "the author's use of repetition."

Identify the Key Words in the Prompt

Of course, the specifics mentioned in the essay prompt are what you should pay close attention to when you read. Just as in the multiple-choice section, where looking at the questions can help you read the passages more actively, identifying precisely what the Readers want you to write about can help you focus on those aspects of the poem or prose.

However, even if you're responding to a modified essay prompt, you should begin just like you're answering the classic one. You want to talk about what meaning you found in the poem or passage, and then use that as a foundation to discuss the topic ETS has specifically asked for in the question.

Let's look at an example. (You don't need the actual passage to understand our discussion of the question here.)

> Read the following passage carefully. Write a well-organized essay that discusses the interrelationship of humor, pity, and horror in the passage.

This seems like a simple enough question—until you try to answer it. How do you go about discussing the interrelationship of humor, pity, and horror? Most students start out something like this:

> The story X by writer Z mixes humor pity and horror in an interesting way. It begins with a father meeting his son. The father seems like a funny guy because of things he does, but then we see that he is actually a person who arouses our pity because he goes too far, so far in fact, that the father becomes almost horrible.

The student who writes this response knows he's basically flailing. He's just trying to answer the question without looking foolish. If the student uses reasonable examples, writes with some organization and only a few grammatical errors, then the student will get a five, a "limbo" score, not passing, not failing.

But the student who understands that this question is a modified form of the classic question and knows how to use the Idea Machine will break it down:

What does the passage mean? What was I supposed to get from it? What did I get from it? Okay, I got that the passage was about a father and son and that the son feels his father is basically embarrassing. Yeah, that sounds about right. Now, let's see, how does the author get that across using humor, pity, and horror?

Notice how this student has taken the question, turned it into the classic question, and simply used the modification to focus on the point to be developed. The student began by describing the meaning of the story. ("The son feels his father is basically embarrassing" is the meaning. Remember the meaning doesn't have to be complicated.) Then this student asked herself, *How does the author get that across using humor, pity, and horror?* This student's opening is going to look something like this:

> In story X, writer Z shows us a son confronted by the embarrassing spectacle of his father. By shifting the son's perspective of his father from humor and pity, to horror, we see and feel the son's fluctuating, uncertain responses to his father's vulgarity and ignorance.

This student is writing about something and it shows. She's on the way to a score of at least seven, and if the essay stays this clear and focused, it's going to earn a score of nine. Do you see how slight an alteration has been made between this response and the one that came before it? Yet there's a world of difference. The first student rephrased the question without really saying anything, and then began to work his way through the points, ticking them off…first humor, then pity, then horror. The second student began by answering the implied question in every essay: *What does this story mean?* Then she began to show how the author brought that meaning across.

The best part is that the second essay is easier to write than the first one. It's easier to write an essay about something than nothing. Writing a bogus essay is like trying to wind up a ball of string with nothing to wrap it around. The second essay is going to wrap itself neatly around the core of the story's meaning—the son's uncertain embarrassment at his father's behavior.

No Fear!

Sometimes the questions can be fairly intimidating. But don't let them throw you. Remember to use the Idea Machine. What does the passage mean? How does that meaning come across?

Once you've got that under your belt you can think about how to focus on the points in a question about a poem. Let's look at an example:

> Read the poem below carefully. Notice that the poem is divided into two stanzas and that the second stanza reapplies much of the first stanza's imagery. Write a well-organized essay in which you discuss how the author's use of language, including his use of repetition, reflects the content and tone of the poem.

That's a hair-raising question, not because it's super hard, but because it's so scary-looking it could mess with your confidence. Again, you should look at it and remember that, as always, *it's just a modified version of the classic essay question*. Your first task is to get at the author's meaning. What does the author want you to get from the whole poem? Once you've answered that for yourself, you can think about how the author got that across with repeated imagery. In fact, this question almost organizes itself once you look at it that way. Your first paragraph would say something about what you get from the whole poem. Your next paragraph would talk about the language of the first stanza and what it means. Then you would write about the second stanza and what it means. Your conclusion would look back at the poem and ensure that you've discussed both of the stanzas and emphasized why and how repetition is important in understanding the overall tone and theme of the poem.

A GREAT START

The key to a great essay is a great start. The key to a great start is having an overall idea of what you're doing. We've shown you how to address the meaning (literal and emotional) of the poem right from the beginning, and that you then have to address the "how" of the author's method. Taken together, these things will form your opening. They form the central idea around which you will write—the idea you will explain and support. If you're already a sharp, sensitive reader, following these instructions will lead you to high-scoring essays.

Sounds easy in principle. But are you ready? Let's go back to that tough, intimidating question we just looked at in the No Fear section, this time along with the poem that goes with it. We'll use our approach to come up with a good first paragraph for a high-scoring essay. Then we'll show you two powerful tools you can use to open up a passage and get the kinds of ideas that blow AP Readers away.

DYLAN THOMAS'S "IN MY CRAFT OR SULLEN ART"

Read the poem below carefully. Notice that the poem is divided into two stanzas, and that the second stanza reapplies much of the first stanza's imagery. Write a well-organized essay in which you discuss how the author's use of language, including his use of repetition, reflects the content and tone of the poem.

In My Craft or Sullen Art by Dylan Thomas

In my craft or sullen art
Exercised in the still night
When only the moon rages
Line And lovers lie abed
(5) With all their griefs in their arms,
I labor by singing light
Not for ambition or bread
Or the strut and trade of charms
On the ivory stages
(10) But for the common wages
Of their most secret heart.

Not for the proud man apart
From the raging moon I write
On these spindrift pages
(15) Nor for the towering dead

With their nightingales and psalms
But for the lovers, their arms
Round the griefs of the ages,
Who pay no praise or wages
(20)   Nor heed my craft or art.

So, where do you begin? Well, before you begin to consider the repetition mentioned in the essay instructions, get the answers to the questions that let you write a classic essay. Use the Idea Machine.

What does the poem say, literally? That shouldn't be too tough to answer, even if you don't know exactly what Dylan Thomas is trying to say. Put it in your own words. What does the poet say about his "craft or sullen art"? Take a moment to think about it, then read on.

You should have come up with something like this: "Dylan Thomas explains that he isn't writing for money or fame but for lovers who don't even care about his writing."

Okay, now what is the feel of the poem? What emotions are conveyed? Is there an overall emotion? Again, think about it a moment before you read on.

It's a tougher question, isn't it? You probably went back to the poem to look at it again, thinking, "Just what emotion was I supposed to get? There's something there, but what?"

You might have picked up on a few aspects of the tone: pride, grief, loneliness, perhaps futility, and also perhaps the opposite of futility—a sense of total purpose. The poem has a truly complex emotional range in it. Don't let that scare you off; it only gives you more to write about.

What is the meaning of the poem for your AP essay? Take your literal sense and your emotional sense, and combine them:

> Dylan Thomas's "In My Craft or Sullen Art" explores the pride, grief, loneliness, futility, and yet sense of total purpose that come from the author's struggle to write not for fame or for wealth but for "the lovers, their arms round the griefs of ages."

So far so good. But don't think we're finished. This sentence is just the answer to question 1 of the Idea Machine—what does the poem mean? If you're particularly astute, you may even notice that we haven't completely answered that question. We've only said what Thomas "explores." We haven't come out and taken a stand on exactly where Thomas's exploration has led him. Don't worry. You don't have to try to pin everything down all at once. If this essay were an assignment due at the end of the week you'd want to write a rough draft so that you could revise carefully later. Here on the AP exam, you don't have the opportunity for careful revision. You don't have to write a perfect essay. The Readers don't expect you to, not even for a score of nine. Just stay with our method: What does the work mean, how does the author achieve his effects, and what does the question ask you to address?

Now you have the second part of our three-part approach to consider:

How does the author achieve his effects? Perhaps in answering that question we can take more of a stand. How does Thomas bring his emotions into his sense of what writing means to him and (because the essay instructions demand we consider it) what does the repetition have to do with it?

How indeed? Thomas gets his message across in so compact a fashion you may feel a little lost and overwhelmed. Remember, you're just trying to write a 40-minute essay on a poem you've never seen before. The Readers don't expect perfection or profound originality. They want to see you focus on saying *something*, and then they want you to say it as clearly as you can. In brief, they want to see you confidently develop your ideas as best you can.

Here's how we'd complete our opening statement and answer the question of how Thomas explores his sense of what, to him, it means to write:

Dylan Thomas's "In My Craft or Sullen Art" explores the pride, grief, loneliness, futility, and yet sense of total purpose that come from the author's struggle to write not for fame or for wealth but for "the lovers, their arms round the griefs of ages." Thomas gives us an image of himself, laboring alone "by singing light" and contrasts this with an image of self-contained completeness, of lovers wrapped in each other's arms, oblivious to all the world and even to his poetry. By repeating these images, and key words like "moon," "rage," and "grief," he emphasizes the power of his emotions and the intensity of his need to define himself and the purpose of his art.

This opening puts our essay off to a great start. Of course, you might have had different ideas, and you undoubtedly would have phrased your ideas another way, even if you saw exactly what we saw in the poem. You might even have written two or three better sentences—although you wouldn't have had to in order to score well. This brings up our next point.

Have Confidence in Your Answer

Many other insights about Dylan Thomas's poem are waiting between the lines. It all depends on what you got from it. If you ask yourself, "How can I describe the subject of this poem in one word?" You will find that your answer, in this case, reflects the title of the poem. It is his writing. Then, ask yourself: "What is Dylan Thomas saying about the craft of writing?" The answer to this question is the theme of the poem. If you look at the last few lines of the poem, you will discover the answer in those lines. Usually, if you look at the title of the poem, the last few lines of the poem, and combine that with the one word that accurately describes the subject of the poem, you are on your way to accurately describing the theme of the poem. You want to make sure that you are on track with your interpretation because the Readers want to see that you have understood the point of the poem and that you can explain how this understanding helps you answer the essay question.

Use that literary vocabulary you've been building by studying the glossary. The readers are paying attention to your craft of writing as you address the question. They want to see how the literary work you've been asked to write about acted on your imagination and how well you've managed to convey the impressions you've received.

IMAGERY AND WORDS

Speaking of *imagination*, notice what we've done in the "how" part of our opening paragraph about the Dylan Thomas poem. We've discussed imagery. We chose to mention the contrasting images of the author working alone and of the lovers in their self-enclosed togetherness. You might have chosen something else. The point to remember is: *It's always a safe bet to talk about imagery.* The most important, most open-ended, most easily discussable aspect of a poem is almost always the imagery.

In writing (as opposed to cinema or theater or painting) an image is made of words. Is that obvious? Yes, it is. But just because it's obvious doesn't mean all students pay attention to that important fact. On the AP essays your job is to discuss writing. Remember then, whenever you're discussing the imagery in a passage, you're discussing words. If a word sticks out as unusual or particularly vivid, think about it. Ask yourself, why did the author use *that* word? What effect does that word have? If you can think of something to say about the words an author has used to create an image and the specific effect those words have, by all means put it in your essay. You'll have the AP Readers eating out of your hand. One easy method of discussing imagery is to try to create a short film clip with your words based on what the poet has written.

Notice that in our sample opening we zeroed in on the two most striking word choices in the poem. *Rage* and *grief*. It's odd (and poetic) to say lovers have their arms around their griefs. And when was the last time you saw the moon raging? A lot of students run from unusual language like that. They think that the poet is just being a typical crazy artist who can't really be understood or that they'll misinterpret the phrase anyway and look dumb. But when you see unusual usages like that, consider them. Why that word? What does that word do to the feel of the piece? Thinking that way, you'll jog ideas loose and come up with the material that makes for great AP essays. Notice also that both *rage* and *grief* have strong emotional content. Writing about the emotional content is the best way to let the Reader know you're really reading and not enacting some dry, mechanical exercise.

OPPOSITION

If you've been following our discussion so far, you should see that you need to be able to pull ideas from the text you're working with, so that you have ideas for your essay. Considering imagery and word choice is a good start, but there's one more concept we want you to think about as you read. This concept should really help you find the ideas that you need to write a great essay.

How can you get to the heart of what you read on the AP English Literature Exam? How can you find something interesting and important to say about a passage quickly? What do you look for to see what makes a passage or a poem "tick?"

The answer is *opposition*.

Attune your reading to seeing opposition and you'll open up AP passages like cans of sardines. You'll have something around which to center your discussion of the way an author uses language and imagery and tone to make her point. If you carefully read the question, you will notice that there is usually a comparison or contrast that it directs you to address. Sometimes it is subtle, but sometimes you are directed to focus your answer on a comparison or contrast noted within the passage or two passages.

Some people call opposition *conflict*, but we think that's too narrow a term. *Conflict* sounds like two people having a fight. Don't be crude. Be subtle. Opposition is everywhere in good writing, and the passages on the AP test will always be good sources. Seek out opposition, count on it being there and look for it, because opposition leads you to the important parts of a passage or poem.

So, What's Opposition?

Opposition occurs when any pair of elements contrast sharply. Another way to think about opposition is tension—think of the two opposing elements as if they were magnetized poles, attracting and repelling each other. Opposition provides a structure underneath the surface of the poem, which you will unlock by discovering the oppositional elements. Opposition might be as blatant as night and day. Or it might be less obvious: a character who's naïve and a character who's sophisticated. Opposition might be found in a story that begins with a scene in a parlor but ends with a scene around a campfire, which would be the opposition of indoors and outdoors. It would be easy to miss if you weren't looking for it. Opposition can often be found between the author's style and his subject. For example, a cerebral, intellectual style that's heavy on analysis in a story about a hog farmer would be opposition. Your essay would want to address why the author wrote that way and what effect it has on the story. Keep an eye out for any elements that are in contrast to each other: They'll often lead you to the heart of the story.

Let's look at that Dylan Thomas poem again. Notice what we went after in our opening paragraph: the image of the author working alone and the image of lovers in each other's arms. That's an opposition. Do you see how it's not exactly a conflict? It's a pairing of images whereby each becomes more striking and informative when placed against the other. Doesn't that pair of images seem central to the poem? Doesn't it seem there's something to talk about there? What exactly it means is open to interpretation, and that's exactly what you should do when you see elements opposed to each other: *interpret*. Don't worry about getting it right; there is no single right answer. The AP Reader will see that your searching intelligence has found the complexity of the material and is making sense of it. That's exactly what the Reader wants you to do. (And it's what very few students attempt to do.)

Opposition creates tension and mystery. What's the most mysterious line in "In My Craft or Sullen Art"? We think it's "And lovers lie abed / With all their griefs in their arms." That line alone has an opposition: If they're lovers, why do they have their griefs in their arms?

So your job is to figure out what Thomas means by that. The answer is: Nothing simple, but something you can write about. Realize that you don't have to resolve opposition. You don't have to interpret that line (or the poem) in a final way that makes absolute perfect sense. It's a poem, not a riddle.

Our opening paragraph mentioned a third opposition: Thomas's sense of futility and his sense of total purpose. The sense of futility in the poem comes from the statements that the lovers "pay no praise or wages," nor do they heed Thomas's "craft or art." Describing how Thomas gets across his deep sense of purpose is more difficult, even though it is the stronger of the two impressions. In many ways the entire poem is about conveying the sense of purpose Thomas feels when writing poetry. An AP essay won't get to all of these oppositions; it shouldn't try to. But you can be sure we'll mention that repetition plays a part.

We found these things because we looked for the oppositions. Some oppositions are obvious. Like a tiger in a bus station, they catch your attention immediately and make you wonder what's going on. Good writers boldly toss together mismatched concepts, objects, and tones all the time. But good writers also work with quiet oppositions that aren't nearly so easy to spot. If you aren't paying attention, you'll feel what's going on without realizing where it's coming from. Many literary oppositions come from within one character. The character who wants two totally opposite things at the same time is a classic case of opposition, as is the character who badly wants something that he just isn't cut out for. Another important opposition is *tone*. Some writers will write about the silliest thing possible in a deadly serious way. (This is generally done to make a situation funnier.) Still another opposition, one that is often handled with supreme delicacy and with seemingly infinite repercussions, is *time*. Writers will often let the past stand in opposition to present. The story of a once proud family that has fallen on hard times is an example of a plot that uses the changes time brings to develop oppositions.

We could come up with hundreds of specific examples of oppositions in literature, but those examples won't do you any good if you haven't read the works referred to. Our point here is to give you a tool with which to generate ideas for your AP essays.

You're probably still a little unclear as to how to apply this concept of oppositions to a short AP essay, but don't worry. The samples and examples in Chapter 10 will take you through several AP passages and point out how you might use oppositions to find ideas (and boost your essay scores into the eights and nines).

AFTER THE FIRST PARAGRAPH — DO AN ESSAY CHECK

Look back at our overall approach to the Essay section and you'll see that the second to last point is the recommendation to do an essay check. That sounds fancy, but all it means is that you should think briefly about the points you need to make in your essay.

The time to do this thinking is after you've written that first paragraph. The first paragraph comes from using the Idea Machine: discussing the meaning of the passage or poem (remember, the newspaper version plus emotion) and beginning to talk about how the author gets her point across. This method gives you a first paragraph that establishes the foundation on which the rest of your essay will be built. If it's hyperfocused, it will already set out the overall points you intend to cover, but even if it just gives you a general platform on which to build, you've got plenty, enough to put you miles ahead of the majority of other (flailing) students. The essay check is just a spot check, a place to pause and make sure you're on the right track and haven't forgotten anything important. When you've finished your first paragraph, stop and ask yourself:

- What points does my first paragraph indicate I'm going to cover?
- Do those points address the specifics the essay question calls for?
- In what order am I going to put my points?

When you've decided in what order to put your points, get back to writing. Your check shouldn't take more than a minute. The least important part of the check is deciding what order to put your points in. It's the closest thing to an outline you need to do, and don't overdo it. As long as you've paused to think about addressing the question it makes sense to form a rough plan of how you'll proceed. But the idea is to make it easier for you to write, not to suffocate your writing. Be flexible. If it's convenient to change the order of your points as you write, change them. If you think of new things to say, say them!

DON'T CRAMP YOUR STYLE

As you write, you'll notice things that you hadn't seen at first. These are things that will depart from your original ideas and take you in unexpected directions. Should you include these things? YES!

Many, many students are intimidated by the test. They think their writing has to be truly organized and tight. These students end up writing short, dry, little essays: Essays that receive a score of five. Go with the flow. It is impossible to write a tight, well-organized essay in 40 minutes—*impossible*. As long as your ideas have some faint connection to the question ETS has asked, include them. Write a great first paragraph that sets you out in the right direction and then loosen up—you'll score high.

DEVELOPING YOUR ESSAY

Once you've finished your first paragraph and your essay check, it's time to develop your essay. When it comes to development, each essay is unique. The best way to study development is through examples. The next chapter is devoted to sample essays; we'll show you how to put our method (and your ideas) into practice.

SUMMARY

- If you can get off to a good start, you're more than halfway to a great score.

- Use our approach:
  - Note the time. Remember, 40 minutes per essay.
  - Pick the essay (prose, poetry, open) you want to write.
  - Identify the key words in the essay prompt.
  - Skim the passage.
  - Work the passage, making notes and identifying quotations you will want to use.
  - Use the Idea Machine to plan your first paragraph.
  - Support and develop the points you made in your first paragraph in your body paragraphs.
  - Get a solid conclusion on the page.
  - Repeat the process with the other essays.

- Don't write an outline.

- Identify key words in the prompt.

- Understand the question and how to turn the question into an *essay idea*.

- There is a basic format for the classic essay question that ETS uses:

  > Read the following work carefully. Then write a well-organized essay in which you discuss the manner in which the author conveys ideas and meaning. Discuss the techniques the author uses to make this passage effective. Avoid simple summary.

- You probably won't see the classic question word for word; you'll see a modified version that asks you to focus on a specific element or two from the passage.

- Use the Idea Machine:
  - What is the meaning of the work?
    Meaning is literal meaning plus the emotions the work evokes.
  - How does the author get that meaning across?
    important images
    specific words or short phrases
    opposition

- The Idea Machine is the tool that helps you to apply your skills specifically to a 40-minute essay.

- Any student who can write a five-scoring essay can write a seven-scoring essay or better.

- Don't worry about being wrong. Have confidence in your interpretation.

- Unusual language and imagery are great places to find essay ideas.

- *Opposition* is created when any pair of elements in a story or poem contrast sharply or subtly.

- Look for elements that are in opposition. They'll lead you to the heart of the passage and give you material for the kinds of ideas that make AP Readers give out nines.

- Go with the flow. It is impossible to write a tight, well-organized essay in 40 minutes. Write a great first paragraph that sets you out in the right direction, and then loosen up. Don't digress, however, and start talking about irrelevant topics. Always stay focused on the text.

10

Sample Prose and Poetry Essays

Here's a poem that relies a great deal on irony, similar to Robert Browning's *My Last Duchess*, which you worked on back in Chapter 4. This time, the poem we are studying comes with an essay question. Read the question and the poem and think about how you might write a response.

SAMPLE ESSAY ON POETRY
MARGARET ATWOOD'S "SIREN SONG"

ESSAY (SUGGESTED TIME — 40 MINUTES)
Read the following poem carefully, and then write a well-organized essay in which you discuss the author's use of language to convey her themes.

Siren* Song

This is the one song everyone
would like to learn: the song
that is irresistible:

Line   the song that forces men
(5)   to leap overboard in squadrons
even though they see the beached skulls

the song nobody knows
because anyone who has heard
it is dead, and the others can't remember.

(10)   Shall I tell you the secret
and if I do, will you get me
out of this bird suit?

I don't enjoy it here
squatting on this island
(15)   looking picturesque and mythical

with these two feathery maniacs,
I don't enjoy singing
this trio, fatal and valuable.

I will tell the secret to you,
(20)   to you, only to you.
Come closer. This song

is a cry for help: Help me!
Only you, only you can,
you are unique

(25)   at last. Alas
it is a boring song
but it works every time.

* A siren is a character in classical Greek mythology, half woman
and half bird, who lured sailors to their deaths by singing a seductive song.

From *Selected Poems* by Margaret Atwood. Houghton Mifflin Co., 1987.

Poetry Answers in General

Before we delve into this specific poem, we want to discuss some differences between prose and
poetry. Poems are special cases; they deal in compressed language. Lyric poems (most of the poems
on the AP English Literature exam are lyric poems) often use a convention, simple on the surface but
infinite in its varieties and depth. In this convention, the speaker of the poem (the "I") is addressing
the reader directly, as prompted by a certain occasion or dramatic situation. If you pay attention to
this lyric convention and its component parts, you may be able to understand a seemingly difficult

poem more quickly. Not all poems on the AP exam will completely fit into this convention, but most will. The one we've chosen to discuss, *Siren Song* by Margaret Atwood, absolutely does.

In the previous chapter, we introduced the Idea Machine; three questions to consider when looking at a work of literature. Do you remember them? They are:

1. What does the poem or passage mean?

2. How did the author get you to see that?

3. How do the answers to question 1 and 2 direct your knowledge to adequately answer the question?

The same three questions also apply to the poetry essay. Question 2, however, should be considered more as a kind of drop-down menu when you are writing about poetry. Here are the three Idea Machine questions modified for the poetry essay:

What does the poem mean?

How did the author get you to see that?

- What is suggested by the title?

- Who is the speaker and who is the audience?

- What is the dramatic situation that prompted the speaker to speak?

- What problem is being explored in the poem, and does the poem find a solution?

How do the answers to the first two questions direct your knowledge to adequately answer the exam question?

You don't have to ask or answer all of the secondary questions under question 2, but the more answers you can find to these questions, the better your essay will be. Let's see how this method works by looking at a specific poem.

Discussion of Siren Song by Margaret Atwood

As with many poems, this poem could be the focus of a long discussion. A full class period could be spent analyzing it, as a group of interested students slowly circled it, discovered small details about it, and found ways to express their discoveries to each other. You don't have that time.

We won't be delving deeply into the many possible interpretations of this poem. The point here is to figure out what you could say about this poem in order to write an essay that answers the question ETS has given you. Let's use the poetry essay Idea Machine—the simple, orderly process that you should apply to every AP English Literature essay.

First, tackle the question.

What's the literal meaning of the poem?

It is the classic AP essay question. That makes our lives a little easier. The Idea Machine will work perfectly here.

Here is some background that may prove helpful to your understanding of the poem. The speaker is a siren, a creature from Greek mythology. These creatures were notorious for using their "honey-voiced" song to attract sailors toward their island. When the sailors, entranced by the siren's voices, came in close to the island to try and catch a glimpse of the singers (who kept their hideous bird-shaped bodies out of sight), the sailor's ship would be dashed on the dangerous rocks and all the passengers would die. This entire poem is an allusion to Homer's *The Odyssey*. Odysseus, the main character, wants to hear the sirens' song but does not want to die before he can return to his home. He puts wax in the ears of his oarsmen and has them tie him to the mast so he cannot react to the song. Odysseus is nearly driven mad by the experience, but he and his ship pass the island safely.

If the AP test writers were to use this poem, or another that relies heavily on allusions, the chances are that they would not provide the background that we just did. They might place an asterisk after the word "Siren" in the title and define it in a few words like we did, but unless you've read the original work of literature that the selected poem is referencing, the allusion will be mostly lost on you. For this reason, we are going to work with this poem as if you did not have any outside information about Homer or *The Odyssey*. Fortunately, you don't need to grasp the allusion to understand this poem well enough to write a high scoring essay about it. Recognizing the allusion helps, and if you do recognize an allusion, you should develop it in your essay as thoroughly as time permits, but the AP test writers will never choose a poem that relies on an allusion for its very sense.

Here's a quick summary of what you should have in your mind after reading the poem. We will only refer to information actually on the page.

The song being described in the first four stanzas has four main qualities: Everyone wants to learn the song; the song cannot be resisted once it is heard; the song causes men to leap out of their ships, into the sea and to their deaths; the song is unknown because those who have heard it are all dead.

The next three stanzas of the poem (lines 10–21) provide important information about the speaker. The speaker is willing to trade a secret for the reader's help in getting her out of her bird suit. The speaker reports being unhappy with her life. She does not like "squatting" or "looking picturesque and mythical." She seems unsatisfied with the company she keeps, calling them, "feathery maniacs." She even maintains that she doesn't get any joy from singing, which seems to be her main occupation. She characterizes her song as a "trio, fatal and valuable." In other words, the siren song is sung with three voices and causes the death of those men throwing themselves overboard, who were mentioned in line 5.

The penultimate lines of the poem (lines 19–25) represent a shift in tone, as the speaker stops musing on her fate and directly addresses the reader. She is calling us closer to her, promising exclusive knowledge of this valuable secret she harbors, and she is claiming that only we can successfully answer her "cry for help."

The closing lines of the poem shift tone again. The speaker contradicts her earlier statement about the song's irresistibility by claiming that it is "boring," despite its efficiency. The reader is to understand that the song has worked, insofar as the reader is now dashed and dead amongst the "beached skulls" of the other folks who responded to this siren song in the past.

The four paragraphs preceding this one are a summary of the poem; they are not an essay. In fact, you can use these four paragraphs as a good example of what not to write on your AP essay. This literal reading is only a first step, a first step that will happen internally for you if you practice it. Nothing is more mechanical or commonplace than a simple retelling of the passage. This kind of essay is going to score in the range of a 4 or a 5. If we apply the rest of the Idea Machine to this literal reading, we can move the score much higher. Let's continue with the Idea Machine:

What is suggested by the title?

Who is the speaker and who is the audience?

What is the dramatic situation that prompted the speaker to speak?

What problem is being explored in the poem, and does the poem find a solution?

What feelings do you get from the poem?

What is the overall effect of the poem?

Let's take these questions one by one:

What is suggested by the title? For only two words, the title is complex. It uses alliteration (in this case, repetition of sibilant "S" sounds at the beginning of each word) and allusion (already discussed above). But more important for our current purposes, the title seems to call attention—through its use of the word "song"—to the idea that we may be reading lyrics which are meant to be sung, for all or part of the poem. Another function of the title might be to clue us in to the fact that the poem is describing the sensual characteristics of a siren's song. We'll have to see, as we explore the other questions, which interpretation of the title seems more in keeping with our other answers.

Who is the speaker and who is the audience? The answer to this question is crucial for many poems, and especially important for this one. The speaker is a siren. You might say that her audience is the reader, and you'd be correct, but you could also correctly observe that the author projects a role onto the reader—that of a sailor lost in the siren's song. This strategy is a common one in lyric poems. A reader of a Shakespearean sonnet, for example, might find himself being addressed directly, as if the reader were Shakespeare's lover. The reader is meant, of course, to use his imagination. The reader is not supposed to respond to the poem and actually agree to marry the speaker of a four hundred year old sonnet. The reader is instead supposed to understand that he is being directly addressed as if he were part of a dramatic situation.

What is the dramatic situation that prompted the speaker to speak? If you can put the dramatic situation of this poem into your own words, you are off to a good start. We know from our reading of literature that first-person narrators are not always trustworthy. How much do we trust this speaker, who complains of being trapped in a bird suit, singing with two other feathery maniacs, and who promises us the answer to a secret? To what extent does her cry for help seem genuine? Because we have read the poem several times, we have the benefit of knowing the final three lines, where she comes out from behind her mask and reveals that "it works every time." The "it" is her song. The secret she has been promising us, which has kept us in suspense, has caused our death in the dramatic situation of the poem. We are yet one more group of sailors taken in. She has even told us that we would not be able to resist it, but we were somewhat fooled by this appearance of sincerity. Maybe we were immune. After all, wasn't she the victim here? Her life was unenjoyable. She needed our help. "Come closer," she said, and we did, and we became "unique / at last," at the very moment that we became like every other sailor who has had his skull beached because he could not resist the song.

What problem is being explored in the poem and does the poem find a solution? Once you read the last three lines of this poem, you can easily realize that the earlier twenty-four lines were a performance. If the speaker was only saying "Help me!" in order to seduce the reader/sailor closer to the rocks, then the speaker was using irony, saying one thing while meaning another, to trap the reader. This observation is true, but the slippery nature of irony rarely stops at the first observational level. Isn't it also possible to read "Help me!" as a sincere request? Couldn't the speaker be fed up with the "boring song" of her seductive conquests? To what extent should a reader read past the first ironic level to a deeper, true level within the irony, where the speaker is stuck in a "bird suit" and can't get out, where the speaker is doomed to fatally seduce all passersby? The problem of this poem has to do with the places where point of view and tone intersect. How much should the reader trust the speaker? Which part of the poem is more believable, the first 24 lines or the last 3? Why? How? The poem does not find an easy solution to these questions, so lets move on to the feelings the reader gets from this poem.

What feelings do you get from this poem? You probably already noticed how the tool of "finding oppositions," the tool we discussed at great length in the preceding chapter, is coming into play in our discussion of this poem. The title has two possible meanings. The speaker has two mutually exclusive possible intentions. And the feelings a careful reader pulls from this poem are probably going to be in opposition also. Don't let such discoveries unnerve or confuse you. The AP exam will feature complex poems, full of these kinds of tensions. If they didn't, you'd have nothing to write about.

Readers of this poem often feel coaxed. For part of the poem, at least, the reader is likely to feel pleasure at being the object of someone else's intense, intimate need. The speaker, after all, wants to share a secret with us. A secret establishes a bond between those who know the secret, and this speaker wants to create such a bond with us. We may be flattered, even if we recognize the foreshadowing in phrases such as "leap overboard," "beached skulls," and "fatal and valuable." Some secrets are terrible and devastating, yet we understand ourselves to be privileged to hear this secret. The speaker has chosen us, believes us worthy. By listening to this secret, we may even be able to do some good. We feel a good deal of pity for this speaker, trapped as she is in a bird suit. She is squatting, which seems to make her vulnerable or maybe undignified. She is directly playing to our sympathies, begging us for help. How can we resist such persuasion?

If the reader feels compelled to learn the siren's secret to satisfy his own curiosity and to help the speaker out of a sense of generosity, then the reader, for the first 24 lines, is responding in a similar manner—with keen interest—to apparently opposing forces: selfishness and selflessness. Combined, they make a powerfully magnetizing force that weakens only as the final three lines expose the preceding 24, as if a curtain were pulled back to reveal the mundane inner workings of an otherwise impressive spectacle. To go back to the allusion, these final three lines are analogous in form and content to the way that the sailors, drawn by the honey voices of the hidden sirens, see the hideous appearance of the sirens moments before their inevitable deaths. The reader usually feels tricked and cast off during the last three lines. The speaker, who had previously seemed so thoroughly interested, is now yawning, bored with the certainty of her own success.

What is the overall effect of this poem? Many readers have found great depth in this poem because it deals so ambivalently with seduction. The speaker has great power, but she seems trapped by that power. The song she sings is irresistibly fatal, yet she finds it to be dull and repetitive. The speaker, almost against her will, plays the victim in order to be the victor, but her performance of the part of the victim seems humiliating to her, and the victory is hollow.

We came to all these points by thinking about the answers to the questions in italics and by looking for oppositions. But we also had the time we needed, and we've had some practice at this kind of thing before. So…

Relax

Are you supposed to get all this in one or two readings in between checking your watch to make sure you have time for the next two essays? Not likely. We wanted to show you how much there is to unearth in a typical AP exam passage or poem and how much our techniques can dig up for you. All you'd need to see about this poem on the actual test is that the speaker is in some kind of opposition with herself. If you saw that and looked for the ways that Atwood got that opposition across, you'd find enough to write a great essay.

A Strong Beginning

You should be ready to formulate your opening. Here's an example:

> "Siren Song" is a deceptively simple title that calls attention to the idea that human beings are sometimes undone by their desires, forced "to leap overboard in squadrons." By the end of the poem, the speaker seems conflicted about her desires also.

Is this great writing? No. It won't win any prizes. But for the AP English Literature Exam, such writing is well on its way to a high score. Anything beyond this will blow your Reader away. Let's take it apart for a moment, and then we'll finish the essay.

The beginning paragraph is a first stab at talking about meaning. We wanted to start with something more original than, "In 'Siren Song' by Margaret Atwood…" Starting that way is okay, and if the rest of your essay is good, you'll score high, but the readers like to see you try something a little more daring. So, we connected the title to a feeling—the overall feeling of the poem—and it seemed to work. We connected the concrete image of the men forced to leap overboard in large groups with an abstract corollary: the idea that human desire can lead us into dangerous situations. Then we made a link back to the speaker's own dilemma. This kind of work justifies our effort at an original beginning. The reader would be impressed that you arrived so quickly at a main (but by no means obvious) point of the passage.

Unfortunately, we ran out of steam before we could satisfy the overall goal of our beginning: to get at the meaning of the poem (literal and emotional) and explain how Atwood gets it across (we barely started this process).

Keep Going

Because our first paragraph began with such originality, we can begin our second paragraph, "Atwood's poem," without fear of seeming dull or mechanical. We'll start describing (not summarizing) what Atwood's poem is, what it does, and how it does it. This is a song with a double meaning. Whenever you can show that a writer has created a double meaning, you have already risen in the estimation of the Reader, who has likely been dealing with single meanings for most of the last hour of her reading assignment. We can't stop there; we have to say what both meanings are. We might have analyzed any number of double meanings, but we chose to stick with the speaker's dilemma, which is one of the central contrasts of this poem. The poem is a song in two parts: The first part is a persuasive performance, and the second part comments back on that performance, revealing it to be artificial and predictable. Now we are talking about two things at once, and on the road to a higher score.

> Atwood's poem is a song in two parts: the first part (lines 1–24) is a persuasive performance, and the second part (lines 25–27) comments back on that performance, revealing it to be artificial and predictable. The speaker is a Siren, and by her nature, has to entice people to their death. She admits this role to her reader, complains about it, asks for the reader's help in releasing her from that role and then causes the death of the reader to ostensibly occur, even as he lives long enough to have the trick of it revealed in the final lines.

Not bad. Let's do an essay check. Is the product of our Idea Machine complete? Not yet. We still haven't said enough about how Atwood shaped the poem, and we haven't addressed our specific intention of writing about Atwood's use of irony. Next, we need to commit ourselves to a statement about how Atwood shapes her imagery. What comes next is the most "mechanical" part of our opening, but such a formula is necessary as it will launch us into the rest of the essay.

> Through the use of an ironic, untrustworthy, first-person speaker and through the careful use of tonal contrast, Atwood gives the reader a sense of the ambivalence human beings often have when they are involved in presenting manipulative, persuasive speech and actions.

There. We've said something. We've called attention to the persuasive performance, the ambivalence of the speaker and the literary tricks and methods that Atwood uses to communicate these aspects of the poem to the reader. Now it's time to check again and pause briefly to consider what points we'll make, and how we'll address the specifics of this essay question.

...And Going

What's left? Let's see. We are pretty thin on specifics. We've made assertions about irony and tonal contrast, but we should still support these assertions with concrete developed examples from the text. We have said that there are no checklists for the Readers to use, but one aspect of your writing that every reader will look for is your fluid use of specific evidence to prove your point. Without evidence, your essay is an empty series of assertions. With evidence, your essay starts, at least, to follow through on your argument.

Here's the rest of our essay.

> Who is being manipulated in the poem? The answer is not entirely clear. On the first level of irony, the level where the speaker pleads "Help me," the reader is being manipulated to feel pity for the speaker and to "come closer" in order to provide some relief. The fact that the speaker has already provided the gruesome imagery of "beached skulls" as what results if one were to follow her "irresistible" song only makes the manipulation more impressive. It is as if a salesmen told you about other customers he had bilked before cheating you, and you were still powerless in the face of his persuasive force. Atwood, however, is not only interested in this first level of irony. She also wants to draw the reader's attention to the condition of the manipulator. The Siren asks for the reader's pity, ironically, as a way of seducing the reader, but then earns the reader's pity, more sincerely, in the last three lines when she reveals how tedious the whole process is for her. This tonal contrast, "boring" as opposed to the earlier "irresistible" provides the main shape of Atwood's poem. The writer wants the reader to feel complex and mutually exclusive allegiances. The reader will momentarily sympathize with the men forced to "leap overboard in squadrons" to their deaths, but feel a deeper, more compelling pity for the speaker trapped in a "bird suit," who reports that she does not enjoy her fatal role in life, even as she efficiently performs it. After giving in to the urge to "come closer" to hear the Siren's secret and to help her escape her plight, the reader is likely to feel cheated because the speaker suddenly shifts her tone: "Alas / it is a boring song / but it works every time." After the speaker moves beyond the feeling of being cheated — the reader is not actually dashed against the rocks — he can better appreciate the ironic pain of the Siren, who is doomed to victimize others through her natural singing voice.

That's the end of our essay. It's not that long; much more could be said. But that's it. That's all the time we had. So we wrote that and moved on. We checked our watch, and it said that we had used up 40 minutes. Is it the best piece of writing we've ever done? No. But will it earn a high score? Yes, high enough. Why?

First, as we said, the AP readers are forgiving of some mistakes. The opening of the essay lets the Readers know we understand some of the main aspects of the poem and are able to put these understandings into fairly clear sentences. Second, the essay continues to make good points. It talks about irony and the speaker's trustworthiness and the tonal contrast in the last few lines of the poem. We spread out well-chosen examples from most of the stanzas of the poem and we draw attention to the manipulative aspects of the tone. We might have overdone the bit about the salesman, but so what? We didn't digress for long, and we weren't being overly repetitive. The Readers want to see your ideas. By making these insights clear and obvious to the Reader, you make it easy for the Reader to give you a better score.

Is this a well-organized essay? Not by the standards of the writing process. If you were writing for a take home essay, this would be more like a free-writing, brainstorming session on the journey to a finished project, but by AP standards, this essay is pretty good. The essay begins with a clear direction, moves on to a consideration of double meanings and oppositions, and finishes with specifically developed examples of imagery, irony, and tonal contrast. For a first draft done in just 40 minutes top to bottom, the essay is admirable and will probably receive a 7.

SAMPLE ESSAY ON PROSE

Let's look at another sample. If you've got paper and pencil handy, try the question that follows and time yourself. At the very least, before you go to our sample essays (we've written two sample responses to this passage, one great and one fair) think about your first paragraph and try writing it in your head. But you really should practice writing a whole essay under time restraints.

Essay (Suggested Time—40 Minutes)

Read the following passage carefully. Write a well-organized essay that discusses the author's use of the resources of language to dramatize the speaker's experiences of life at sea as well as to dramatize the character of that speaker.

Ultramarine by Malcolm Lowry

Puella mea[1]…No, not you, not even my supervisor
would recognise me as I sit here upon the number six
hatch drinking ship's coffee. Driven out and com-

Line pelled to be chaste. The whole deep blue day is before

(5) me. The breakfast dishes must be washed up: the
forecastle and the latrines must be cleaned and
scrubbed—the alleyway too—the brasswork must be
polished. For this is what sea life is like now—a
domestic servant on a treadmill in hell! Labourers,

(10) navvies, scalers rather than sailors. The firemen[2] are
the real boys, and I've heard it said there's not much
they can't do that the seamen can. The sea! God, what
it may suggest to you! Perhaps you think of a deep
gray sailing ship lying over in the seas, with the hail

(15) hurling over her: or a bluenose skipper who chewed
glass so that he could spit blood, who could sew a
man up alive in a sack and throw him overboard, still
groaning! Well, those were the ancient violences, the
old heroic days of holystones; and they have gone

(20) you say. But the sea is none the less the sea. Man
scatters even farther and farther the footsteps of exile.
It is ever the path to some strange land, some magic
land of faery, which has its extraordinary and un-
earthly reward for us after the storms of ocean. But it

(25) is not only the nature of our work which has changed,
Janet. Instead of being called out on deck at all hours
to shorten sail, we have to rig derricks, or to paint the
smokestack: the only thing we have in common with
Dauber, besides dungarees, is that we still "mix red

(30) lead in many a bouilli[3] tin." We batter the rusty scales
off the deck with a carpenter's maul until the skin
peels off our hands like the rust off the deck…Ah well,
but this life has compensations, the days of joy even
when the work is most brutalising. At sea, at

(35) this time, when the forecastle doesn't need scrubbing,
there is a drowsy calm there during the time we may
spend between being roused from our bunks and
turning out on deck. Someone throws himself on the
floor, another munches a rasher; hear how Horsey's

(40) limbs crack in a last sleepy stretch! But when bells
have gone on the bridge and we stand by the
paintlocker, the blood streams red and cheerful in the
fresh morning breeze, and I feel almost joyful with
my chipping hammer and scraper. They will follow

(45) me like friends, throughout the endless day. Cleats
are knocked out, booms, hatches, and tarpaulins
pulled away by brisk hands, and we go down the
ladder deep into the hold's night, clamber up along

the boat's side, where plank ends bristle, then we sit
(50) down and turn to wildly! Hammers clap nimbly
against the iron, the hold quivers, howls, crashes, the
speed increases: our scrapers flash and become
lightning in our hands. The rust spurts out from the side
in a hail of sharp flakes, always right in front of
(55) our eyes, and we rave, but on on! Then all at once the
pace slackens, and the avalanche of hewing becomes a
firm, measured beat, of an even deliberate force, the
arm swings like a rocking machine, and our fist
loosens its grip on the slim haft—

(60) And so I sit, chipping, dreaming of you Janet, until
the iron facing shows, or until eight bells go, or until
the bosun comes and knocks us off. Oh, Janet, I do
love you so. But let us have no nonsense about it.

[1] My girl (Latin).
[2] The men that tend the steam engines and boilers of the ship.
[3] bouillion

DISCUSSION

Did you practice writing the essay on this passage? Did you time yourself? If so, great; if not, we hope you at least read the passage carefully and thought about how you would go about writing your first paragraph.

Oddly enough, writing about prose can actually be more difficult than writing about poetry. Poetry often presents many difficulties to the reader, difficulties caused by the density and complexity of poetic language. However, once interpreted, those same difficulties give you material to write about. Prose presents the opposite problem. In general, assimilating the passage is not too hard; the challenge is finding something worth saying about it. It is useful to remember that the literary devices you look for in poetry can also be pointed out in your prose essays.

As always, start out with the classic question and let the Idea Machine guide your thinking process. Of course, make sure that you allow the actual ETS question to focus the development of your essay, and also note the time so that you don't go overboard and come up short on the last essay.

Below you'll find two responses to the passage. One is excellent, and one is mediocre. We'll discuss both responses after the samples are given. By the way, in these two essays we've taken out the annoying errors of diction and spelling that creep into every student's essay. We want you to read the essays for what they say and how they say it without distracting errors. The sentence construction reflects student writing, but in reality, both essays would have more language mistakes.

Sample Response to *Ultramarine* — Essay 1

In the passage, Malcolm Lowry effectively uses the resources of language to create an interior monologue (a mental speech) to dramatize the adventures a young English boy has aboard a ship, and shows the character of the boy, Dana Hilliot, as well. He uses vivid imagery and many details from the boy's life to show who Hilliot is and what he thinks, and captures the different rhythms of life aboard a ship.

First Hilliot thinks that no one, "not even my supervisor would recognise me..." This shows that Hilliot thinks that he has changed and that life at sea has changed him. But he's happy, he likes the change, as he says, "The whole deep blue day is before me." But there are many conflicting feelings in Hilliot as he sits and drinks his coffee. For he quickly screams out, "this is what sea life is like now—a domestic servant on a treadmill in hell!" This shows the conflict that Hilliot undergoes. He doesn't know whether he thinks life at sea is great or a stinking hell. Lowry shows this by switching all the time between images that are pleasant, and images that are full of misery and despair and heartbreak. He really misses Janet and it shows. A sailor's life is lonely, and Lowry shows that. Lonely and boring sometimes, as hard as that may be to believe. But the boredom is broken up by danger and hardship. "We batter the rusty scales off the deck with a carpenter's maul until the skin peels off our hands like the rust off the deck..." is an example of the hardship. But immediately, the conflict shows up again. The very next sentence is, "Ah well, but this life has compensations, the days of joy even when the work is most brutalising."

Through it all though, Hilliot thinks of Janet. He begins thinking of her "Puella mea...," which is Latin for "my girl" and ends saying "Oh, Janet, I do love you so." This tells us a great deal about Hilliot. He misses his girlfriend and is probably homesick for England too. These are normal reactions for the character of a young Englishman far from home, and by framing the story between these statements Lowry shows that the character of Dana Hilliot hasn't changed as much as he thinks it has. Hilliot is still a lonely young man with a great deal to learn.

Sample Response to *Ultramarine* — Essay 2

Who hasn't dreamed of throwing everything away and running off to sea? And yet very few people actually do run off to sea, probably because, at least in part, they realized (around the time they're packing all those wool sweaters into a duffle bag) that life at sea isn't just dropping anchor at exotic ports and gazing at the moon setting over the Indian Ocean. It's a hard, dangerous life. Better unpack the sweaters.

The passage shows the inner thoughts of one young man who actually did run off, and as he sits and thinks of the life he's leading and the life he's left behind, we get a picture of what a young sailor's life is really like. We get something else as well, a detailed portrait of a young, confused man, Dana Hilliot, and all the swirling emotions that he carries in his young heart. Hilliot is lonely, defiant, excited, bored, romantic, and cynical all at once.

The passage begins, "Puella mea..." Although that's Latin for "my girl," the translation isn't so important as the fact that it's Latin. Right from the beginning, Lowry shows us a fish out of water. Dana's educated, but how many of Dana's shipmates speak Latin? Probably none. Dana talks about how unrecognizable he's become. Maybe he really is unrecognizable to his old friends, but it's more likely that he can't recognize himself. He's gotten more than he bargained for, "this is what sea life is like now—a domestic servant on a treadmill in hell!" This is one of the recurring themes of the passage. Hard, dull, work. Polishing brass. Chipping paint. Scrubbing and cleaning. It isn't a very romantic scenario. This theme tells us not just about sea-life, but about Dana. He must have been pretty naïve to not know that a sailor works from daybreak into the night, and it's all manual labor.

Lowry gives us a picture of the wild, terrifying, intense life that Dana thought he was going to lead. He describes it to his girlfriend, to correct her and tell her the truth, but you can be sure that these were Dana's ideas of life at sea before he came to the ship. "Perhaps you think of a deep gray sailing ship lying over in the seas, with the hail hurling over her: or a bluenose skipper who chewed glass so that he could spit blood…" Well, Dana has learned that it isn't anything like that at all. His romantic dreams have been squashed, all except the sea. He still finds poetry in the sea. It is "ever the path to some strange land, some magic land of faery…" This is the beauty that Dana really got on board for.

The passage then takes us even deeper into Dana's character. In the beginning, he talked about how horrible it was to be just a lackey, scrubbing decks. As he thinks deeper though, we see a real change in him. He loves the moments of calm, and is such a sensitive experiencer of the life around him that he even notes the way one of his fellows' joints crack, but the amazing thing is that he's learned to love the work. He describes it with relish, "I feel almost joyful with my chipping hammer and scraper. They will follow me like friends…The rust spurts out from the side in a hail of sharp flakes, always right in front of our eyes, and we rave, but on on!" The work, the hard relentless work, is the real adventure, and in those words "on on!" you can hear almost hear Dana's amazement at the fact that he can do it, he can keep going on.

In the end Dana's loneliness, cut off from his familiar life, returns him to being a moody "Romeo," dreaming of his girlfriend, imagining sweet-talking her. It wells up in him with the line, "Oh, Janet, I do love you so." But then comes the very last line of the passage, another abrupt change, "But let us have no nonsense about it." He's still a young person, pouring out his love to his girlfriend but then a second later he's pretending to be a tough guy, a sailor, who wants "no nonsense." By putting these lines, one after the other, Lowry shows Dana in the midst of growing up, and pretending to be more hardened than he is.

DISCUSSION OF SAMPLE RESPONSES 1 AND 2

It shouldn't be too difficult to tell which is the better of the two responses. Essay 1 is clearly an average response. It shows an intelligent student struggling to write a response about a passage he didn't get much from. Notice the mechanical repetition of the question, and the mechanical, plodding way he works through the passage, not so much interpreting as it is summarizing. He did manage to address the question somewhat, and did pull together a few simple insights into the passage. He would receive a score of five. Not a terrible score by any means, but you can do better.

The biggest mistake the author of the first essay made was to choose to emphasize the life-at-sea aspect of the question. Unless an author is just setting the stage for what is to come, or planting some enormous symbol, almost every sentence in a novel or a story *is intended to reveal character*. This is especially true of the kind of masterful writers you'll be dealing with on the AP exam. When you read prose on the AP test always ask yourself what the sentences tell you about the people in the passage. In the Lowry passage, everything Dana thinks tells us something about Dana. The first student missed most of the psychological details of the passage and ended up floundering.

The author of the second essay worked with the Idea Machine. She asked herself about both the literal and emotional content of the passage. She kept an eye out for strong imagery and evidence of opposites. In doing so she saw that the passage was filled with conflicting images. Dana loves Janet, but then wants "no nonsense." Dana thinks the work is beneath him ("domestic servant"—Dana's the kind of kid who's used to having servants, not being one) and makes his shipboard life hell, but at the same time he realizes that when he's lost in the physical frenzy of the labor, he finds the work exhilarating. The author of the second essay tried to put these oppositions together in a meaningful way. Most important, she knew to focus on character. By tying everything back to Dana's character she assured herself of a high score. In fact, the second essay would be scored a nine—the top score.

Also notice that the second passage does not begin with the typical restatement of the question. That doesn't mean that a Reader would look at essay 2's beginning and think, "Oh my, what an original opening—this essay gets a high score." A nice opening isn't enough. You still have to write the essay. But, the Reader would think, "Hmm, this kid isn't writing like a robot...now if she can show me she understood the passage and communicate her understanding with anything like the flair of this opening, I'll give her a high score." In other words, yes, your opening can be a little stiff and dull (yes, you can paraphrase the question if you want to) if you write an otherwise good, insightful essay, but an original, interesting opening is better, if you can write one without wasting a lot of time.

Essay Dos and Don'ts to Remember

After reviewing some sample essays, you probably have a good sense of what you need to accomplish to achieve a solid score. Some of this may seem basic and verge on the formulaic. Remember that your good ideas do need to be clear and well-organized. The following are tips for reviewing your own practice essays.

Your first paragraph should

- grab the reader (don't worry if you can't do this, but it helps)
- answer the question in the prompt
- preview the evidence you'll use to support your ideas

Your first paragraph should not

- go off on a tangent
- ignore the prompt
- merely restate the wording of the prompt

Your body paragraphs should

- have clear transitions and topic sentences
- provide evidence, in the form of quotations from the prompt, that supports your opinion
- explain how that evidence supports your point of view

Your body paragraphs should not

- rely on plot summary
- let quotation outweigh analysis
- ramble

Your conclusion should

- exist
- sum up the evidence for the jury
- contain any profound insights about the work which may have occurred to you while writing

Your conclusion should not

- suggest you didn't budget your time
- merely restate the introduction or prompt

SUMMARY

- Avoid summary.
- Get a feel of the passage.
- Notice imagery.
- Notice oppositions.
- Your essay doesn't have to be great, but you do have to show command of the English language. An AP essay that scores a nine might not even be an A paper in English class. Of course not. It's a 40-minute essay on a story or poem you've never seen before.
- Whenever possible, show your verbal flare.
- It's okay to establish the foundation of your essay in two or three short opening paragraphs, if necessary.
- Your first paragraph should be free of error, but nobody writes an error-free paper. That doesn't mean be careless and sloppy. It means write as well as you can and don't worry about mistakes.
- If the question gives you the opportunity, write about character. The writing in AP passages almost always says something about character. This is especially true in the dialogue of a character, or in a first-person narration.
- A nice opening is icing on the cake.

The Open Essay

HOW DO YOU PREPARE FOR AN ESSAY ON *ANYTHING*?

The open essay usually appears as the last of the three essays on the AP test. Unlike the prose or poetry essays, the open essay does not give you a text to work with; you must write an essay on a given theme using support drawn from your own reading.

Most people assume that the open essay is the most difficult of the three essays. This assumption is false. Even though the average score on the open essay tends to be a little lower than on the other two essays, a close look at the data suggests that students who attempt the open essay earn higher scores. Many students skip this essay altogether, so there are more scores of NR and 0 here than on the prose and poetry essays. On the other hand, more students earn scores of 8 and 9 on this essay than on the other two. The scores still tend to bunch up around the middle (the mean), but they spread out more across all the score ranges (a greater standard deviation). All the same, the open essay is the most dreaded and anticipated portion of the AP exam. It isn't worth any more than the other questions, but unlike the rest of the test, the open essay question feels like the one you *have to* study for. At the same time, it's the question that most students feel like they *haven't* studied for, at least not enough.

We've shown you that you can and should study for the rest of the test. We *hope* we've shown you that knowing what you're doing on the Essay section is the way to shoot your scores through the roof. Now, what about the open essay—how do you prepare for it?

The answer is simple. Use all the techniques we've already described for writing the prose and poetry essays. Use the Idea Machine to direct your thoughts and answer the classic question as you go about answering the specifics of the ETS question. The open essay is no different from the other essays. There's just one more bit of preparation you need for the open essay: three well-chosen works of literature that you know backward and forward.

WHAT ETS REALLY WANTS FROM YOUR OPEN ESSAY

You can, should, and *must* study a literary work for the open essay. But what if the open essay question asks for a theme that the work you've prepared doesn't address? Don't worry. ETS isn't trying to persecute you (although it does feel that way sometimes). Follow our instructions and you'll be prepared.

What ETS would really like to do is say, "Write an essay about any major literary work that you enjoyed. We just want to see how well you can write on a longer work that you've read and studied." Unfortunately, they can't ask you that directly because there would be no way to stop students from writing essays ahead of time (or having dear Aunt Toni, the Pulitzer Prize–winning novelist, write an essay ahead of time) and memorizing them. The open essay question is just a way of making sure that the student hasn't prepared the whole essay in advance.

However, ETS doesn't want to ask open essay questions that are too restrictive, either. They won't ask a question that points to just a handful of literary works, for example. They won't ask for an essay about "a character who may or may not be insane and who sees ghosts that may or may not be there." A few hundred students would get nines by writing about Henry James's *The Turn of The Screw*. A few thousand would struggle to make this question make sense for *Hamlet* or *Macbeth*. The rest would just leave it blank.

ETS goes out of its way to make sure the open essay question is truly open and provides an opportunity for a student who has read challenging literary works to write a good essay.

Let's look at the kinds of themes the open essay question asks for. Remember, you can see real, previously asked essay questions at **www.collegeboard.com/student/testing/ap/english_lit/samp. html?englit**.

SAMPLE THEMES FOR THE OPEN ESSAY

- Discuss the function of a character who does not appear or appears only briefly in a novel or play, and yet is a significant presence in the work.

- Discuss the function of a character who serves as the main character's sympathetic listener, or confidant(e).

- Discuss a scene or character that provokes "thoughtful laughter."

- Discuss a novel or play in which much of the action occurs internally, within the consciousness of a character or characters in the work.

- Discuss the use of contrasting settings in a novel or play.

- Discuss parent-child conflict in a novel or play.

As you can see, these themes are broad, and any one of them can be applied to thousands of literary works. At the same time, these themes are specific enough that you couldn't just go ahead and write an essay ahead of time, as not every work applies to each theme equally well. The key to a great open essay is having the right work for the theme, and knowing it cold.

So what works should you study?

PREPARING FOR THE OPEN ESSAY

To be really ready for the open essay, you should know at least three works very well. Two of them should be longer works that you've studied in class. We'll call these the *primary* works. The third work is a safeguard in case, for some reason, you can't apply your knowledge of the first works to the question at all, or in case you need to back up your points with another example. The Reader will be hugely impressed if you can adeptly discuss not one, but two or three pieces of literature. We'll provide you with a list of short *secondary* works which are useful for the AP exam.

THE PRIMARY WORK

Have two primary works that you know well. Your primary works should be fairly hefty. One of Shakespeare's plays or a thick, complex novel will do. The full-length works of the following authors are all good choices: Jane Austen, James Joyce, Joseph Conrad, Emily or Charlotte Brontë, Charles Dickens, Nathaniel Hawthorne, Herman Melville, Toni Morrison, Thomas Hardy, George Eliot, Fyodor Dostoyevsky, and Thomas Mann. The object in choosing your primary works is to come up with two novels or plays that are so rich in incident and form that no matter what the open essay question asks, you have something to say.

Choose a Work You Already Know (and Love)

You've already studied some literary works in school. Pick two and go over your notes. Read the books again, or at least spend a few hours looking them over thoroughly. Pick your favorite work. If you fell in love with Shakespeare's *Hamlet*, great, use *Hamlet*. If you felt sleepy every time the word Shakespeare was mentioned but thought Dostoyevsky's *Crime and Punishment* might change your life, then that's the work to use.

There are just a couple of exceptions to the favorite-work rule. Do not pick a short story, a work of nonfiction, or a poem. The ETS open essay questions, as a rule, say, "Choose a play or a novel: Do not choose a poem or short story." There have been very few exceptions to this rule, and the exception is that they'll allow complete epic poems. Now, if your favorite work of literature is really-honestly-no-kidding-I-loved-it Milton's *Paradise Lost* or Spenser's *The Faerie Queene*…well, okay, you could prepare those novel-length poems for the open essay, but you'd still be better off with a novel. Short stories are wonderful reading material, but they are practically useless for the AP exam. ETS just won't let you use them. They don't want students preparing to write essays on short stories; they think it's too easy.

If you don't have a usable favorite work, or are for some reason undecided about what to choose for your primary work, we highly recommend Shakespeare's plays, particularly *Hamlet*, *A Midsummer Night's Dream*, *King Lear*, *Othello*, and *The Tempest*. All of these plays are intricately plotted, all contain elements of comedy and tragedy, and all are incredibly rich in the kind of material about which open essays are written. The object in choosing your primary work is to find a work that can support any number of questions, and Shakespeare's works fit that bill better than any others of comparable length. As tough as Shakespeare's plays can be to read, they are considerably shorter than say, *Crime and Punishment* or *David Copperfield*. If you decide to go with Shakespeare, you could easily prepare to write about two plays in the time it takes to prepare to write about a longer novel. Just remember, we said we recommend Shakespeare. If you already know the work of another writer better, by all means prepare something else. But remember that we strongly recommend using a book you've already studied in class. During the 2007–2008 school year, the College Board conducted an audit of AP English Literature classes. All AP English Literature teachers submitted their course syllabi to the Board for approval. Thus, all current AP teachers are teaching books that are approved by the College Board—yet another great reason that books you've studied in class are a safe bet.

While we're getting a bit more specific, we have one more important recommendation: There are a few works that seem to crop up on students' open essays every year, and the Readers do not look on them favorably: *Night* by Elie Wiesel and *To Kill a Mockingbird* by Harper Lee. While these are both phenomenal books, *Night* is a work of non-fiction (a no-no) and *To Kill a Mockingbird* is considered to be below the level of "literary merit" that the College Board would like. If a student selects a book considered to be below this level, no matter how well-written or insightful the essay, the best score that the essay can receive is a 5. Do yourself a favor and simply steer clear of writing about either of these titles.

You'll be happy to know that in the past few years many contemporary books have appeared on the list of accepted sources for the open essay. *Kite Runner* by Khaled Hosseini, *Life of Pi* by Yann Martel, *Reading Lolita in Tehran* by Azar Nafisi, and *The Bonesetter's Daughter* by Amy Tan are a few contemporary works that fall outside of the traditional primary works list, but might be strong choices as one of your primary works.

SUGGESTIONS FOR PRIMARY WORKS

Here are some other books we think make for good primary works. This list is not even close to complete, but it's a start. If you happen to know and love another long work inside and out, that's fine.

Emma by Jane Austen

Jane Eyre by Charlotte Brontë

Wuthering Heights by Emily Brontë

Don Quixote by Miguel Cervantes

White Noise by Don Delillo

Bleak House by Charles Dickens

David Copperfield by Charles Dickens

Great Expectations by Charles Dickens

A Tale of Two Cities by Charles Dickens

Crime and Punishment by Fyodor Dostoyevsky

Invisible Man by Ralph Ellison

The Sound and the Fury by William Faulkner

Tess of the D'Urbervilles by Thomas Hardy

The Scarlet Letter by Nathaniel Hawthorne

Their Eyes Were Watching God by Zora Neale Hurston

Sons and Lovers by D. H. Lawrence

The Magic Mountain by Thomas Mann

One Hundred Years of Solitude by Gabriel García Márquez

Moby Dick by Herman Melville

The Catcher in the Rye by J. D. Salinger

The Grapes of Wrath by John Steinbeck

Of Mice and Men by John Steinbeck

Anna Karenina by Leo Tolstoy

The Adventures of Huckleberry Finn by Mark Twain

The Bonesetter's Daughter by Amy Tan

Kite Runner by Khaled Hosseini

THE SECONDARY WORK

The secondary work is your just-in-case work, and perhaps a bit more. The question just may not fit any aspect of your primary works. This is highly unlikely, but if this happens, you need to have something prepared. You don't want to be stuck trying to remember some book you haven't looked at since ninth grade. The other reason to prepare a secondary work is simply to have more options. If the question fits your secondary work perfectly, you'll want to use it. Prepare your secondary work well, and, in effect, you have three primary works. With well-chosen and well-prepared primary and secondary works you would have to be extremely unlucky to find yourself faced with an open essay question that did not fit any of the works.

Choose Something Different from Your Primary Works

Ideally, you want your secondary work to be as different as possible from your primary works. If you pick *Hamlet* as one of your primary works, you don't want to pick another Shakespearean tragedy starring a messed-up, confused, violent hero. In other words, don't pick *Macbeth*. You'd be much better off picking a comedy such as *A Midsummer Night's Dream*. Even better would be to pick a twentieth-century comic novel like *Catch-22* by Joseph Heller or *A Confederacy of Dunces* by John Kennedy Toole. If you pick an extremely male-oriented work for one of your primary works, say *Invisible Man*, then Kate Chopin's *The Awakening* makes an excellent choice for a secondary work, as would Henry James's *The Turn of the Screw*, both of which feature female main characters.

SUGGESTIONS FOR SECONDARY WORKS

We've put together a list of secondary work books. These are all short novels, novellas, and plays which are acceptable to the AP Readers. Some works are not acceptable. Writing about *The Family Guy*, episode 56, will result in a low score, as will writing about a Danielle Steele or Stephen King novel. Don't push it. You may think William Gibson's *Neuromancer* is a great book, but the AP committee probably won't be impressed, and they'll lower your score.

The books on the list below were chosen according to the following guidelines: They're all recognized classics of which the AP Readers will highly approve. They're all short. Most important, they're all works that have been perfect fits with many open essay questions.

We strongly recommend studying at least one of the works listed here. If you've read one of these works in class (and there's a good chance you have), by all means look it over again and prepare it for the AP exam. An asterisk (*) means that the work is most highly recommended reading for the exam. These marked items are the AP open essay superstars. Pick one and you won't go wrong.

Finally, if you really don't feel comfortable with any of the longer works that you've studied in class, or if you're thinking of taking the AP exam without having taken an AP course, or if you, well, slacked off in class—don't try to prepare a longer work for the AP exam. Go straight to the list below and knock off two or three or four titles (remember, these are short works). You'll be prepared.

Novellas and Short Novels:

The Stranger by Albert Camus

The Awakening by Kate Chopin*

Heart of Darkness by Joseph Conrad*

Notes from the Underground by Fyodor Dostoyevsky

The Great Gatsby by F. Scott Fitzgerald*

The Old Man and the Sea by Ernest Hemingway

The Turn of the Screw by Henry James*

Death in Venice by Thomas Mann

Ballad of the Sad Café by Carson McCullers

Billy Budd by Herman Melville

A Sentimental Journey by Lawrence Sterne

The Death of Ivan Ilyich by Leo Tolstoy

Candide by Voltaire

Plays:

Waiting for Godot by Samuel Beckett

A Man for All Seasons by Robert Bolt

The Cherry Orchard by Anton Chekhov

The Seagull by Anton Chekhov

Uncle Vanya by Anton Chekhov

Medea by Euripides*

A Doll's House by Henrik Ibsen*

Hedda Gabler by Henrik Ibsen*

The Crucible by Arthur Miller

Death of a Salesman by Arthur Miller

Emperor Jones by Eugene O'Neill

Hughie by Eugene O'Neill

Long Day's Journey Into Night by Eugene O'Neill

Antigone by Sophocles*

Oedipus Rex by Sophocles*

A Streetcar Named Desire by Tennessee Williams

The Glass Menagerie by Tennessee Williams

WHAT DOES "PREPARE THE WORK" MEAN?

We keep telling you to *prepare* your primary and secondary works. What does this mean? It means two things:

- Study the work as thoroughly as you can.

- Write a first paragraph based on the classic question for each work you prepare.

Studying Your Primary and Secondary Works

Study the works you've chosen. Take notes. Record impressions. Map out different themes and examples of these themes within the work. Imagine important scenes as movies in your head. If you're reading this book early in the school year or in the summer before your AP English course begins, you should consider prepping every work you read for class. (The College Board suggests to your teacher that you should read at least 12 works closely in class.) This strategy not only will give you a broad array of works to select from on test day, but also will improve your study habits. If you have a few months or a few weeks to prepare, then selecting two or three works you have studied will put you in a good place. If it's the week before the test, looking over the books to remind yourself of the plot lines and the names of the main characters might forestall those moments you lose when you're racking your brain, thinking, "Gatsby's girlfriend's name…Rose…Iris…Violet?"

How should you prepare the works?

- Reread your primary and secondary works within four weeks of the test. You want to have each one fresh in your mind.

- Work from critical editions. The books you should prepare for the AP test are the kinds of works that have been studied and restudied over the years. Although you can easily find your chosen texts in small, inexpensive reading editions, you should look for them in larger, critical editions that contain full introductions, notes, annotations, and sometimes appendices containing background material, biographical information, and samplings of past critical commentary. Whenever possible, use these fuller editions. Read as much of the supplementary material as you can stand. If you can put the work in a cultural context and discuss the political or sociological happenings of the time, the Readers socks will undoubtedly be knocked off. No AP Reader is going to downgrade your essay because the points you make about the novel seem influenced by the opinions of other authors and critics. On the contrary, they'll think you're a genius. One student in a hundred actually bothers to read literary criticism about the book he or she has prepared, but that's about the percentage of students who score a 9 on the open essay. Coincidence?

- Write your own study guide. As much as your teachers disparage those booklets from Acme Notes, they can be an invaluable supplement to your own study. (Note that we said "supplement." You still need to read the books.) Even better than a store-bought study guide, however, is one you've written yourself. You'll accomplish a lot of your review just by writing it. Moreover, once you're done, you'll have a study guide that highlights the aspects of a work that you find most interesting— and those are the things you're most likely to write about on the exam.

Your custom study guide should be no longer than one page and should contain the following:

- Plot—In your essay, you want to avoid plot summary, but it's still important to remember what happens—and *why*. Chapter by chapter or scene by scene, note what happens, but focus on the major conflicts of the book. The details help you remember the specific chronology of the narrative; thinking about the larger conflicts puts the story into perspective.
- Character—Who's who? This list could be as simple as remembering how they spell their names (very useful indeed if a Chekhov play or a Tolstoy novel is one of your works) or it can be as detailed as you want it to be.
- Themes—What's the message or moral of the story? Avoid oversimplification.
- Symbols—Scarlet letters, green lights, white whales: what do they stand for and how do they help the author achieve his or her purpose?
- Quotations—"If you have tears, prepare to shed them now." (That's from *Julius Caesar*, in case you were wondering.) In the open essay, it's important to provide support for your assertions, and even more important to avoid plot summary. Quoting your chosen work and explaining how the quote relates to the prompt demonstrates to the reader that you know and understand the work. Memorizing the quotes—and understanding what each means—allows you to write with more confidence.

A sample page of your self-made study guide might look like this:

> *The Seagull* by Anton Chekhov
>
> Act I—Lots of complaining (Masha's in mourning for her life, Treplev's mother Arkadina doesn't love him) as preparations are made for Treplev's play, starring Nina. The chain of unrequited lovers is introduced. Treplev loves Nina, Nina has a crush on Trigorin, Arkadina's acknowledged lover. Masha's mother Polina has the hots for Dorn, the local doctor. The play is experimental and a flop. Arkadina laughs at it, and Treplev's feelings are hurt. Trigorin takes an interest in Nina. Masha confesses to Dorn that she loves Treplev.
>
> Act II—Midsummer squabbles on the estate—can Arkadina take the horses out or not. Nina thinks the great actresses' demands are the most important thing. Treplev shoots a seagull and lays it at Nina's feet, threatening that one day he will do the same to himself. Nina dismisses his concerns, and Trigorin promptly begins seducing her. The dead seagull inspires Trigorin—a young girl lives by the lake like a seagull, but one day a man comes along and, for lack of anything better to do, destroys her.
>
> Act III—Three big scenes: Masha tells Trigorin she's going to destroy her love for Treplev by marrying Medvedenko, the schoolmaster who pines for her. Arkadina changes Treplev's bandages (he's attempted suicide offstage between the acts). Arkadina fights with Trigorin, who wants to stay behind and complete his seduction of Nina, but Arkadina wants him out of there. As they're

leaving together, Trigorin goes back for his walking stick. Nina goes to him; she's run away from home and heading to Moscow to become an actress. Trigorin gives her his address and asks her to come to him.

Act IV—Two years later. Masha has married Medvedenko, but she's still in love with Treplev and miserable. She's hoping Medvedenko's transfer will tear the love from her heart. Treplev brings Dorn up to date on Nina. She had a child by Trigorin, who managed to stay with Arkadina the whole time, and has returned to her. Meanwhile, Nina's acting career has been a disaster. Trigorin and Arkadina arrive. Trigorin is kind to Treplev's face, but behind his back, disparages his writing. After a quick game of lotto, the party relinquishes the study to Treplev. He struggles with his writing, then is surprised by Nina. He's been trying to see her. They reminisce about old times, and Nina compares herself to a seagull. She leaves as abruptly as she arrived. Treplev tears up his manuscripts and exits, just as Shamreyev shows Trigorin the stuffed seagull. A shot is heard offstage. Treplev has shot himself.

Characters

ARKADINA, an actress. 42 years old. Petty, vain, involved with writer Trigorin.
CONSTANTINE TREPLEV, Arkadina's son, an aspiring writer.
SORIN, Arkadina's brother and the owner of the estate where the play is set.
NINA, a young local girl and aspiring actress. Romantically involved with Treplev at the outset, later falls in love with Trigorin.
SHAMRAYEV, Sorin's estate manager.
POLINA, Shamrayev's wife. In love with Dorn.
MASHA, Shamrayev's daughter. In love with Treplev, but will marry Medvedenko.
TRIGORIN, a writer. Spineless.
DORN, a doctor.
MEDVEDENKO, a schoolteacher. Obsessed with money.

Themes

Unrequited love and lots of it. Idealistic youth spoiled by the corruption of the real world. Struggle to create new art forms (Chekhov creating a new kind of drama in this play).

Symbols

The seagull: symbolic of youth. Trigorin sees it as emblematic of Nina and her innocence, which he will proceed to spoil. Treplev, who has shot a seagull, thinks it represents himself, and he shoots himself at the end of Act IV, just as he threatened when he laid the seagull at Nina's feet in Act II. Nina is a little confused about if she's the seagull or not, as we see in her Act IV monologue.

Quotations

"I'm in mourning for my life; I'm depressed."—Masha, Act I. Opening lines of play, sets tone for what is to follow.
"I am a seagull; no, that's not it; I am an actress"—Nina, Act IV.

This study guide isn't perfect—it isn't very thorough—but it forces you to think about how the work is structured and how the author achieves his effects. While prepping this, you might note that each act begins with Masha, a minor character. In looking at criticism about the play, you might note that it was a failure when originally produced, possibly because Chekhov's effects are so subtle. Finally, after prepping the work in this way, you'll be certain about the names of the characters and what happens when, which will allow you to write with more clarity.

Prepare for the Open Essay Ahead of Time

In addition to prepping the works, you should also write the first paragraph of an open essay a couple of nights before the test. (Remember to use the Idea Machine: What does the work mean? What are the emotional contents of the work?) Writing the first paragraph shouldn't take you longer than 30 minutes, and when you consider how much time and stress it will save you on test day, surely you can see why it's a winning strategy.

True, you have no idea what aspect of the work the prompt will ask you to address, but we've supplied you with plenty of sample prompts with which to practice. Once you've seen a few, you'll be familiar with the kind of questions that appear on the exam and should see how altering one or two sentences in your sample introduction will probably save the day. And, even if you do end up writing an entirely new introduction on test day, you'll write with more confidence and skill if you've had some recent practice.

SUMMARY

- When writing the open essay, use all the techniques we've already described for writing the prose and poetry essays.

- Don't worry about having to face an open question that doesn't apply to the works you've prepared. ETS tries to make its open essay questions broad enough that you won't be lost…as long as you have *something* prepared.

- Prepare two primary works and a secondary work.

- If you've studied Shakespeare's work in class (and enjoyed it), we strongly recommend using a Shakespeare play as one of your primary works. His plays are chock-full of the material open essays call for.

- Choose a work that you've already studied in class.

- Our list of secondary works suggests novellas and plays that have proven useful on many AP open essays in the past.

- Your secondary work should be as different as possible from your primary works. For example, if one of your primary works is a Shakespearean tragedy, pick a modern comic novella for your secondary work.

- If possible, reread your primary and secondary works within four weeks of the test. Otherwise, at least skim the book and look over any class notes you have. Use critical editions if you can find them.

- Write a sample first paragraph of the open essay ahead of time. It's great practice.

PART IV

The Princeton Review AP English Literature and Composition Practice Tests and Explanations

12

Practice Test 1

ENGLISH LITERATURE AND COMPOSITION

SECTION I

Time—1 hour

<u>Directions:</u> This section consists of selections from literary works and questions on their content, form, and style. After reading each passage or poem, choose the best answer to each question and then fill in the corresponding oval.

<u>Questions 1–15.</u> Choose your answers to questions 1–15 based on a careful reading of the following passage.

Phraxos lay eight dazzling hours in a small steamer south of Athens, about six miles off the mainland of the Peloponnesus and in the center of a landscape as
Line memorable as itself: to the north and west, a great fixed
(5) arm of mountains, in whose crook the island stood; to the east a gently peaked archipelago; to the south the soft blue desert of the Aegean stretching away to Crete. Phraxos was beautiful. There was no other adjective; it was not just pretty, picturesque, charming—it was
(10) simply and effortlessly beautiful. It took my breath away when I first saw it, floating under Venus like a majestic black whale in an amethyst evening sea, and it still takes my breath away when I shut my eyes now and remember it. Its beauty was rare even
(15) in the Aegean, because its hills were covered with pine trees, Mediterranean pines as light as greenfinch feathers. Nine-tenths of the island was uninhabited and uncultivated: nothing but pines, coves, silence, sea. Herded into one corner, the north-west, lay a
(20) spectacular agglomeration of snow-white houses round a couple of small harbours.

But there were two eyesores, visible long before we landed. One was an obese Greek-Edwardian hotel near the larger of the two harbours, as at home on Phraxos
(25) as a hansom cab in a Doric temple. The other, equally at odds with the landscape, stood on the outskirts of the village and dwarfed the cottages around it: a dauntingly long building several storeys high and reminiscent, in spite of its ornate Corinthian facade, of
(30) a factory—a likeness more than just visually apt, as I was to discover.

But Lord Byron School, the Hotel Philadelphia, and the village apart, the body of the island, all thirty square miles of it, was virgin. There were some silvery
(35) olive-orchards and a few patches of terrace cultivation on the steep slopes of the north coast, but the rest was primeval pine-forest. There were no antiquities. The ancient Greeks never much liked the taste of cistern-water.
(40) The lack of open water meant also that there were no wild animals and few birds on the island. Its distinguishing characteristic, away from the village, was silence. Out on the hills one might pass a goatherd and his winter flock (in summer there was no grazing)
(45) of bronze-billed goats, or a bowed peasant-woman carrying a huge faggot, or a resin-gatherer; but one very rarely did. It was the world before the machine, almost before man, and what small events happened— the passage of a shrike, the discovery of a new path,
(50) a glimpse of a distant cacique far below—took on an unaccountable significance, as if they were isolated, framed, magnified by solitude. It was the last eerie, the most Nordic solitude in the world. Fear had never touched the island. If it was haunted, it was by
(55) nymphs, not monsters.

I was forced to go frequently for walks to escape the claustrophobic ambiance of the Lord Byron School. To begin with there was something pleasantly absurd about teaching in a boarding school (run on
(60) supposedly Eton-Harrow lines) only a look north from where Clytemnestra killed Agamemnon. Certainly the masters, victims of a country with only two universities, were academically of a far higher standard than Mitford had suggested, and in themselves the
(65) boys were no better and no worse than boys the world over. But they were ruthlessly pragmatic about English. They cared nothing for literature, and everything for science. If I tried to read the school eponym's poetry with them, they yawned; if I taught the English names
(70) for the parts of a car, I had trouble getting them out of class at lesson's end; and often they would bring me American scientific textbooks full of terms that were just as much Greek to me as the expectant faces waiting for a simple paraphrase.
(75) Both boys and masters loathed the island, and regarded it as a sort of self-imposed penal settlement where one came to work, work, work. I had imagined something far sleepier than an English school, and

GO ON TO THE NEXT PAGE

instead it was far tougher. The crowning irony was
(80) that this obsessive industry, this mole-like blindness to
their natural environment, was what was considered
to be so typically English about the system. Perhaps to
Greeks, made blasé by living among the most beautiful
landscapes in the world, there was nothing discordant
(85) in being cooped up in such a termitary; but it drove me
mad with irritation…

Soon I took to the hills. None of the other masters
even stirred an inch farther than they needed to, and
the boys were not allowed beyond the *chevaux de frise**
(90) of the high-walled school grounds except on Sundays,
and then only for the half-mile along the coast road
to the village. The hills were always intoxicatingly
clean and light and remote. With no company but my
own boredom, I began for the first time in my life to
(95) look at nature, and to regret that I knew its language
as little as I knew Greek. I became aware of stones,
birds, flowers, land, in a new way, and the walking, the
swimming, the magnificent climate, the absence of all
traffic, ground or air—for there wasn't a single car on
(100) the island, there being no roads outside the village, and
aeroplanes passed over not once a month—these things
made me feel healthier than I had ever felt before. I
began to get some sort of harmony between body and
mind; or so it seemed. It was an illusion.

* literally a "horse of plank" or a wooden horse

―――――――
Excerpt from *The Magus* by John Fowles (pp. 52–53).
Copyright © 1978, Dell Books.

1. The word "itself" (line 4) refers to

   (A) "Phraxos" (line 1)
   (B) "landscape" (line 3)
   (C) "mainland" (line 2)
   (D) "Peloponnesus" (line 3)
   (E) "desert" (line 7)

2. The narrator's first impression (lines 8–17) was best
   emphasized by his use of

   (A) pretentious hyperbole
   (B) elusive metaphors
   (C) metaphysical speculations
   (D) whimsical onomatopoeia
   (E) symbolic similes

3. The tone the narrator reflects in his description of
   the island primarily helps to

   (A) describe the beauty of the sea and the
       mountains
   (B) verbalize his anticipation of the representation
       of the "Corinthian facade"
   (C) reinforce the contrast between intellectual
       pursuits and natural passions
   (D) provide a pedantic explanation for the lack of
       towns on the island
   (E) analyze his affinity for the physical
       surroundings

4. The word "obese" (line 23) refers to the

   (A) proximity of the hotel to the water
   (B) correlation between the size of the hotel and
       the island
   (C) analogous comparison of a taxi to a hotel
   (D) intrusion of an ostentatious manifestation of
       the modern world on the enticing beauty of
       the island
   (E) concentration of buildings on the "north-west"
       section of the island

5. The second paragraph helps to establish the
   narrator's

   (A) acceptance of the contrast of civilization and
       nature on the island
   (B) uneasiness with his first impression of the
       island
   (C) understanding of the significance of the
       facade of the buildings in terms of his future
       experiences on the island
   (D) perspective of the conflict of his inability to
       escape the trappings of a proper education
   (E) critical analysis of the island's beauty

6. The speaker establishes the tone of the passage in
   the fourth paragraph by

   (A) describing the feeling of solitude the island
       evoked
   (B) comparing the isolation of the village with the
       absence of wild life
   (C) reflecting on the island's ability to permeate his
       understanding of reality
   (D) associating his life in school with feelings of
       depression
   (E) stressing the pedagogy to which he adheres

GO ON TO THE NEXT PAGE ⟶

7. The allusions to Clytemnestra and Agamemnon serve to

(A) establish an underlying conflict between the pursuits of intellect and those of passion
(B) prepare the reader for the surreptitious events that follow
(C) explain the influence of myth on the history of the island
(D) provide an image of grandeur that the island exuded
(E) communicate an atmosphere of antiquity and violence

8. The speaker implies that education on Phraxos is

(A) superficially mediocre
(B) annoyingly archaic
(C) overzealously superfluous
(D) disconcertingly adequate
(E) perplexingly inconsequential

9. The speaker's attitude toward his assignment can best be described as one of

(A) frustration
(B) elation
(C) confusion
(D) trepidation
(E) disappointment

10. The speaker's use of "mole-like blindness" (line 80) implies

I. the shortcomings of the British educational system
II. the myopic interests of the students
III. the consequence of the apathy of the island's inhabitants
IV. the conundrum of teaching on the island

(A) I and II
(B) I, II, and III
(C) II and III
(D) III and IV
(E) I, II, III, IV

11. The attitude of the speaker is emphasized by the use of

(A) parody
(B) apostrophe
(C) imagery
(D) repetition
(E) hyperbole

12. The use of the metaphor "termitary" (line 85) helps to reinforce all of the following EXCEPT

(A) the atmosphere of the school is the epitome of a British education
(B) the attitude of the Greeks on the island provides a paradoxical contrast to the students in the school
(C) the masters and the students seem oblivious to their surroundings
(D) the school directs their attention to the pragmatic rather than the romantic application of knowledge
(E) the students and masters are task oriented in their approach to life

13. The reader can infer from the last paragraph that the hills make the speaker feel

(A) laconic
(B) languid
(C) apathetic
(D) congenial
(E) impatient

14. "It was an illusion" (line 104) implies

(A) the speaker's harmonious feelings would confront inner turmoil
(B) the weather on the island would soon become dreary
(C) the speaker would learn the true meaning of the Greek language
(D) there was a war about to break out between the English and the Greeks
(E) he would no longer enjoy his moments of solitude in the hills

15. The elements that help reinforce the theme of this passage include all of the following EXCEPT

(A) imagery
(B) allusion
(C) diction
(D) metaphor
(E) paradox

GO ON TO THE NEXT PAGE

Questions 16–27. Choose your answers to each of the following questions based on careful reading of the following poem by Christina Rossetti.

Passing away, saith the World, passing away:
Chances, beauty and youth sapped day by day:
Thy life never continueth in one stay.
Line Is the eye waxen dim, is the dark hair changing to gray
(5) That hath won neither laurel nor bay?
I shall clothe myself in Spring and bud in May:
Thou, root stricken, shalt not rebuild thy decay
On my bosom for aye.
Then I answered: Yea.

(10) Passing away, saith my Soul, passing away:
With its burden of fear and hope, or labor and play;
Hearken what the past doth witness and say:
Rust in thy gold, a moth is in thine array,
A canker is in thy bud, thy leaf must decay.
(15) At midnight, at cockcrow, at morning, one certain day
Lo the bridegroom shall come and shall not delay:
Watch thou and pray.
Then I answered: Yea.

Passing away, saith my God, passing away:
(20) Winter passeth after the long delay:
New grapes on the vine, new figs on the tender spray,
Turtle calleth turtle in Heaven's May.
Tho' I tarry, wait for Me, trust Me, watch and pray.
Arise, come away, night is past and lo it is day,
(25) My love, My sister, My spouse, thou shalt hear Me say.
Then I answered: Yea.

16. How many speakers does the poem directly present?

 (A) One
 (B) Two
 (C) Three
 (D) Four
 (E) Five

17. "Laurel" and "bay" (line 5) are allusions to

 (A) flowers highly prized for their rarity which
     bloom briefly and beautifully and then die
 (B) spices which add flavor to food and,
     metaphorically, to life
 (C) leaves traditionally woven into wreaths to
     honor poets
 (D) traditional symbols for Homer and Ovid
     respectively
 (E) traditional symbols for true faith and pious
     conduct, respectively

18. Lines 6–7 suggest that

 (A) the principal narrator is faced with a choice
     between the afterlife that true faith offers
     or the physical corruption that awaits the
     unbeliever
 (B) although the World has regenerative powers,
     the principal narrator of the poem does not
 (C) paradoxically, life can sometimes emerge from
     death
 (D) there is a natural cyclical pattern of renewal
     that the principal narrator has forsaken
 (E) the principal narrator is gravely ill and certain
     to die before the spring

19. Which of the following lines contains an image NOT
 echoed closely elsewhere in the poem?

 (A) Line 6
 (B) Line 7
 (C) Line 13
 (D) Line 14
 (E) Line 21

20. Which of the following choices best characterizes
 the speaker's attitude in each of the poem's three
 stanzas, respectively?

 (A) Realization of death's inevitability; fear of
     physical decay; passive acceptance of what
     cannot be escaped
 (B) Nostalgia for the earthly world that must be
     left behind; fear of physical decay; welcome
     acceptance of the afterlife
 (C) Realization that death will come before one's
     ambitions have been achieved; dismay
     over the visible signs of physical decay;
     supplication for the healing powers of divine
     intervention
 (D) Sorrow and mild surprise at the arrival of
     early death; deepening awareness of death's
     certainty; hopefulness for a place in the
     afterlife
 (E) Acknowledgment of death's inevitability;
     understanding of the need to prepare oneself;
     happiness at the prospect of union with the
     divine

GO ON TO THE NEXT PAGE

21. In the context of the poem "a moth is in thine array" (line 13) is intended to imply that the

(A) narrator's attire is being eaten by moths
(B) narrator's body is being consumed by cancer, or a cancer-like disease
(C) narrator's soul contains a destructive element which, unless the narrator takes some action, will render it unworthy of the afterlife
(D) narrator's soul is corrupted with sin that only death can purge
(E) narrator's body is being gradually destroyed by the silent and natural processes of life

22. Lines 7 and 8 provide an example of

(A) apostrophe
(B) doggerel
(C) enjambment
(D) mixed metaphor
(E) simile

23. In the third stanza "winter" can be taken to represent

(A) long disease
(B) earthly life
(C) the coldness of the grave
(D) spiritual despair
(E) aging and loss of vigor

24. Which of the following statements most accurately characterizes the relationship of the imagery in the third stanza to that of the first and second stanzas?

(A) The third stanza weaves together the wedding-day imagery of the second stanza and the springtime imagery of the first stanza, thereby reconciling those earlier stanzas' differing views.
(B) Through its imagery, the third stanza further develops the themes which were advanced by the first stanza and then questioned by the second stanza.
(C) The third stanza echoes much of the first two stanzas' imagery, but recasts that imagery so that what earlier had been likened to decay is instead characterized as renewal.
(D) By echoing the imagery of the earlier stanzas, the third stanza reaffirms and repeats the views advanced by those stanzas.
(E) By introducing the terms "love" and "sister," the third stanza continues the progression by which each stanza proposes its own unique central metaphor around which to further the poem's exploration of the themes of death and renewal.

25. Lines 15 and 16 suggest that

(A) the principal narrator's final hour will come, despite the small uncertainty of knowing exactly what hour that will be
(B) the bridegroom mentioned in line 16 will arrive at three distinct times
(C) the hour when a deadly illness first infects the principal narrator cannot be avoided
(D) a mysterious and evil stranger will arrive at some time between midnight and morning
(E) the principal narrator's soul prophesies that she will eventually meet the man who will become her beloved husband

GO ON TO THE NEXT PAGE

26. In context, the word "spray" (line 21) most nearly means

(A) tree
(B) blanket
(C) a small branch
(D) a liquid mist
(E) a holy spirit

27. The grammatical subject of the sentence that begins at line 24 is

(A) "Arise"
(B) "night is past and lo it is day"
(C) "My love, My sister, My spouse"
(D) "thou"
(E) "Me"

GO ON TO THE NEXT PAGE →

Questions 28–40. Read the following passage carefully before you choose your answers. The selection is an excerpt from the novel *Barchester Towers* by Anthony Trollope.

It is not my intention to breathe a word against Mrs Proudie, but still I cannot think that with all her virtues she adds much to her husband's happiness. The truth
Line is that in matters domestic she rules supreme over her
(5) titular lord, and rules with a rod of iron. Nor is this all. Things domestic Dr Proudie might have abandoned to her, if not voluntarily, yet willingly. But Mrs Proudie is not satisfied with such home dominion, and stretches her power over all his movements, and will not even
(10) abstain from things spiritual. In fact, the bishop is henpecked.

The archdeacon's wife, in her happy home at Plumstead, knows how to assume the full privileges of her rank, and express her own mind in becoming tone
(15) and place. But Mrs Grantly's sway, if sway she has, is easy and beneficent. She never shames her husband; before the world she is a pattern of obedience; her voice is never loud, nor her looks sharp; doubtless she values power, and has not unsuccessfully striven to acquire it;
(20) but she knows what should be the limits of a woman's rule.

Not so Mrs Proudie. This lady is habitually authoritative to all, but to her poor husband she is despotic. Successful as has been his career in the eyes of
(25) the world, it would seem that in the eyes of his wife he is never right. All hope of defending himself has long passed from him; indeed, he rarely even attempts self-justification; and is aware that submission produces the nearest approach to peace which his own house can
(30) ever attain.

One other marked peculiarity in the character of the bishop's wife must be mentioned. Though not averse to the society and manners of the world, she is in her own way a religious woman; and the form in which
(35) this tendency shows itself is by a strict observance of Sabbatarian rule. Dissipation and low dresses during the week are, under her control, atoned for by three services, an evening sermon read by herself, and a perfect abstinence from any cheering employment
(40) on the Sunday. Unfortunately for those under her roof to whom the dissipation and low dresses are not extended, her servants namely and her husband, the compensating strictness of the Sabbath includes all. Woe betide the recreant housemaid who is found
(45) to have been listening to the honey of a sweetheart in the Regent's park, instead of the soul-stirring discourse of Mr Slope. Not only is she sent adrift, but she is so sent with a character, which leaves her little hope of a decent place. Woe betide the six-foot hero
(50) who escorts Mrs Proudie to her pew in red plush breeches, if he slips away to the neighbouring beer-shop, instead of falling in the back seat appropriated to his use. Mrs Proudie has the eyes of Argus for such offenders. Occasional drunkenness in the week may be
(55) overlooked, for six feet on low wages are hardly to be procured if the morals are always kept at a high pitch, but not even for grandeur or economy will Mrs Proudie forgive a desecration of the Sabbath.

28. Which of the following descriptions is an example of the narrator's use of irony?

(A) "It is not my intention to breathe a word against Mrs Proudie" (lines 1–2)
(B) "the bishop is henpecked" (lines 10–11)
(C) "doubtless she values power, and has not unsuccessfully striven to acquire it" (lines 18–19)
(D) "it would seem in the eyes of his wife he is never right" (lines 25–26)
(E) "a perfect abstinence from any cheering employment on the Sunday" (lines 38–40)

29. Mrs Proudie's authoritarian character is shown most pointedly in the phrase

(A) "not satisfied with such home dominion" (line 8)
(B) "knows how to assume the full privileges of her rank" (lines 13–14)
(C) "submission produces the nearest approach to peace" (lines 28–29)
(D) "the soul-stirring discourse of Mr Slope" (lines 46–47)
(E) "has the eyes of Argus for such offenders" (lines 53–54)

30. The use of the word "titular" in line 5 is an example of

(A) hyperbole
(B) metonym
(C) onomatopoeia
(D) zeugma
(E) irony

GO ON TO THE NEXT PAGE

31. In the context of the passage, the phrase "if not vol-untarily, yet willingly" (line 7) is used to show Dr. Proudie's attitude toward

   (A) the duties that the clergy are expected to assume
   (B) entering the institution of marriage
   (C) strict Sabbatarianism
   (D) granting his wife some power
   (E) the hiring of domestic help

32. The description of Mrs Grantly serves to

   (A) provide another example of the power of the aristocracy
   (B) prove that Mrs Grantly henpecks her husband
   (C) imply specific faults of Mrs Proudie
   (D) suggest a rivalry between her and Mrs Proudie
   (E) assert why women should be seen and not heard

33. The narrator's attitude toward Mrs Proudie can best be described as one of

   (A) pity
   (B) objectivity
   (C) emotional judgment
   (D) sardonic condemnation
   (E) jaded disgust

34. Which of the following best describes Dr Proudie's relationship to his wife?

   (A) Morally devoted
   (B) Completely servile
   (C) Awkwardly tender
   (D) Thoroughly uxorious
   (E) Bitterly tyrannical

35. The author attributes Dr Proudie's attitude and behavior most clearly to

   (A) ambition
   (B) pride
   (C) pacifism
   (D) spirituality
   (E) feudalism

36. In context, the adjective "recreant" (line 44) is best interpreted as meaning

   (A) unfaithful and disloyal
   (B) engaging in a pastime
   (C) refreshing
   (D) craven and cowardly
   (E) depraved

37. What is the effect of the repetition of the phrase "Woe betide…" in the final paragraph?

   (A) It retards the tempo of the prose.
   (B) It satirizes the fate of the servants.
   (C) It highlights the drama of the situation.
   (D) It changes the point of view of the narrator.
   (E) It emphasizes the moral consequences of the action.

38. In context, the word "character" (line 31) is best interpreted as meaning

   (A) dubious personage
   (B) reference
   (C) antagonist
   (D) conscience
   (E) footman

39. Which of the following best describes the effect of the last paragraph?

   (A) It suggests a cause of Mrs Proudie's moral transformation.
   (B) It introduces Mr Slope as an observer of Mrs Proudie's actions.
   (C) It illustrates how Mrs Proudie's religious beliefs reflect her character.
   (D) It counters speculations about Mrs Proudie's character.
   (E) It shows how hard it is to hire household servants.

40. The style of the passage as a whole can best be described as

   (A) humorless and pedantic
   (B) effusive and subjective
   (C) descriptive and metaphorical
   (D) terse and epigrammatic
   (E) witty and analytical

GO ON TO THE NEXT PAGE

Questions 41–55. Read the poem below carefully, and then choose answers to the questions that follow.

Mother, picked for jury duty, managed to get through
A Life of Voltaire in three volumes. Anyway, she knew
Before she half-heard a word, the dentist was guilty.

Line As a seminarist whose collar is his calling
(5) Chokes up without it, baring his naked neck,
The little furtive dentist is led across the deck
Mounts the plank, renders a nervous cough.
Mother frowns, turns a page, flick a fly-speck
With her fingernail. She will push him off!
(10) Call to her, Voltaire, amid the wreck
Of her fairmindedness; descended from a line
Of stiff physicians; dentists are beyond
The iron palings, the respectable brass plate,
Illegible Latin script, the chaste degrees.
(15) Freezing, she acknowledges the mechanic, welder,
wielder
Of pliers, hacker, hawker, barber—Spit it out, please.
Worst of all, this dentist advertises.

Gliding through Volume II with an easy breast stroke,
(20) Never beyond her depth, she glimpses him,
Formerly Painless, all his life-like bridges
Swept away; tasting brine as the testimony
Rises: how he chased his siren girl receptionist,
Purse-lipped, like a starlet playing nurse
(25) With her doll's kit, round and round the little lab
where full balconies of plaster teeth
Grinned at the clinch.

New musical chimes

Score their dalliance as the reception room fills.
(30) Pulling away at last from his mastic Nereid,
He admits a patient; still unstrung,
Stares past the tiny whirlpool at her, combing
Her silvery hair over his silver tools, runs the drill—
Mark this!—the drill through his victim's tongue.
(35) Mother took all his easy payments, led the eleven
Crew-members, docile, to her adamantine view:
He was doomed, doomed, doomed, by birth, profession,
Practice, appearance, personal habits, loves…
And now his patient, swollen-mouthed with cancer!

(40) Doves

Never cooed like Mother pronouncing sentence.
She shut Voltaire with a bang, having come out even,
The last page during the final, smiling ballot,
The judge, supererogated, studying the docket
(45) As Mother, with eleven good men in her pocket
And a French philosopher in her reticule, swept out.

Nice Mrs. Nemesis, did she ever look back
At love's fool, clinging to his uneasy chair,
Gripping the arms, because she had swooped down,
(50) And strapped him in, to drill him away, then say,
"Spit out your life, right there."

Imposing her own version of the Deity
Who, as the true idolaters well know,
Has a general practice, instructs in Hygiene &
(55) Deportment,
Invents diseases for His cure and care:
She knows him indispensable. Like Voltaire.

Carolyn Kizer "A Long Line of Doctors" from Mermaids in the Basement

41. Overall, the mother's attitude toward the trial related in the poem shows her to be

  (A) interested in seeing that all the relevant facts be uncovered and considered
  (B) completely unaware of the duties imposed upon her by her situation
  (C) one who believes that those brought to trial are almost always guilty
  (D) unconcerned with taking her responsibilities as a juror too lightly
  (E) one who considers herself above the law

42. The phrase "half-heard" (line 3) serves to

  (A) characterize the mother as elderly
  (B) reinforce the fact that the mother pays as much attention to reading as the trial
  (C) show that the mother does not hear well
  (D) emphasize the speed with which the mother reaches her decision
  (E) suggest the very quiet tone in which the guilty dentist speaks

43. In the second stanza, the dentist is most directly implied to be

  (A) a man suffering from a terminal illness
  (B) a fly-speck
  (C) a seminarist
  (D) a man who will be made to "walk the plank"
  (E) a victim of circumstances over which he has had no control

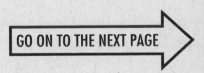
GO ON TO THE NEXT PAGE

44. Which of the following best conveys the meaning in context of "Freezing, she acknowledges the mechanic, welder, wielder/ Of pliers, hacker, hawker, barber" (lines 15–17)?

    (A) The mother thinks of other tradesmen she dislikes as much as she does dentists.
    (B) The mother thinks of professions similar to dentistry.
    (C) The mother thinks of the diverse and distasteful aspects of the dentist's profession.
    (D) The mother thinks of trades which, like dentistry, she recognizes as necessary although disagreeable.
    (E) The mother thinks of the control typically male professions exert upon her and how in this instance the tables are turned.

45. The phrase, "this dentist advertises" (line 18) principally suggests that

    (A) the dentist is unscrupulous
    (B) the dentist is not professionally qualified
    (C) the dentist's lack of skill causes him to constantly seek new clientele
    (D) the dentist is a newcomer to the area
    (E) the dentist offends the mother's sense of propriety

46. The poem states or implies which of the following?

    I.   To a large degree the mother finds the dentist guilty because he is a dentist.
    II. The jury finds the dentist guilty.
    III. The dentist should be found innocent.

    (A) I only
    (B) II only
    (C) III only
    (D) I and II only
    (E) I, II, and III

47. In the fourth stanza, the dentist is portrayed as

    (A) comically lecherous
    (B) brutally vicious
    (C) calculatingly criminal
    (D) timidly amorous
    (E) angrily frustrated

48. The phrase "tasting brine" (line 22) indicates the dentist's

    (A) desire for the trial to be over quickly
    (B) anger at the falsehoods offered as testimony against him
    (C) shame at the revelations of his unprofessional behaviour
    (D) fear of being imprisoned for his acts
    (E) sense of the growing likelihood of a guilty verdict

49. Which word is used as a metaphor for reading?

    (A) Dreaming
    (B) Walking
    (C) Conversing
    (D) Swimming
    (E) Flying

50. Which stanza suggests that the mother's treatment of the dentist could be seen as "poetic justice?"

    (A) 4
    (B) 5
    (C) 6
    (D) 7
    (E) 8

51. "Nice Mrs. Nemesis" (line 47) is an example of

    (A) understatement
    (B) hyperbole
    (C) irony
    (D) personification
    (E) onomatopoeia

GO ON TO THE NEXT PAGE

52. The poem's final stanza suggests which of the following?

    I.   The mother's vision of God is deeply held but unsophisticated.

    II.   The mother believes that God's views are similar to those of Voltaire's.

    III. The mother believes that God shares her belief in the need for social decorum.

(A) I only
(B) II only
(C) III only
(D) I and III only
(E) II and III only

53. Grammatically, "swept out" (line 46) takes as its subject

(A) "The judge" (line 44)
(B) "Mother" (line 45)
(C) "eleven good men" (line 45)
(D) "French philosopher" (line 46)
(E) "her reticule" (line 46)

54. The mother disapproves of the dentist for all of the following reasons EXCEPT

(A) his religious beliefs
(B) his profession
(C) his affair with his assistant
(D) his demeanor
(E) his mistreatment of a patient

55. Which one of the following choices best describes the poet's attitude toward the mother's jury service?

(A) Frustrated anger
(B) Anxious shame
(C) Scornful displeasure
(D) Cold indifference
(E) Amused ambivalence

STOP

END OF SECTION I

IF YOU FINISH BEFORE TIME IS CALLED, YOU MAY CHECK YOUR WORK ON THIS SECTION.
DO NOT GO ON TO SECTION II UNTIL YOU ARE TOLD TO DO SO.

ENGLISH LITERATURE AND COMPOSITION

SECTION II

Total Time—2 hours

Question 1

(Suggested time—40 minutes. This question counts as one-third of the total essay score.)

The passage that follows is excerpted from Don DeLillo's novel *Libra*, (1988), a fictional treatment of the young Lee Harvey Oswald, who as an adult would assassinate President John F. Kennedy. Read the passage carefully. Then write a well-organized essay concerning the methods by which the author has portrayed the subject and the substance of the portrait itself. Be sure to consider such literary elements as diction, imagery, and point of view.

He returned to the seventh grade until classes
ended. In summer dusk the girls lingered near the
benches on Bronx Park South. Jewish girls, Italian girls
Line in tight skirts, girls with ankle bracelets, their voices
(5) murmurous with the sound of boys' names, with song
lyrics, little remarks he didn't always understand. They
talked to him when he walked by making him smile in
his secret way.
   Oh a woman with beer on her breath, on the bus
(10) coming home from the beach. He feels the tired salty
sting in his eyes of a day in the sun and water.
   "The trouble leaving you with my sister,"
Marguerite said, "she had too many children of her
own. Plus the normal disputes of family. That meant I
(15) had to employ Mrs. Roach, on Pauline Street, when
you were two. But I came home one day and saw
she whipped you, raising welts on your legs, and we
moved to Sherwood Forest Drive."
   Heat entered the flat through the walls and
(20) windows, seeped down from the tar roof. Men on
Sundays carried pastry in white boxes. An Italian was
murdered in a candy store, shot five times, his
brains dashing the wall near the comic-book rack.
Kids trooped to the store from all around to see the
(25) traces of grayish spatter. His mother sold stockings in
Manhattan.
   A woman on the street, completely ordinary, maybe
fifty years old, wearing glasses and a dark dress,
handed him a leaflet at the foot of the El steps. Save the
(30) Rosenbergs, it said. He tried to give it back thinking
he would have to pay for it, but she'd already turned
away. He walked home, hearing a lazy radio voice
doing a ballgame. Plenty of room, folks. Come on out
for the rest of this game and all of the second. It
(35) was Sunday, Mother's Day, and he folded the leaflet
neatly and put it in his pocket to save for later.
   There is a world inside the world.
   He rode the subway up to Inwood, out to
Sheepshead Bay. There were serious men down there,
(40) rocking in the copper light. He saw, beggars, men
who talked to God, men who lived on the trains, day
and night, bruised, with matted hair, asleep in patient

bundles on the wicker seats. He jumped the turnstiles
once. He rode between cars, gripping the heavy chain.
(45) He felt the friction of the ride in his teeth. They went
so fast sometimes. He liked the feeling they were
on the edge. How do we know the motorman's not
insane? It gave him a funny thrill. The wheels touched
off showers of blue-white sparks, tremendous hissing
(50) bursts, on the edge of no-control. People crowded in,
every shape face in the book of faces. They pushed
through the doors, they hung from the porcelain straps.
He was riding just to ride. The noise had a power and
a human force. The dark had a power. He stood at the
(55) front of the first car, hands flat against the glass. The
view down the tracks was a form of power. It was a
secret and a power. The beams picked out secret things.
The noise was pitched to a fury he located in the mind,
a satisfying wave of rage and pain.

GO ON TO THE NEXT PAGE

Question 2

(Suggested time—40 minutes. This question counts as one-third of the total essay score.)

Carefully read the following poems by Sylvia Plath and William Blake. Then, in a well-organized essay, analyze how the speakers use imagery to reveal their attitudes toward infancy.

Morning Song

Love set you going like a fat gold watch.
The midwife slapped your footsoles, and your bald cry
Took its place among the elements.

Line
(5) Our voices echo, magnifying your arrival. New statue.
In a drafty museum, your nakedness
Shadows our safety. We stand round blankly as walls.

I'm no more your mother
Than the cloud that distills a mirror to reflect its own slow
Effacement at the wind's hand.

(10) All night your moth-breath
Flickers among the flat pink roses. I wake to listen:
A far sea moves in my ear.

One cry, and I stumble from bed, cow-heavy and floral
In my Victorian nightgown.
(15) Your mouth opens clean as a cat's. The window square

Whitens and swallows its dull stars. And now you try
Your handful of notes;
The clear vowels rise like balloons.

—Sylvia Plath

Infant Sorrow

My mother groaned, my father wept;
Into the dangerous world I leapt,
Helpless, naked, piping loud,
Like a fiend hid in a cloud.

Line
(5) Struggling in my father's hands,
Striving against my swaddling bands,
Bound and weary, I thought best
To sulk upon my mother's breast.

—William Blake

GO ON TO THE NEXT PAGE

Question 3

(Suggested time—40 minutes. This question counts as one-third of the total essay score.)

"When a true genius appears in the world, you may know him by this sign, that the dunces are all in confederacy against him."

—Jonathan Swift
"Thoughts on Various Subjects, Moral and Diverting"

In some works of literature, the main character often finds himself or herself in conflict with the social or moral values of his environment. Choose one novel or play of literary merit in which the character is at odds with the people around him or her, or with society at large. Write an essay in which you explain how these conflicts are essential to the overall meaning of the work.

You may select a work from the list below, or you may choose to write upon another work of comparable literary merit.

The Awakening
As I Lay Dying
Catch-22
Crime and Punishment
The Duchess of Malfi
A Fan's Notes
Hamlet
Heart of Darkness
Hunger
I Know Why the Caged Bird Sings
The Idiot
The Iliad
Invisible Man
King Lear
Long Day's Journey Into Night

Man's Fate
Marat/Sade
Medea
Miss Lonelyhearts
Moby-Dick
Native Son
Nausea
Old Goriot
One Flew Over the Cuckoo's Nest
The Scarlet Letter
The Turn of the Screw
Under the Volcano
Waiting for Godot
Wuthering Heights

STOP
END OF SECTION II
IF YOU FINISH BEFORE TIME IS CALLED, YOU MAY CHECK YOUR WORK ON THIS SECTION.

13

Practice Test 1: Answers and Explanations

This passage from the beginning of *The Magus*, a novel by British author John Fowles, is a selection that exhibits a sophistication of style that you will find on the AP English Literature Exam. This exam tests your knowledge, not only of literary elements, but of how well you comprehend the effect of those elements on the selection as a whole.

The voice of the narrator is important in this piece, as it is in every piece. But after you have finished reading this selection, you should be able to recognize that the narrator's realization of his situation is reflected in the setting.

1. **A** You may have read answer choice (A), which is a straightforward answer, and thought, "Oh, that's the answer," and then puzzled over the other choices wondering if you'd missed something. Perhaps (B) and (C) seemed to be possible answers also. Most of the time a pronoun refers to the last noun that has been named, but there are exceptions to this rule. In this case, the narrator is telling us that Phraxos, which is in the center of the landscape (B), is as memorable as the landscape is. When you looked at choice (C) again, you would have seen that "mainland" was used for location rather than imagery. Choice (D) could not have been the correct choice because a noun must precede the pronoun, not the other way around. Your only logical choice then was (A).

2. **E** Remember that when you are given choices that contain two words, both words must correctly answer the question. If one of the words is not accurate, then the entire choice must be eliminated. This question also tests your knowledge of literary terminology. Choice (A) could have been eliminated immediately because the narrator states that it was "simply and effortlessly beautiful." That alone would have eliminated choice (A) because "pretentious" indicates it was showy and not simple. The description is also not a form of a hyperbole. Choice (B) could have been a close choice because of the term "metaphor." In the phrase "amethyst evening sea," the adjective "amethyst" can be seen as a color or as a gem. However, the term "elusive" eliminates the answer because "elusive" indicates that it is intangible and mysterious. The concrete comparisons that are used in lines 5–10 would also help to eliminate this answer. Choice (C) indicates that the comparisons that are made are farfetched and do not have any concrete references. This is not the case. Choice (D) indicates that there is no depth to the impression the landscape has made on the narrator. This is the exact opposite of what has occurred. (E) is the correct answer. The comparisons used in these lines are predominately similes, and when you continue reading, it is evident that the use of Venus and the use of the whale are symbolic. Venus, the brightest planet in the sky, is used in contrast with a black whale in an evening sea. Also, Venus is symbolic of passion and romantic notions, whereas the whale is a symbol of earthly and pragmatic ideals.

3. **C** Make sure you understand what this question is asking. To answer it, you need to first think about what the narrator's tone is as he describes the island. He is clearly awed by its beauty. Now, what is the effect of this awe? Choice (A) seems pretty redundant and does not really address how the tone advances something else. Does it advance his anticipation of the one "facade?" This choice is only partially correct; the narrator is expressing something about the setting. However, he is not offering a logical explanation of the lack of towns on the island (D); this does not really suit the tone of awe and beauty. Same thing with (E)—the narrator is not offering a cold, objective analysis. So what does his awed description of the island's beauty *do*? It highlights the contrast between nature and the intellect, choice (C).

4. **D** This question requires that you take the time to refer to the line in which the word "obese" appears. If you rely on the definition you might erroneously choose (B) because the answer indicates a size. Don't forget, if you are given a line number, you must check to see how the word is used. Read at least one sentence before the word appears and one sentence after the word appears to get a better understanding of the meaning of the word in context. Rarely will you be asked for a textbook definition of a word, although it might happen. Choice (A) deals with the location of the hotel in relation to the water, which does not answer the question. Choice (C) does reflect a comparison to the analogy that the narrator makes, but it does not answer the question. The question is asking what the word "obese" is being used to describe. Choice (E) is a detail found in the previous paragraph that has to do with location. The remaining choice is (D). The word "obese" implies a very large object that is evidently out of place. This hotel is the result of modern commercialism and an intrusion on the landscape. Even if you did not know the meaning of all of the words in this selection, through POE, you should have arrived at choice (D).

5. **C** This question asks you to reflect on the importance of the second paragraph to the selection as a whole. The narrator recognizes that the building has a "facade." He later learns that this is not the only thing that has a disguise. He learns that the feelings of harmony he has are also an "illusion." Choice (A) is not accurate. The word "acceptance" is not true of this passage. When he arrives on the island he sees it in terms of simple beauty and considers the modern buildings to be "eyesores." The word "uneasiness" in choice (B) is not an accurate description of his impression. The second paragraph does not help to establish choice (D), even though this may be true of your understanding of the passage. Remember that you must select the choice that best completes the statement or answers the question. The second paragraph offers a critical analysis of the island's beauty, but this paragraph does more than that; it sets up a comparison that is expanded upon to great effect later in the passage. Therefore, (C) is correct.

6. **C** Once again, you must take a look at the entire paragraph before you make a decision. In order to establish tone, you must consider the word choice and the imagery that the author has provided. In this case choice (A) only refers to the description of the solitude of the island. Choice (B) refers only to one of the comparisons the narrator states. Choice (D) does not provide an accurate picture of the narrator's attitude in this paragraph, which is evident by his use of the words "significance," and "eerie." Neither of those words indicates depression. With the mention of nymphs and monsters in the last sentence, it is evident that a scholarly tone is not being used in this paragraph. Choice (C) is the best answer for this question. It provides a more in-depth understanding of what the narrator is trying to express.

7. **A** This question provides you with the fact that the names of Clytemnestra and Agamemnon are allusions. If you do not know their place in Greek tragedy and mythology then you might not understand what is being asked of you. Clytemnestra was the wife of Agamemnon, a Greek warrior who accompanied Odysseus to Troy. Prior to his departure, he sacrificed his daughter Iphigenia to the gods in order that he might return home safely. He rationalized his decision to kill his daughter. His wife, Clytemnestra, also sister to the infamous Helen of Troy, vowed revenge on Agamemnon for the murder. Agamemnon returned home safely, only to be murdered by his wife. This conflict provides the correct answer to this question. You should not have chosen choice (B) because there are no surrepti-

tious events that follow in this passage, as is evident by the narrator's understanding of the misconception of the harmony he felt. If you chose (C) you may have recognized the names from Greek mythology, but there is no mention of the history of the island by the narrator. If you chose (D), you may have recognized the Greek names in relationship with a kingdom, but the word "grandeur" is not the word that would be used to describe the island. It is its natural beauty that captivates the narrator. You could eliminate choice (E) because nowhere in the passage is there a reference to violence. Once again, you might have been able to make the correct choice using the Process of Elimination.

8. **D** This question requires you to have an understanding of the vocabulary used in the choices. Once again, you must remember that both words must accurately describe the speaker's impression of education on the island. In this case, choice (A) can be eliminated because the education is a solid and practical British education, not superficial. You can also eliminate choice (B) because it may be annoying to the narrator, but it is not archaic, merely adequate and current. Choice (C) does not provide you with any choices that are accurate. Choice (E) may provide you with the idea that the education one receives there is inconsequential, but it is not perplexing to the speaker. He understands that the education is adequate, but he is frustrated that it does not involve more of a romantic notion of education. Therefore, the best answer is choice (D).

9. **A** The speaker finds the school constricting and the students exasperating. They preferred to talk about cars rather than poetry. He found this preference of theirs frustrating, so choice (A) is correct. If you had chosen (E), you chose an answer that was close to correct, but it was more than disappointment that the narrator felt; it was frustration, as shown by the way he developed his examples in a repetitive, almost sarcastic manner.

10. **A** This type of question posses the most difficulty for students. Once again, you need to look carefully at the question and the choices you are given. Eliminate the choices that do not supply the correct implications. It is true that the narrator believes that there are shortcomings in the British educational system. The education fostered an interest for science and little for literature. If you decided that choice I was a correct answer, you are on the right track. You can eliminate choice (C) and choice (D). If you look at choice II you will see that the "myopic" (limited) vision of the students who only want to learn scientific information and not that of literature, also makes selection II a valid statement. Because the choices that are left all include II, you have to look at III and IV to determine whether or not they also apply. Selection III may be true, but you need to refer to line 80 to make sure you understand what the object of reference is to "mole-like blindness." You can easily determine that this reference loosely applies to education. In that case, you can eliminate selection III because it refers to all inhabitants of the island. We do not know if this statement is true based on this selection. Now you can also eliminate choices (E) and (B). Choice IV is not true, and therefore you are left with choice (A).

11. **C** This question requires you to know some basic literary terminology. Parody is not evident in this passage; you can eliminate choice (A). Apostrophe, which is often used in poetry, is not used in this passage. You can eliminate choice (B). Repetition is often used by good writers, but choice (D) indicates that the attitude of the speaker is emphasized by their usage. So choice (D) is not the best answer for this question. Take a look at (E). Hyperbole is not used. Now, you need to decide between choice (C) and choice (D). This passage, like most literary passages, does depend on the author's use of imagery to make his point. So keep choice (C). That leaves (C) as the correct answer.

12. **B** You may say, "I don't know the meaning of *termitary*" (a nest of termites). But remember that this is an EXCEPT question. Take a look and see if the statements are true, even if you don't understand the term. You do know that the statement in choice (A) is true. The atmosphere of the school on Phraxos is the same as it is in England. You know that the attitude of the Greeks on the island is not in contrast to those of the students in school (B). The Greeks may not pay attention to their surroundings, but the students in the school are also Greek and receiving a British education. This statement, therefore, cannot be true. A look at the other choices indicates statements that you have already recognized as accurate in other questions. Choice (C) indicates that masters and students do not appreciate their surroundings. This choice is a true statement. Choice (D) is implied when the narrator states that the students devoured any scientific information that the masters provided. Choice (E) implies the same response as choice (D). Therefore, the answer is (B).

13. **D** Choice (A), "laconic," means uncommunicative. You could possibly infer that the speaker did not communicate with others based on this selection; however, you need to read the statement carefully. You are asked to infer how the hills made the speaker feel. They made him feel harmonious with nature. Choice (B) indicates they made him feel weak. This is not true. You can eliminate it. Choice (C) is the opposite of what the speaker felt. You can eliminate (C) as well. Although the speaker may have felt impatient at times, the hills did not make him feel that way. You can eliminate (E). Choice (D) is the best answer.

14. **A** Don't forget the reference line: "It was an illusion" refers to the speaker's feelings of harmony between body and mind. The closest answer for the question is (A). You can eliminate (B) because the choice indicates that the climate was an illusion. That is not true. You can also eliminate (C) because it deals with the Greek language and the narrator previously indicated that he knew very little Greek. This is a detail and not a sufficient response to the statement. Choice (D) indicates a feeling of animosity between the two cultures. This is incorrect. Choice (E) indicates that the speaker will not enjoy his time in the hills. That is not what the speaker says previously. Remember, in a reference question, you must look at what comes just before the line and what comes after it, if appropriate. Without a doubt, (A) is the correct answer.

15. **E** Once again, you are quizzed on your knowledge of terminology. Refer to the back of the book if you are not familiar with the literary terms that have been used in these questions. The key to understanding what is being asked of you is to look at the question. The question is not asking you what literary elements are used in the passage—it is asking what elements help to reinforce the meaning of the selection. In this case, all but (E) are correct.

QUESTIONS 16–27

The passage is by Christina Rossetti (1830–94), and was written when she was in her early thirties. The poem's spiritual, death-haunted theme is typical of Rossetti, who was beset with ill-health her entire—yet relatively long—life.

The Rossettis, Christina and her brothers, William Michael and Dante Gabriel, were at the center of an influential mid–nineteenth-century arts movement called the Pre-Raphaelite Brotherhood. Pre-Raphaelite painting and writing were concerned with medieval themes, with romance (often tinged with self-destruction or death), nature, nostalgia, and vivid imagery and color.

Christina's brother Dante (arguably the leader of the Pre-Raphaelite movement) is guilty of one of the truly cheeseball acts of narcissism in literary history. When Dante Gabriel Rossetti's wife died, the painter-poet buried the manuscripts of several of his poems in the casket with her. Ah, love. Seven years later he decided maybe it wasn't such a good idea and had the mess dug up so he could get his poems back. The last laugh, however, is on Dante, whose literary reputation is waning. His sister Christina, however, has acquired a growing respect from the literary world after many years spent in her brother's shadow.

The poem on the test (like almost everything Christina Rossetti wrote) is a meditation on the transience of life and the inevitability of death. When, in the third stanza, God promises to come for the poet when her hour arrives, the poem becomes an avowal of faith.

Although the bulk of the poem's meaning is accessible to most readers, the questions asked on the test lay several traps for the unwary. When reading and interpreting poetry, be on guard against making assumptions that can't be justified. Several questions have incorrect choices that suggest the principal narrator is on her deathbed. You should not reason that the poem's intense contemplation of death indicates the speaker is gravely ill or about to die; those are unwarranted assumptions.

Another difficulty you face when answering the questions on the Rossetti passage is that the questions ask about some of the poem's subtler points. There are several questions, for example, about the important shift in the recurrent nature imagery that occurs in the poem's final stanza. Complications also rise from the presence of multiple speakers in the poem.

This long-standing tradition of conversing with the spiritual forces of the cosmos may seem a hopelessly old-fashioned device, but poets up to the present day continue to create interesting and important works using this convention. The Rossetti poem, however, not only has the speaker in dialogue with the metaphysical world, but takes matters a degree further in the second stanza by having the Soul speak with the voice of the past. Following the line "Hearken what the past doth witness and say:" the Soul presents what the past has to say about human mortality. You needed to understand that in this stanza the past is *not* being directly presented as a speaker. In fact, the past is probably not even being quoted; the Soul is interpreting the past for the benefit of the principal narrator. This is a tangled piece of rhetorical construction and causes most students some problems.

Overall, the passage, taken together with its questions, is at the difficult end of the spectrum of work you will see on the AP English Literature and Composition Exam.

16. **D**   As noted in the general notes to the passage, this is a tough question. Most students choose answer choice (E), five. But the past is not a speaker. The past is being interpreted for the principal narrator by the Soul. Another choice that sophisticated readers sometimes pick is (A), one. The reasoning behind choosing (A) is usually that only the poet is speaking; the Soul, World, and God represent elements and ideas within the poet. In this reading, the poem is a kind of internal monologue in which the poet sorts out her feelings about death and the afterlife. This interpretation is absolutely plausible (Rossetti certainly did not intend for you to think she had actually held a conversation with the World or with God). The problem is that it is an *interpretation*. The question asks, "How many speakers does the

poem present?" The emphasis is on what the poem presents, not what the poem might suggest. The question is not asking for an interpretation but simply for what the poem presents. It presents four speakers.

17. **C**   This is one of the relatively rare knowledge questions on the test. You either know it or you don't. Eighty to ninety percent of the test is about your ability to understand the material you read, both the details and the larger picture. But there are some facts which ETS feels they can expect you know. They expect you to know the basic terminology of literary criticism and form (i.e., simile, metaphor, sonnet, couplet, etc.), and they occasionally ask about those literary historical references a well-read individual should recognize. This question is an example of the latter.

In ancient Greek and Roman society, a garland of laurel and bay leaves was awarded in recognition of triumph in sports, war, or poetry. The original "gold medal" of the Olympics was a laurel wreath, as is that wreath you always see framing Julius Caesar's bald pate. The reason the answer specifically mentions poets is that laurel (bay is a variety of laurel) was the symbolic flower of Apollo, patron God of poetry. Even today, when people are honored as the national poet their title is *poet laureate.* Speaking of honors, graduation from college with a bachelor's degree will mean that you have earned your bacca*laureate*, a term derived from the medieval university tradition of crowning graduates with laurel.

18. **B**   The lines in question here, "I shall clothe myself in Spring and bud in May:/ Thou, root stricken, shalt not rebuild thy decay," contrast the cyclical progress of the seasons with the linear trajectory of human life. Line 7 is a troublemaker line for many students, who frequently pick up on "root stricken" as indicating that the principal narrator is deathly ill. What root-stricken refers to is the fundamental presence of death in human life. The author and humans in general are "root stricken" in the sense that death is imminent from birth; or to use another plant metaphor, we carry the seed of death within us from conception.

19. **C**   The incorrect answers all make use of imagery that draws on living things, especially plants, and of the changing seasons. In line 13, the image of "Rust in thy gold" is the one image of the poem that draws neither on the seasons nor on living things.

20. **E**   In this question the key was to use POE, reading each answer choice carefully for what makes it *wrong*. An answer that gets the meaning of two out of three stanzas correct is still wrong. In these kinds of questions, pay close attention to the wording of the answer choices. In (B), for example, you should reason that for stanza 1, "nostalgia for the earthly world that must be left behind" is close enough to accept, and "welcome acceptance of the afterlife" for stanza 3 is substantially correct. However, "fear of physical decay" for stanza 2 is only half-correct. Physical decay is certainly contemplated, but fear is much too strong a term. This makes the answer wrong. Cross it off. Working this way you should find yourself, without too much trouble, left only with the correct answer, (E).

21. **E**   The question shouldn't have given you too much trouble. Basically, you were asked what "a moth in thine array" is meant to signify metaphorically. The image is yet one more description of the natural aging process. The incorrect choices offer various misreadings, either seeing illness where none is present, or spiritual anxieties that neither the line in question, nor the poem as a whole, is concerned with.

22. **C** The line runs on from 7 to 8. This is another terminology question. If it gave you any trouble you should refer to our section on literary terms for the AP English Literature and Composition Exam. Also, remember to use POE to get rid of those answers you are sure are wrong and guess with what's left. No blanks!

23. **B** This is a question that many students get wrong. Always return to the passage. The third stanza presents a dramatic reversal in the poem's meaning and direction by refiguring imagery from the previous stanzas with an antithetical meaning. In the first two stanzas, Spring and all the imagery of Spring are used to represent youth, energy, and life. You might easily think then that Winter, as Spring's opposite, represents (E) aging and loss of vigor, or perhaps (C) the coldness of the grave, that is, death itself. But the question asks for the meaning of winter in the *third* stanza. In this stanza God says that now "winter passeth after the long delay." What follows are images of spring now clearly tied to death and the afterlife. Spring in the final stanza is a metaphor for the joy of reunion with God. In the final stanza, God offers death as a joyous springlike occasion. It is earthly life, separate from the Maker, which is the long Winter.

24. **C** As with all questions with longer answers, you must read carefully and eliminate when an answer is partially correct. Partially correct means all wrong. Otherwise, the reasoning behind this question is fully covered in the explanation to question 23.

25. **A** Understanding the lines in question is not as much about the lines themselves as it is about letting them make sense in the overall context of the poem. If you understood the bulk of the poem, then this question shouldn't have been difficult. If the poem itself gave you trouble, this question might have as well. The incorrect choices offer various misreadings and over interpretations.

26. **C** One of the easiest questions on the test. This is essentially a vocabulary question, but chances are you were unfamiliar with the passage's usage of the word "spray." Figure out the meaning from the context. None of the incorrect answers makes sense in context except possibly (A), and we hope that between (A) and (C), you chose (C).

27. **D** You are certain to see a question (or two or three) like this one on your test. If you got this question wrong, brush up on your skills with our section on grammar for the AP English Literature and Composition Exam (page 53). As outlined in that section, the best way to figure out the construction of the kind of sentence ETS likes to ask about is to rewrite the sentence (in your mind—you shouldn't need to actually write it down) into a more natural form. The sentences ETS chooses are never straightforward "subject, verb, direct-object, indirect object" sentences like "Jack threw the ball to me." The sentence that begins on line 24 "Arise, come away, night is past and lo it is day, My love, My sister, My spouse, thou shalt hear me say," should be rewritten:

"Thou shalt hear me say, 'Arise, come away, night is past and lo it is day,
My love, My sister, My spouse.'"

Notice we've put quotation marks around what God reports he will say. This is how the sentence would normally be punctuated. If you rewrite it in this manner, you should be able to see that "Thou" is the subject.

This passage is from Anthony Trollope's novel *Barchester Towers*, the second of his Barsetshire novels. It was written in 1857 and, unlike many Victorian novels, was more concerned with the topics of the day than the recent past. However, like the Victorian prose you are apt to see on the test, the sentences can be somewhat convoluted, with multiple negations and other forms of twisted syntax. Tone isn't always easy to discern. Close reading is essential.

28. **A** The narrator states, "It is not my intention to breathe a word against Mrs Proudie," but then spends several paragraphs doing just that. Choice (B) is a colloquialism derived from figurative language describing a domineering wife. Because domineering is precisely what Mrs. Proudie is said to be, there is no irony here. Choice (C) is the juxtaposition of Mrs. Grantly, the archdeacon's wife, but there isn't enough said about her to know if this is ironic or not. Choice (D) might be construed as hyperbole, but it certainly is not the opposite of the author's intended meaning. Choice (E) is close; one might detect some sarcasm, also known as verbal irony, but the author doesn't mean the opposite of what he has stated, so (A) is the best answer.

29. **C** Although it describes Dr. Proudie, it does so in the context of how Mrs. Proudie's despotic behavior has cowed him. Choice (A), while tempting, refers much more closely to Mrs. Proudie's ambitions and how they extend beyond the normal sphere of the wife of a bishop. Choice (B) refers to Mrs. Grantly, not Mrs. Proudie. Choice (D) refers to something Mrs. Proudie expects those under her roof to submit to, but it is not as pointed an example of her authoritarian nature as (C). Choice (E) uses a mythological allusion to a watchful, not authoritarian, character.

30. **E** Dr. Proudie is, in name, the lord of Mrs. Proudie, but as the passage explains in great depth, it is Mrs. Proudie, in actuality, who lords over her husband. The situation is the opposite of what it is in name. Choice (A) doesn't have much going for it, other than a big word that students who aren't adequately familiar with literary terms won't understand. Hyperbole is exaggeration, and (A) is not an exaggeration. Choices (B) and (D) do much the same thing, but with even fancier words. Choice (C) might appeal to a student who knows that onomatopoeia has something to do with how words sound, and "titular" does sound funny—but it's not a noun or verb, so it can't really sound like the noise made by the thing it describes.

31. **D** The phrase states that in domestic matters, he would not have offered the power to his wife, but was happy to cede it. Choice (B) and (E) are based on careless reading of the phrases "domestic" or the vague memory that the passage was about his marriage. Choices (A) and (C) take deceptive language from further afield in the passage.

32. **C** In the context of the passage, which is devoted to describing Mrs. Proudie's character, the example of Mrs. Grantly, the archdeacon's wife, is used to describe Mrs. Proudie by contrast. Mrs. Grantly's virtues are laid out in contrast, and the transition into the subsequent paragraph, "Not so Mrs. Proudie," makes the author's intention clear. Choice (A) is a trap answer, designed to snare the careless reader who sees the words "the full privileges of her rank," which actually pertain to her role as a clergyman's wife. Choice (B) is another use of deceptive language. The transition into the paragraph, "In fact, the bishop is henpecked," refers to Dr. Proudie, not the archdeacon, Mrs. Grantly's husband. Choice (D) is probably the most evil of all trap answers, one designed to catch the rare student who may have read

this novel or its sequels, in particular, *Framley Parsonage*, in which the rivalry of Mrs. Grantly and Mrs. Proudie is given substantial attention. It certainly is not the author's intention to suggest a rivalry, although he may have intended to foreshadow it. Choice (E) has some merit. From the description of Mrs. Grantly, it certainly seems as if the author favors women who exert their power domestically and privately. The passage states, "before the world she is a pattern of obedience; her voice is never loud … she know what should be the limits of a woman's rule." Nevertheless, the language in the answer choice, "assert why women should be seen and not heard," suggests that the author provides evidence for a position stronger than the one he actually takes.

33. **D** *Pity*, answer choice (A), is best used to describe how the author feels toward Dr. Proudie, "her poor husband." Although the narrator may feign an appearance of *objectivity*, answer choice (B), his opening comments make it clear that what he presents is his subjective opinion. Given that, answer choice (C), *emotional judgment*, might be tempting, but his language is strong enough to justify (D), *sardonic condemnation*. He is certainly mocking Mrs. Proudie, and his judgment of her does condemn her behavior. It is choice (E) that is too extreme for the passage.

34. **B** We get no sense of Dr. Proudie's devotion to his wife or of his moral compass, no matter what we might want to infer from knowing his profession, so answer choice (A) is out. Answer choice (B) is supported by the text of the third paragraph. Choice (C) and (D) suggest a happy and loving marriage, not the picture painted by this paragraph. (E) might describe Mrs. Proudie's relationship to her husband, but not the reverse.

35. **C** He is described as "aware that submission produces the nearest approach to peace which his own house can ever attain." Choices (A) refers most nearly to a quality best attributed to Mrs. Proudie. Choices (B) and (E) are not supported by the text. Choice (D) is a trap answer for those who read quickly and saw that the passage was about the clergy and religious matters.

36. **A** The maid in question has been unfaithful to her duty. As is par for the course, on a single phrase or word question, the primary dictionary definition, choice (D) is offered as an answer choice, as is a word it kind of sounds like, choice (B). The other choices have no merit whatsoever.

37. **C** The repetition of the phrase "Woe betide" accentuates the seriousness of the servants' situation. It neither slows down the prose, as in (A), nor does it satirize or mock the servants' fate, as in (B). The phrase is consistent with the narrator's attitude throughout the rest of the passage, so (D) is incorrect. Choice (E) is too extreme.

38. **B** Even if you weren't familiar with the Victorian use of "character" as shorthand for "character reference," you could derive the meaning from the context of the passage—the maid has been dismissed, and because of this "character," she is unable to find decent employment. Choices (A), (C), and (E) all prey on a reader's familiarity with the dictionary definitions of the word, as opposed to the contextual meaning. Choice (D) is a trap for the careless reader who sees "character" and "foot" near each other in the passage and overinterprets—perhaps thinking that the footman is sent to escort the housemaid from the premises.

39. **C** The point of the paragraph is to illustrate Mrs. Proudie's hypocrisy. The paragraph does so by showing how strict she is in applying the rules to others when it comes to this single point of religious belief, although she is given to "[d]issipation and low dresses" the rest of the time. Choice (A) might be tempting because of the religious aspect, but in no place does this paragraph suggest a transformation for the domineering Mrs. Proudie. Choice (B) also has its merits, as this paragraph is where Mr. Slope is introduced, but no mention is made of him observing Mrs. Proudie (quite the contrary, one is expected to observe Mr. Slope). For similar reasons—the mention of religion—(D) might be attractive, but as mentioned above, it doesn't counter speculation about her despotic reign. It extends it beyond her husband to her household staff…which she might have a hard time hiring, as (E) suggests, but that would not be the point of the paragraph.

40. **E** The author analyzes Mrs. Proudie in an amusing way, mocking her cleverly by pointing out her flaws, first in contrast to a social equivalent, then by exposing her hypocrisy. Most of the other answers fall into the half-right, half-wrong category, and aggressive POE will save the day here. Choice (A) is wrong on both counts—the passage is neither humorless nor pedantic. Although the passage is certainly subjective, it is hardly emotional, so as long as you know the definition of effusive, you can eliminate (B). Choice (C) starts out stronger; the passage is certainly descriptive. Alas, a few metaphors do not a metaphorical passage make. If you chose (C), or even kept it on your first pass through the answer choices, don't kick yourself. Close answer choices are one of the ways a question can be made more challenging. Lacking both terseness and epigrams, though, choice (D) should be an easy candidate for elimination.

QUESTIONS 41–55

The passage is the poem "A Long Line of Doctors" by contemporary American poet Carolyn Kizer. Overall, the questions shouldn't have caused you too many problems as long as you had a working sense of the general content of the poem and kept the poem's main idea in mind.

Essentially, the poem describes a character called Mother (we shouldn't presume that the poem is in fact about Kizer's mother, the poem might narrate an entirely fictional trial and fictional people) who serves on the jury at the trial of a dentist. The mother takes a strange and not particularly honorable approach to her duties; she simply finds the dentist guilty from the moment she lays eyes on him, and so pays as much attention to the book she's reading as to the trial itself. If you got this much from the poem you would be off to a good start. Using POE carefully should have solved most (or all) of your problems.

41. **D** This question called for you to interpret the answer choices carefully. You needed to pay strict attention to the wording of the choices. Choice (A) should have been an easy first elimination. It describes an attitude completely opposite to that of the mother's. The other three incorrect answers were a little bit tricky. In (B), was she "completely unaware?" Take the statement literally. Does she not know that she will be called upon to deliver a verdict? Of course she does. She may be unaware of some of the ethical duties imposed on her, but that doesn't make her "completely" unaware. Eliminate (B). Similarly, in (C), just because the Mother judges the dentist according to her own rather than legal standards we can't assume that she would face every jury situation this way, nor in fact does she hold the dentist's status as accused against him. She just doesn't like creepy little dentists. (E) shouldn't have been too tough to eliminate. The mother certainly considers herself superior to the dentist (and probably a lot of other people as well), but how she feels the law applies to her

we don't know. Eliminate (E). This leaves only (D). Yes, it's fair to say that the mother takes her responsibilities too lightly, and her certainty about the whole affair tells us that she has no doubts about her fitness as a juror.

42. **B** This question should have been a piece of cake. You did not need to read too much into the phrase "half-heard." Don't let the power of suggestion steer you down false paths. The mother half-hears because she's reading. If the poet wanted to suggest age or poor hearing she would have returned to those ideas to make them clearer. Here, she wants to reinforce the impression that the mother has made up her mind so fully that she barely bothers with the details of the trial.

43. **D** This is an extremely tricky question. Many students pick answer choices (B) or (C). But the dentist is not said to be a seminarian (a clergyperson). The dentist is uncomfortable, like a priest without the white collar of that profession. The rest of the stanza relates the court-room to a ship (e.g., the "plank," the "deck"). The dentist isn't compared to a condemned sailor, but is described as though he is one when the mother pushes the fly-speck from the page and says "she will push him off." This statement refers to the way in which she will push him from the plank. It also suggests that she thinks of him as easily dismissed and as insignificant as a fly, and perhaps as repulsive. But the poet does not describe the dentist as a fly-speck. Choice (E) may or may not be true, but it is found neither in the stanza, nor in the poem. Only (D) is correct.

44. **C** Here you needed to understand that the poem is about the mother and the dentist, not about other people. That is, you needed to stay with the main idea. The phrase in question refers only to the dentist; in fact, choice (C) summarizes it nicely. The dentist is the "hacker, wielder of pliers," etc. Yes, some of the items in the list are a bit confusing, but use your imagination. How is the dentist a "barber"? Well, think of the hydraulic chair you have to sit in, or the bib the dentist pulls around your neck; aren't those things reminiscent of being in a barbershop?

45. **E** Here you needed to stay with the main idea and not get drawn toward a silly answer. Throughout the poem, the mother feels herself to be superior to dentists in general and to this dentist in particular. The mother is a tremendous snob; she considers dentists to be lowlifes. Advertising is just one more thing that her-kind-of-people just don't do. You might have had some difficulty if you didn't know the word "propriety." It refers to what is proper or polite. POE should have led you to the right answer anyway, however, so long as you saw that other answers all involved reading much too deeply into the passage.

46. **D** This is a super POE question and it should have been pretty easy. Choices I and II should have been obvious. The mother finds the dentist guilty simply because he is a dentist, and she then persuades the rest of the jury that he is guilty. Using POE you are then left with just choices (D) and (E). So, does the poem imply that the dentist should have been found innocent? Not at all. All it implies is that the dentist is an unattractive creep who drilled a patient through the tongue. Does this action make him guilty? Who knows? Innocent? Again: Who knows? We're never told with what exactly the dentist has been charged.

47. **A** ETS has a way of sneaking some vocabulary into the test, and this question is a good example. It is also a good example of a question that lends itself to POE and the principle of half-bad = all-bad. You didn't have to know what *lecherous* meant in (A) to say that the dentist could be seen as comically chasing his assistant around the chair while molded plaster teeth grin from the shelves, and there's something sickly funny too about his being so out of it with love that he drills right through a patient's tongue. So, if you didn't know what lecherous meant you'd leave (A) for a guess. For (B) to be correct, the dentist would had to have deliberately drilled through his patient's tongue. That's wrong, so eliminate (B). For exactly the same reason eliminate (C), the dentist was not calculating. In (D) you find more vocab. What's *amorous*? If you know, great, but you don't need to know to eliminate the choice. You could eliminate by simply using the half-bad = all-bad principle. Is the dentist timid? No. He chased his assistant around the chair. He sounds more like a maniac. Eliminate (D). Finally there's (E). The dentist drilled his patient's tongue in a moment of dreamy contemplation, not anger. Eliminate (E). Thus, using POE, we're left with only (A). So what does lecherous mean? Well, essentially, it means lustful, with strong overtones of slime.

48. **E** The phrase "tasting brine" continues the doomed-sailor-forced-to-walk-the-plank metaphor of the second stanza. Again, vocabulary helps: "brine" is seawater. The dentist has begun to realize that things are not going well, that he will be found guilty. Metaphorically then, he will walk the plank and end up with a mouthful of seawater. It's worth pointing out how nicely Kizer sets this image of "tasting brine." It refers back to the earlier sailor metaphors, but it also works as a fresh rephrasing of a stale idea: that one finds a bitter taste in one's mouth in the face of unpleasant prospects. Along similar lines, and just because artistry is worth pointing out wherever you find it, note Kizer's use of the word "rises" in the phrase "as the testimony rises." It's an unusual/striking verb in this context, but perfectly suited to the moment. "Rises" implies an increase in sound and in passion. It is also the verb of choice to refer to deepening water, as in a rising tide—or even more appropriately—to the effect an approaching storm has on the seas, as in the seas' rise. In the poem, Kizer has found a use for "rise" where all three meanings—increasing sound, increasing emotion, rising (metaphorical) water—come into play. Does seeing this specifically help you answer the question? Not really. But we wanted to point out the kind of sensitivity to language you want to develop in order to fully appreciate poetry (and everything else you read). Developing a keen ear for language brings pleasure and success far beyond the AP exam (though it helps you there, too).

49. **D** The key to this question was to go back and find where the poem attaches a metaphor to reading. The question gives no line reference, but you shouldn't have had too much trouble spotting line 19, where the mother reads with "an easy breaststroke." (Of course, to do this kind of spotting, you needed to have an idea of what a metaphor is. We've mentioned it a couple of times already, but here it is again: Make sure you can define the terms *simile* and *metaphor*, and make sure you can tell the difference between them. Both concepts are defined in our glossary of literary terms.) This was a very easy question so long as you went back to the passage. The disastrous mistake was to not go back to the passage and instead try to figure out the answer based on memory and common sense. Even if you didn't get the question wrong you'd actually end up wasting time, and you'd probably get it wrong.

50. **D** This is primarily a term question, but you could have arrived at a correct guess without knowing that "poetic justice" refers to punishment that reflects the crime. (For example, a counterfeiter buying an expensive old painting with bogus money only to discover later that the painting is a forgery.) In the seventh stanza, the poet describes the dentist now in the position of a patient, gripping the arms of his chair and being most uncomfortably drilled. This sort of reversal also falls under the category of poetic justice. If you were unfamiliar with the term poetic justice you could have arrived at a perfectly good guess by reading the question carefully. It refers to "Mother's treatment" of the dentist. In which stanza is the mother most directly involved with the dentist himself (and not simply the legal process)? In the seventh stanza, where she "strapped him in, to drill him away." This understanding should have made (D), the most attractive guess. *Guess.* By the way, there's another more technical definition of poetic justice, which ETS will probably not use. We cover that definition in our glossary.

51. **C** There's our old friend irony again. In the phrase "Nice Mrs. Nemesis" the irony is not very delicate; in fact, it has almost become irony's nasty little brother, sarcasm. To answer this question, it helped a great deal to know that a "nemesis" is an archenemy. (In the poem, Kizer actually refers to the Greek goddess, Nemesis, who represented righteous anger.) If you knew that a nemesis is an archenemy, or even just something negative (which you could have figured out from context), you could have reasoned that "Nice Mrs. 'something nasty'" contains the kind of contradiction that makes for irony. Barring that understanding, you should have worked with the terms you knew and used POE. All the terms in the answer choices are covered in our glossary of terms.

52. **D** These I, II, III questions are made for POE. After reading through the items, you should have gone back to the final stanza and reread it. Then look at the items again. Which choice is easiest to decide upon? Choice II should look weird—eliminate it. The stanza discusses the mother's idea of God; Voltaire is an afterthought, and all that's said is that she finds him "indispensable." What Voltaire's views are, the poem doesn't say (and ETS does not expect you to know Voltaire's philosophy). With item II gone, choices (B) and (E) are gone as well. What about item III? Social decorum refers to polite behavior. In the last stanza, the mother mentions that God instructs in "hygiene and deportment," that is, in necessary social graces. Item III is a keeper. Even if you didn't know what decorum meant, which makes more sense: the mother believes God agrees with her, or disagrees? If you got the general drift of the poem you should know that the Mother thinks God shares her views. Keeping item III means you can eliminate (A). All that's left are choices (C) and (D). Okay, let's look at item I. Here you needed to read closely. She says God is "indispensable." That's good enough to justify the "deeply held" part of item I. What about "unsophisticated." Is it a sophisticated conception of the Divine to think that God cares about hygiene? Not really. Furthermore, Kizer's comparison of the mother to "true idolaters" reinforces the unsophisticated idea. Does the mother think she's unsophisticated? Not at all! She thinks she's hot stuff reading Voltaire and all! But the question doesn't ask what the mother thinks of herself. It asks about what the poem says about her. In the final stanza Kizer has some fun at the mother's expense. Item I is a keeper, which makes the right answer (D).

53. **B** This should have been a truly easy grammar question. In fact, it really isn't a grammar question at all, just a disguised comprehension question. Basically, it asks who "swept out"? The answer is Mother. You should have gone back to the poem and read the sentence carefully. ETS likes to ask grammar, or pseudogrammar questions like this one, when the elements in question are widely separated. In this instance, the only difficult aspect of the question is that several words intervene between "Mother" and "swept out." Don't let that throw you. Subject and verb do not have to come close to one another. ETS likes it when they don't. You've probably also been taught that modifiers should be placed next to the word(s) they modify. That's true, but ETS likes to ask questions about sentences that are exceptions to that rule.

54. **A** The lines "He was doomed, doomed, doomed by birth, profession,/ Practice, appearance, personal habits, loves…/ And now his patient swollen-mouthed with cancer!" gave this question away. All you had to do was to work through the choices using those lines to eliminate (remember this is an EXCEPT question!). In the end, all you are left with is the correct answer. The dentist's religious beliefs are never mentioned.

55. **E** This is a tone question. As you read the poem, you probably found yourself thinking the mother is being pretty harsh and unfair in condemning a man for being a dentist. And it's true. By conventional ethical standards the mother has behaved abominably. Kizer knows it but never passes judgment. Mostly, Kizer has fun with the situation. She's impressed with the mother's strength (and arrogance) even as she calls upon Voltaire to rescue the "wreck of [the mother's] fairmindedness." Kizer's sympathetic to the mother, but not entirely so, not when she refers to the mother as "Nice Mrs. Nemesis," and not when she relates the mother's vision of the deity. These statements are lightly critical. The whole thing is softened by the fact that the dentist does sound like a creep who deserves what he gets, so the mother's cavalier attitude doesn't have tragic consequences. All of this reasoning adds up to (E), amused ambivalence. The situation might have been shocking, but Kizer prefers to see the underlying humor in the clash of the mother's snooty sense of proper conduct, the dentist's low life self-presentation, and the irony that neither of them are actually conducting themselves well. The incorrect choices all call up emotional states that are too extreme to be justified, and should have been pretty easy to eliminate, so POE should have gotten you the right answer even if the term "ambivalence" in choice (E) puzzled you.

HOW TO SCORE PRACTICE TEST 1

Section I: Multiple Choice

_____ – (1/4 × _____) = _____
number correct   number wrong   **Multiple-Choice Score**

Section II: Free Response

(See if you can find a teacher or classmate to score your essays using the guidelines in Chapter 7.)

_____ + _____ + _____ = _____
essay 1   essay 2   essay 3   **Free-Response Score**
(out of 9) (out of 9) (out of 9)

Composite Score

_____ × 1.23 = _____
Multiple-Choice Score   **Weighted Section I Score**

_____ × 3.06 = _____
Free-Response Score   **Weighted Section II Score**

_____ + _____ = _____
Weighted Section I Score   **Weighted Section I Score**   **Composite Score**

AP Grade Conversion

Composite Score	AP Grade
107–150	5
93–106	4
73–92	3
43–72	2
0–42	1

14

Practice Test 2

ENGLISH LITERATURE AND COMPOSITION

SECTION I

Time—1 hour

<u>Directions:</u> This section consists of selections from literary works and questions on their content, form, and style. After reading each passage or poem, choose the best answer to each question and then fill in the corresponding oval.

<u>Questions 1–15.</u> Choose your answers to questions 1–15 based on a careful reading of the following passage.

An Invective Against Enemies of Poetry

With the enemies of poetry I care not if I have a bout, and those are they that term our best writers but babbling ballad-makers, holding them fantastical fools,
Line that have wit but cannot tell how to use it. I myself
(5) have been so censured among some dull-headed divines, who deem it no more cunning to write an exquisite poem than to preach pure Calvin or distill the juice of a commentary in a quarter sermon. Prove it when you will, you slow-spirited Saturnists, that
(10) have nothing but the pilferies of your pen to polish an exhortation withal; no eloquence but tautologies to tie the ears of your auditory unto you; no invention but "here it is to be noted, I stole this note out of Beza or Marlorat"; no wit to move, no passion to urge, but
(15) only an ordinary form of preaching, blown up by use of often hearing and speaking; and you shall find there goes more exquisite pains and purity of wit to the writing of one such rare poem as "Rosamund" than to a hundred of your dunstical sermons.
(20) Should we (as you) borrow all out of others, and gather nothing of ourselves our names should be baffuld on every bookseller's stall, and not a chandler's mustard pot but would wipe his mouth with our waste paper. "New herrings, new!" we must cry, every
(25) time we make ourselves public, or else we shall be christened with a hundred new titles of idiotism. Nor is poetry an art whereof there is no use in a man's whole life but to describe discontented thoughts and youthful desires; for there is no study but it doth illustrate and
(30) beautify.
To them that demand what fruits the poets of our time bring forth, or wherein they are able to prove themselves necessary to the state, thus I answer: first and foremost, they have cleansed our language from
(35) barbarism and made the vulgar sort here in London (which is the fountain whose rivers flow round about England) to aspire to a richer purity of speech than is communicated with the commonality of any nation under heaven. The virtuous by their praises they
(40) encourage to be more virtuous; to vicious men they are as infernal hags to haunt their ghosts with eternal infamy after death. The soldier, in hope to have his high deeds celebrated by their pens, despiseth a whole army of perils, and acteth wonders exceeding all
(45) human conjecture. Those that care neither for God nor the devil, by their quills are kept in awe.
Let God see what he will, they would be loath to have the shame of the world. What age will not praise immortal Sir Philip Sidney, whom noble Salustius
(50) (that thrice singular French poet) hath famoused; together with Sir Nicholas Bacon, Lord Keeper, and merry Sir Thomas More, for the chief pillars of our English speech. Not so much but Chaucer's host, Bailly in Southwark, and his wife of Bath he keeps such a
(55) stir with, in his *Canterbury Tales*, shall be talked of whilst the Bath is used, or there be ever a bad house in Southwark. Gentles, it is not your lay chronographers, that write of nothing but of mayors and sheriffs and the dear year and the great frost, that can endow
(60) your names with never-dated glory; for they want the wings of choice words to fly to heaven, which we have; they cannot sweeten a discourse, or wrest admiration from men reading, as we can, reporting the meanest accident. Poetry is the honey of all flowers,
(65) the quintessence of all sciences, the marrow of wit and the very phrase of angels. How much better is it, then, to have an elegant lawyer to plead one's cause, than a stuttering townsman that loseth himself in his tale and doth nothing but make legs; so much it is better
(70) for a nobleman or gentleman to have his honor's story related, and his deeds emblazoned, by a poet, than a citizen.

-Thomas Nashe

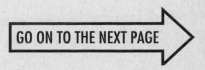

1. In the first paragraph, preachers are accused of all the following EXCEPT

   (A) plagiarism
   (B) stupidity
   (C) dullness
   (D) eloquence
   (E) laziness

2. "Saturnist" (line 9) means

   (A) astrologer
   (B) nymphomaniac
   (C) depressed and depressing person
   (D) pagan
   (E) foolishly optimistic person

3. Lines 20–26 argue that

   (A) poets must take second jobs to make a living
   (B) most people don't respect poets
   (C) there are too many poets
   (D) poets have to work hard to present consistently fresh material
   (E) poetry books are never bestsellers

4. "New herrings, new!" (line 24)

   (A) refers to an implied comparison between the writers of new poems and the sellers of fresh fish
   (B) suggests that poetry is slippery and hard to catch the meaning of, like fish
   (C) implies that poetry is just another commodity
   (D) implies that poetry grows stale rapidly, like fish
   (E) compares poetry to rotten fish

5. In lines 31–39 London is described as

   (A) flooded
   (B) a damp, rainy city
   (C) the main influence on the English language
   (D) a cultural garden
   (E) an important port city

6. The main idea of lines 39–48 is which of the following?

   (A) People are motivated by concern for their reputations.
   (B) Poetry is fair to the virtuous and the evil alike.
   (C) Poetry is inspirational.
   (D) Poetry is most attractive to atheists.
   (E) Poets are very judgmental.

7. Who is Salustius (line 49)?

   (A) A French poet
   (B) Sidney's *nom de plume*
   (C) The Roman god of poetry
   (D) The King of England
   (E) The Wife of Bath

8. What is Bath?

   (A) A state of sin
   (B) A character in Chaucer
   (C) A married man
   (D) A poet
   (E) A town and spa in England

9. In the last paragraph, poets are said to be like

   (A) lawyers
   (B) mayors
   (C) chronographers
   (D) townsmen
   (E) angels

GO ON TO THE NEXT PAGE

10. Line 10 is an example of

    (A) metaphor
    (B) onomatoepeia
    (C) paradox
    (D) alliteration
    (E) apostrophe

11. In line 2, what is the referent of "those"?

    (A) Poets
    (B) The author
    (C) Ballads
    (D) Poems
    (E) Poetry's enemies

12. What are "divines" (line 6)?

    (A) Preachers
    (B) Great writers
    (C) Dead writers
    (D) Fools
    (E) Saturnists

13. The author complains (lines 11–12) that the preachers have no eloquence to hold their audience but only

    (A) repetition
    (B) nonsense
    (C) lies
    (D) irrelevance
    (E) sermons

14. According to the passage, which of the following is NOT a function of poetry?

    (A) To encourage the virtuous
    (B) To purify the language
    (C) To embarrass the villainous
    (D) To illustrate and beautify
    (E) To plagiarize sermons

15. Who first raised the issue of poets' necessity to the state?

    (A) Nashe
    (B) Sidney
    (C) Salustius
    (D) Plato
    (E) Milton

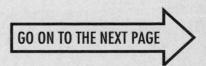
GO ON TO THE NEXT PAGE

Questions 16–28. Choose answers to questions 16–28 based on a careful reading of the following poem by John Donne.

Let me pour forth
My tears before thy face whilst I stay here,
For thy face coins them, and thy stamp they bear,
Line And by this mintage they are something worth,
(5)   For thus they be
          Pregnant of thee;
Fruits of much grief they are, emblems of more—
When a tear falls, that Thou falls which it bore,
So thou and I are nothing then, when on a diverse shore.

(10)   On a round ball
A workman that hath copies by can lay
An Europe, Africa, and an Asia,
And quickly make that, which was nothing, all;
          So doth each tear
(15)   Which thee doth wear,
A globe, yea world, by that impression grow,
Till thy tears mixed with mine do overflow This world;
by waters sent from thee, my heaven disolv'd so.

          O more than moon,
(20) Draw not up seas to drown me in thy sphere;
Weep me not dead in thine arms, but forbear
To teach the sea what it may do too soon.
          Let not the wind
          Example find
(25) To do me more harm than it purposeth;
Since thou and I sigh one another's breath,
Whoe'er sighs most is cruelest, and hastes the other's death.

16. The situation described in this poem is

(A) the end of a romantic relationship
(B) death
(C) the separation of lovers
(D) the end of the world
(E) a pleasure cruise

17. Lines 10–16 are an example of

(A) paradox
(B) dramatic irony
(C) metaphor
(D) metaphysical conceit
(E) dramatic monologue

18. Line 19 is an address to the

(A) moon
(B) world
(C) poet's soul
(D) workmen
(E) beloved

19. To what do lines 14 and 15 refer?

  I. The speaker's tears which reflect the beloved
 II. The beloved's tears
III. The beloved's clothing, which has been torn as a symbol of her grief
IV. The ocean, which is salty like tears
 V. The rain on their faces

(A) I
(B) I and II
(C) I, II, and III
(D) I and IV
(E) All of the above

20. Which of the stanzas do NOT include images of roundness?

(A) Stanza 1
(B) Stanza 2
(C) Stanza 3
(D) Stanzas 1 and 3
(E) None: All of the stanzas contain images of roundness.

GO ON TO THE NEXT PAGE

21. The imagery in this poem can most accurately be described as sustained images of

    (A) worthlessness suggesting the hopelessness of the lovers' situation.
    (B) the globe suggesting the vast distances of the lovers' separation.
    (C) roundness suggesting a perfect circle, and therefore the cosmic and permanent union of the lovers, because circles have no end.
    (D) water suggesting the shifting faithlessness of the lovers.
    (E) water suggesting the sexual bond between the lovers.

22. In line 13, to what does the word "which" refer?

    (A) Copies
    (B) The round ball
    (C) The world
    (D) The workman
    (E) The continents

23. Which of the following is NOT an appropriate association for lines 19–20?

    (A) The power of a goddess
    (B) The relationship between the moon and the ocean's tides
    (C) The round shape of the moon
    (D) The folktale of the man in the moon
    (E) The moon as suggestive of unhappy feelings, the opposite of "sunny disposition"

24. What does "diverse shore" (line 9) mean?

    (A) Heaven
    (B) Hell
    (C) Europe
    (D) A different place
    (E) The ground

25. Which of the following types of imagery is sustained throughout the poem?

    (A) Tears
    (B) Globes
    (C) Coins
    (D) Moon
    (E) Ocean

26. Line 4 can best be paraphrased as

    (A) you are not worth the salt of my tears
    (B) my tears are worth something because they reflect your face
    (C) my tears are emotionally refreshing
    (D) my tears are worth something because they are for your sake
    (E) my grief is a valuable feeling

27. What does the speaker ascribe to his beloved in lines 20–25?

    (A) The power to break his heart
    (B) The power to kill him
    (C) The power to influence the natural elements
    (D) The power to restrain her grief
    (E) The right to seek other lovers

28. In the extended metaphors of this poem, the speaker flatters the beloved through the use of

    (A) hyperbole
    (B) sarcasm
    (C) irony
    (D) parallelism
    (E) eschatology

GO ON TO THE NEXT PAGE

Questions 29–39. Choose answers to questions 29–39 based on a careful reading of the passage below. The passage, an excerpt from a short story by Mary E. Wilkins Freeman, describes a woman about to be married after a long engagement.

Every morning, rising and going about among her neat maidenly possessions, she felt as one looking her last upon the faces of dear friends. It was true
Line that in a measure she could take them with her, but,
(5) robbed of their old environments, they would appear in such new guises that they would almost cease to be themselves. Then there were some peculiar features of her happy solitary life which she would probably be obliged to relinquish altogether. Sterner tasks than
(10) these graceful but half-needless ones would probably devolve upon her. There would be a large house to care for; there would be company to entertain; there would be Joe's rigorous and feeble old mother to wait upon; and it would be contrary to all thrifty village traditions
(15) for her to keep more than one servant. Louisa had a little still, and she used to occupy herself pleasantly in summer weather with distilling the sweet and aromatic essences from roses and peppermint and spearmint. By-and-by her still must be laid away. Her store of
(20) essences was already considerable, and there would be no time for her to distil for the mere pleasure of it. Then Joe's mother would think it foolishness; she had already hinted her opinion in the matter. Louisa dearly loved to sew a linen seam, not always for use, but for
(25) the simple, mild pleasure which she took in it. She would have been loath to confess how more than once she had ripped a seam for the mere delight of sewing it together again. Sitting at her window during long sweet afternoons, drawing her needle gently through
(30) the dainty fabric, she was peace itself. But there was small chance of such foolish comfort in the future. Joe's mother, domineering, shrewd old matron that she was even in her old age, and very likely even Joe himself, with his honest masculine rudeness, would laugh and
(35) frown down all these pretty but senseless old maiden ways.
Louisa had almost the enthusiasm of an artist over the mere order and cleanliness of her solitary home. She had throbs of genuine triumph at the sight of the
(40) window-panes which she had polished until they shone like jewels. She gloated gently over her orderly bureau-drawers, with their exquisitely folded contents redolent with lavender and sweet clover and purity. Could she be sure of the endurance of even this? She
(45) had visions, so startling that she half repudiated them as indelicate, of course masculine belongings strewn about in endless litter; of dust and disorder arising necessarily from a coarse masculine presence in the midst of all this delicate harmony.

(50) Among her forebodings of disturbance, not the least was with regard to Caesar. Caesar was a veritable hermit of a dog. For the greater part of his life he had dwelt in his secluded hut, shut out from the society of his kind and all innocent canine joys. Never had Caesar
(55) since his early youth watched at a woodchuck's hole; never had he known the delights of a stray bone at a neighbor's kitchen door. And it was all on account of a sin committed when hardly out of his puppyhood. No one knew the possible depth of remorse of which
(60) this mild-visaged, altogether innocent-looking old dog might be capable; but whether or not he had encountered remorse, he had encountered a full measure of righteous retribution. Old Caesar seldom lifted up his voice in a growl or a bark; he was fat
(65) and sleepy; there were yellow rings which looked like spectacles around his dim old eyes; but there was a neighbor who bore on his hand the imprint of several of Caesar's sharp white youthful teeth, and for that he had lived at the end of a chain, all alone in
(70) a little hut, for fourteen years. The neighbor, who was choleric and smarting with the pain of his wound, had demanded either Caesar's death or complete ostracism. So Louisa's brother, to whom the dog had belonged, had built him his little kennel and tied him up. It was
(75) now fourteen years since, in a flood of youthful spirits, he had inflicted that memorable bite and with the exception of short excursions, always at the end of the chain, under the strict guardianship of his master or Louisa, the old dog had remained a close prisoner. It
(80) is doubtful if, with his limited ambition, he took much pride in the fact, but it is certain that he was possessed of considerable cheap fame. He was regarded by all the children in the village and by many adults as a very monster of ferocity. Mothers charged their children
(85) with solemn emphasis not to go too near him, and the children listened and believed greedily, with a fascinated appetite for terror, and ran by Louisa's house stealthily, with many sidelong and backward glances at the terrible dog. If perchance he sounded a hoarse bark,
(90) there was a panic. Wayfarers chancing into Louisa's yard eyed him with respect, and inquired if the chain were stout. Caesar at large might have seemed a very ordinary dog, and excited no comment whatever;

GO ON TO THE NEXT PAGE

chained, his reputation overshadowed him, so that he
(95) lost his own proper outlines and looked darkly vague
and enormous. Joe, however, with his good-humored
sense and shrewdness, saw him as he was. He strode
valiantly up to him and patted him on the head, in
spite of Louisa's soft clamor of warning, and even
(100) attempted to set him loose. Louisa grew so alarmed
that he desisted, but kept announcing his opinion in
the matter quite forcibly at intervals. "There ain't a
better-natured dog in town," he would say, "and it's
downright cruel to keep him tied up there. Some day
(105) I'm going to take him out."
　　Louisa had very little hope that he would not, one
of these days, when their interests and possessions
should be more completely fused in one. She pictured
to herself Caesar on the rampage through the quiet and
(110) unguarded village. She saw innocent children bleeding
in his path. She was herself very fond of the old dog,
because he had belonged to her dead brother, and he
was always very gentle with her; still she had great
faith in his ferocity. She always warned people not to
(115) go too near him. She fed him on ascetic fare of corn-
mush and cakes, and never fired his dangerous temper
with heating and sanguinary diet of flesh and bones.
Louisa looked at the old dog munching his simple
fare, and thought of her approaching marriage and
(120) trembled.

29. In overall terms, how is Louisa characterized?

    (A) As a bitter, domineering woman
    (B) As a naive, childish woman
    (C) As a frightened, foolish woman
    (D) As a sheltered, innocent woman
    (E) As a selfish, cruel woman

30. Which statement best describes Louisa's household
    activities (paragraphs 1 and 2)?

    (A) They symbolize the timeless rituals of ancient
        rural harvest deities.
    (B) They demonstrate Louisa's contented
        absorption in a traditionally feminine
        cultural sphere.
    (C) They demonstrate Louisa's mental illness.
    (D) They demonstrate Louisa's repressed artistic
        genius.
    (E) They describe the highest traditional values of
        Louisa's town.

31. Which of the following statements are TRUE?

    The story of Caesar is used in this passage to rein-
    force the idea that

    I.   Louisa has grown too accustomed to her
         circumscribed life to welcome change
    II. cruelty to animals is an indicator of a cruel
         society
    III. marrying is like being conquered by an
         invading emperor
    IV. people can be trapped by unchanging and
         unexamined ideas
    V.   you can't teach an old dog new tricks

    (A) I and IV only
    (B) I, II, and III only
    (C) V only
    (D) All of the above
    (E) None of the above

32. Caesar's "ascetic" diet (paragraph 4)

    (A) reflects Louisa's poverty
    (B) is part of his punishment
    (C) reflects a nineteenth-century theory that bodily
        humors are affected by diet and can change
        disposition
    (D) is part of a religious practice meant to
        encourage celibacy in hermits
    (E) is typical pet food in nineteenth-century homes

33. The word "purity" in line 43 is an example of

    (A) irony
    (B) metaphor
    (C) simile
    (D) oxymoron
    (E) allusion

34. The tone of the description of Caesar (paragraphs
    3 and 4) is

    (A) gently satirical
    (B) indignant
    (C) pensive
    (D) foreboding
    (E) menacing

GO ON TO THE NEXT PAGE

35. The contextual meaning of "sanguinary" (line 117) is

    (A) expensive
    (B) feminine
    (C) masculine
    (D) vegetarian
    (E) bloody

36. Judging from this passage, which of the following best describes Louisa's beliefs about gender relations?

    (A) Men and women naturally belong together.
    (B) Men and women should remain separate.
    (C) Men bring chaos and possibly danger to women's lives.
    (D) Women help to civilize men's natural wildness.
    (E) Men are more intelligent than women.

37. The contextual meaning of "mild-visaged" (line 60) is

    (A) having a calm temper
    (B) having a gentle face
    (C) having an old face
    (D) being confused
    (E) having a kind mask

38. Which of the following are accomplished by the Caesar vignette?

    (A) It shows us Joe's down-to-earth, kindhearted character.
    (B) It symbolically shows us Louisa's fears of the future.
    (C) It serves as a symbol of what happens to those who refuse change.
    (D) It provides a humorous satire of small-town concerns.
    (E) All of the above

39. In line 46, how is the word "indelicate" used?

    (A) To indicate the differences between Louisa and Joe
    (B) To indicate that Louisa considered her thoughts inappropriately sexual
    (C) To indicate the coarseness of Joe's personality
    (D) To indicate the inferior quality of Joe's belongings
    (E) To foreshadow the vision of Caesar's rampage

GO ON TO THE NEXT PAGE ⟶

Questions 40–54. Read the poem below, entitled *Woodchucks* by Maxine Kumin, then choose answers to the questions that follow.

Gassing the woodchucks didn't turn out right.
The knockout bomb from the Feed and Grain Exchange
was featured as merciful, quick at the bone
Line and the case we had against them was airtight,
(5) both exits shoehorned shut with puddingstone,
but they had a sub-sub-basement out of range.

Next morning they turned up again, no worse
for the cyanide than we for our cigarettes
and state-store Scotch, all of us up to scratch.
(10) They brought down the marigolds as a matter of course
and then took over the vegetable patch
nipping the broccoli shoots, beheading the carrots.

The food from our mouths, I said, righteously thrilling
to the feel of the .22, the bullets' neat noses.
(15) I, a lapsed pacifist fallen from grace
puffed with Darwinian pieties for killing,
now drew a bead on the littlest woodchuck's face.
He died down in the everbearing roses.

Ten minutes later I dropped the mother. She
(20) flipflopped in the air and fell, her needle teeth
still hooked in a leaf of early Swiss chard.
Another baby next. O one-two-three
the murderer inside me rose up hard,
the hawkeye killer came on stage forthwith.

(25) There's one chuck left. Old wily fellow, he keeps
me cocked and ready day after day after day.
All night I hunt his humped-up form. I dream
I sight along the barrel in my sleep.
If only they'd all consented to die unseen
(30) gassed underground the quiet Nazi way.

40. What does this poem literally describe?

(A) World War II
(B) The elimination of garden pests
(C) The problems of vegetarians
(D) A dream
(E) Landscape design

41. The theme of the poem would best be described as

(A) the animals are taking over the world
(B) we must be ever-vigilant against the battles of everyday life
(C) raising your own food is essential to independence
(D) the world is essentially violent
(E) violence and persecution are potentials within everyone

42. Which of the following is FALSE?

(A) The poem exploits the Nazi rhetoric of vermin extermination.
(B) The poem draws parallels between Nazi philosophy and contemporary social Darwinism.
(C) The poem suggests that political beliefs are as emotional and irrational as religious beliefs.
(D) The poem suggests that all violence is essentially similar.
(E) The poem suggests that some killing is justifiable.

43. "Darwinian pieties" (line 16) is a good example of

(A) paradox
(B) juxtaposition
(C) oxymoron
(D) truism
(E) metaphor

GO ON TO THE NEXT PAGE

44. All of the following statements accurately describe line 4 EXCEPT

(A) The legal rhetoric of this line reminds us of the historical perversions of the legal system.
(B) "Airtight" puns on its legal meaning and its literal meaning in the context of gassing.
(C) The pronouns in this line establish an "us against them" mindset.
(D) The line proves that the speaker's attitudes are correct.
(E) The aural closure provided by the end rhyme echoes the sealing up of the woodchucks' den and the closed mind portrayed in the poem.

45. Which of the following best describes the tone of the poem?

(A) Righteous outrage
(B) Helpless sorrow
(C) Ironic satire
(D) Indignant protest
(E) Quiet triumph

46. What is the most important thematic point made in the final two lines of the poem?

(A) If only the woodchucks had all been killed, the garden would be safe.
(B) Even garden-variety violence is similar to the atrocities of the Nazis.
(C) If only the woodchucks were all dead, the speaker could sleep better at night.
(D) If only the gassing had killed the woodchucks, the speaker would never have had to confront the violence in his nature.
(E) If only the gassing had killed the woodchucks, the speaker would not have had to see their disgusting deaths.

47. Which of the following statements describing the setting of the poem are true?

I. The stereotypically peaceful garden is an ironic setting for the violence described in the poem.
II. The garden symbolizes nature and thereby enriches the speaker's allusion to Darwin.
III. The garden makes this poem a pastoral poem.
IV. The specific references to the garden provide a realistic setting in which to consider the serious issues raised by the poem.
V. The garden is a symbol of threatened civilization that must be protected from encroaching predators.

(A) I, II, and III
(B) I, II, and IV
(C) III and V
(D) II and III
(E) All of the above

48. The word "Nazi" in the final line of the poem is

(A) a metaphor
(B) an allusion
(C) a simile
(D) a paradox
(E) a metonym

49. The phrase "beheading the carrots" (line 12) is an example of

(A) a metonym
(B) metaphor
(C) personification
(D) anthropomorphism
(E) symbolism

50. "I" in this poem refers to

(A) the poet
(B) the father woodchuck
(C) the narrator
(D) a Nazi
(E) Darwin

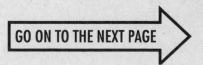
GO ON TO THE NEXT PAGE

51. The function of line 24 is best described by which statement?

(A) The phrase "came on stage forthwith" emphasizes the artificiality of the cultural attitudes under which the speaker is operating.
(B) The adjective "hawkeye" emphasizes the natural predatory role of humans.
(C) The noun "killer" emphasizes the horror of the speaker's actions.
(D) The alliteration of the line is onomatopoeic.
(E) The senselessness of the line demonstrates the speaker's confusion.

52. How does the first line of this poem function?

I. It frames the ensuing narrative.
II. It raises the question of right and wrong.
III. It turns on the ambiguity of the word "right" to mean both "effective" and "moral."
IV. Its understatement ironically foreshadows the conclusion of the poem.
V. It summarizes the poem.

(A) II and V
(B) III and IV
(C) I and II
(D) I, II, III, and IV
(E) I, II, III, IV, and V

53. The word "airtight" (line 4) functions as a

(A) metaphor
(B) oxymoron
(C) pun
(D) allusion
(E) symbol

54. Which of the following best describes the final stanza of the poem?

(A) The narrator endorses fascism.
(B) The slant rhymes indicate the emotional imbalance the speaker is feeling.
(C) It contradicts the rest of the poem.
(D) It makes a strong moral point about environmentalism.
(E) It abandons the verisimilitude of the poem for a surreal dream vision.

55. What does the narrator mean by "the food from our mouths" in line 13?

(A) His family is hungry because it is winter.
(B) He is outraged because the woodchucks are eating the food from his family's garden.
(C) He is angry that the woodchucks are going through his family's garbage.
(D) He is disgusted because the woodchucks are literally eating food out of his mouth.
(E) He will find an animal higher on the food chain to eat the woodchucks.

STOP
END OF SECTION I

IF YOU FINISH BEFORE TIME IS CALLED, YOU MAY CHECK YOUR WORK ON THIS SECTION.
DO NOT GO ON TO SECTION II UNTIL YOU ARE TOLD TO DO SO.

SECTION II

Total Time—2 hours

Question 1

(Suggested time—40 minutes. This question counts as one-third of the total essay score.)

The passage that follows is from *The Secret History* by Donna Tartt (1993). This introduction sets the tone for the rest of the novel. Read the passage carefully. Then write a well-organized essay in which you characterize the narrator's attitude toward Bunny's death. In your essay analyze the literary techniques that the author has used to portray the narrator and his attitude toward the events that followed. Be sure to include specific references to the passage.

The snow in the mountains was melting and Bunny had been dead for several weeks before we came to understand the gravity of our situation. He'd been
Line dead for ten days before they found him, you know. It
(5) was one of the biggest manhunts in Vermont history—state troopers, the FBI, even an army helicopter; the college closed, the dye factory in Hampden shut down, people coming from New Hampshire, upstate New York, as far away as Boston.
(10)   It is difficult to believe that Henry's modest plan could have worked so well despite these unforeseen events. We hadn't intended to hide the body where it couldn't be found. In fact, we hadn't hidden it at all but had simply left it where it fell in hopes that some
(15) luckless passer-by would stumble over it before anyone even noticed he was missing. This was a tale that told itself simply and well: the loose rocks, the body at the bottom of the ravine with a break in the neck, and the muddy skidmarks of dug-in heels pointing the way
(20) down; a hiking accident, no more, no less, and it might have been left at that, at quiet tears and a small funeral, had it not been for the snow that fell that night; it covered him without a trace, and ten days later, when the thaw finally came, the state troopers and the FCI
(25) and the searchers from town all saw that they had been walking back and forth over his body until the snow about it was packed down like ice.
    It is difficult to believe that such an uproar took place over an act for which I was partially responsible,
(30) even more difficult to believe I could have walked through it—the cameras, the universe, the black crowds sprinkled over Mount Cataract like ants in a sugar bowl—without incurring a blink of suspicion. But walking through it all was one thing; walking away,
(35) unfortunately, has proved to be quite another, and though once I thought I had left that ravine forever on an April afternoon long ago, now I am not so sure. Now the searchers have departed, and life has grown
(40) quiet around me, I have come to realize that while for

years I might have imagined myself to be somewhere else, in reality I have been there all the time; up at the top by the muddy wheel-ruts in the new grass, where the sky is dark over the shivering apple blossoms and
(45) the first chill of the snow that will fall that night is already in the air.
    What are you doing up here? Said Bunny, surprised, when he found the four of us waiting for him.
    Why, looking for new ferns, said Henry.
(50)   And after we stood whispering in the underbrush—one last look at the body and a last look round, no dropped keys, lost glasses, everybody got everything?—and then started single file through the woods, I took one glance back through the saplings that
(55) leapt to close the path behind me. Though I remember the walk back and first lonely flakes of snow that came drifting through the pines, remember piling gratefully into the car and starting down the road like a family on vacation, with Henry driving clench-jawed through
(60) the potholes and the rest of us leaning over the seats and talking like children, though I remember only too well the long terrible night that lay ahead and the long terrible days and nights that followed, I have only to glance over my shoulder for all those years to drop
(65) away and I see it behind me again, the ravine, rising all green and black through the saplings, a picture that will never leave me.
    I suppose at one time in my life I might have had any number of stories, but now there is no other. This is
(70) the only story I will ever be able to tell.

GO ON TO THE NEXT PAGE →

(Suggested time—40 minutes. This question counts as one-third of the total essay score.)

Read the following poem carefully. Considering such literary elements as style, tone, and diction, write a well-organized essay that examines the poem's view of patriotism.

"next to of course god america i
love you land of pilgrims' and so forth oh
say can you see by the dawn's early my
Line country 'tis of centuries come and go
(5) and are no more what of it we should worry
in every language even deafanddumb
thy sons acclaim your glorious name by gorry
by jingo by gee by gosh by gum
why talk of beauty what could be more beaut-
(10) iful than these heroic happy dead
who rushed like lions to the roaring slaughter
they did not stop to think they died instead
then shall the voice of liberty be mute?"

He spoke. And drank rapidly a glass of water.

– e. e. cummings

GO ON TO THE NEXT PAGE

Question 3

(Suggested time—40 minutes. This question counts as one-third of the total essay score.)

In some works of literature, mothers or the concept of motherhood play central roles. Choose a novel or play of literary merit and write a well-organized essay in which you discuss the maternal interaction between two characters and how that relationship relates to a larger theme represented by the work.

You may select a work from the list below, or you may choose to write about another work of comparable literary merit.

A Doll's House
The Awakening
As I Lay Dying
Beloved
Black Rain
Bleak House
The Color Purple
Daniel Deronda
Dombey and Son
Fifth Business
The Glass Menagerie
Hamlet

The Joy Luck Club
Medea
Mrs. Warren's Profession
A Room with a View
Pedro Paramo
Pride and Prejudice
The Scarlet Letter
The Seagull
Sons and Lovers
Sophie's Choice
The Sound and the Fury
The Stranger
To the Lighthouse

STOP
END OF SECTION II
IF YOU FINISH BEFORE TIME IS CALLED, YOU MAY CHECK YOUR WORK ON THIS SECTION.

15

Practice Test 2: Answers and Explanations

QUESTIONS 1–15

"An Invective Against Enemies of Poetry" is excerpted from *Pierce Penniless, His Supplication to the Devil*, by English satirist Thomas Nashe (1567–1601). A journalist in London, Nashe published *Pierce Penniless* in about 1592. Although much of his work would now be considered reactionary bigotry, Nashe is admired for his energetic and relatively modern-sounding prose style. In the passage excerpted here, Nashe is defending poetry as a valuable intellectual contribution to society, especially in contrast to the work of preachers and historians.

1. **D** "Eloquence" is the obvious answer here, since it runs contrary to the meaning of the passage. (And you remembered you were looking for the contrary, right? This is one of those "except" questions.) All the other answers are straightforward accusations in the text, except for (E), which is a little obscure. But when Nashe talks about the preachers' "quarter sermon," he means a sermon given once a quarter, only four times a year. The implication is that the preachers really don't work very hard, unlike poets, as the next paragraph goes on to explain.

2. **C** In astrological terms, Saturn was thought to be the planet of depression and gloom, and Saturnists were people ruled by Saturn, hence, depressed, depressing people. Remember that in the sixteenth century, astrology was considered more scientific than it is today. (A) is meant to lure people who recognize that Saturn is a planet and jump to "astrologer" by association. (B), "nymphomaniac," or sex addict, is there to trick people who confuse "Saturnist" with "satyr." (D), "pagan," picks up on the magical associations of astrology, but is certainly the wrong description of a preacher. (E), "optimistic person," means the opposite of the required definition.

3. **D** Unlike the lazy, plagiarizing preachers, poets must have new material all the time or the public won't buy their books. (A) is wrong because the various professions presented in these lines are only implied comparisons for a poet's career, not a list of moonlighting poets. (B) is wrong because Nashe's audience does respect good poets; they only reject bad poets who present stale, recycled material. (C) and (E) are completely irrelevant to the passage, but might tempt those who think in terms of marketplace competition.

4. **A** Nashe is comparing poets to fishmongers, who must constantly keep their product fresh for the marketplace. He is continuing his thought about poets being superior to plagiarizing preachers. You could make arguments in support of (B), the idea that poetry has slippery meanings, but Nashe is not arguing that; he's defending poetry. (C) and (D) are also interesting ideas, but they are not in this passage, and are in fact contradicted in other portions of the reading, which praise the special cultural meaning and lasting fame of poetry. (E) is just ridiculous and completely contradicts the meaning of the passage.

5. **C** Nashe is asserting the purity and beauty of the English language, and argues that London, as the seat of literary culture, influences how English is spoken all over the country, like the streams of a fountain spreading out beyond the fountain itself. Therefore, poets who improve English in London have a national influence. Answers (A), (B), and (E) are just incorrect associations with the watery imagery of fountains. (D) is tempting because it includes the idea that London is the source of culture, but does not include the important concept of national influence.

6. **A** Lines 39–48 describe how people are motivated by what is said about them, by their longing for fame or their horror of shame, and by fear for their reputations. Nashe might agree with (B), but nothing is said about fairness in these lines. (And despite what he may have thought, Nashe was often considered a slanderer during his lifetime, so his contemporaries didn't think he was fair.) (C) is tempting because the passage does mention that soldiers are inspired by poetry, but the concern in this passage is specifically the personal concerns of individuals for their reputations, not the general idea that poetry is uplifting. (D) might trick people who focus on the reference to "those that care neither for God nor the devil," but Nashe is not interested in atheists except as another category of people with reputations to worry about. (E) doesn't really have anything to do with the passage, except for those who overthink and get caught up in why the poets are writing about everyone in the first place. But that's getting far afield from the meaning of the specified lines.

7. **A** This question is actually pretty straightforward; the parenthetical phrase directly following the name Salustius tells you he is a French poet, actually more familiarly known today as Guillaume de Saluste du Bartas (1544–1590). (B) might confuse people who know what *nom de plume* means (it means "pen name"). (C) is simply incorrect but suggested by the Latinate name. (D) is straight out of left field. (E) is for people whose eyes glazed over while reading this passage and got stuck on the Wife of Bath.

8. **E** Bath is an ancient town and spa in England. This is a general knowledge question that you are just expected to know; the town shows up not only in Chaucer but also in Jane Austen. Answer (B) might be confusing because there is a famous character in Chaucer called the Wife of Bath, because she's from Bath, and she is mentioned in this passage. If you were getting very frazzled, the notion of wife might sucker you into choosing (C), because wives have husbands. (D) is there to confuse you if you were getting overwhelmed by this list of poets. (A) is just irrelevant.

9. **A** Nashe says it is better "to have an elegant lawyer to plead one's cause" than a stuttering townsman (lines 67–68), and just so, it is better to have a poet write your history than a historian. (B) is wrong because mayors are not even compared to anything here; they are just something chronographers write about. Chronographers are local historians, and poets are said to be better than chronographers, not like them, so (C) is incorrect. (D) is wrong for the same reason: Lawyers are better than townsmen just as poets are better than chronographers. (E), angels, is a little tricky, because poetry is said to be "the very phrase of angels" (line 66), which might imply that poets are the angels speaking the phrases. But that sentence is talking about Poetry: the Concept, not poets as members of society. And even conceited poets don't generally compare themselves to angels, certainly not in the middle of such a satirical piece. Even if you were confused by that, you should be able to see that lawyers is a direct comparison, while "angels" requires some overreading and stretching.

10. **D** The phrase "the pilferies of your pen to polish" is an example of alliteration, which means using the same initial consonant sound repeatedly in a line. All the other answers are just wrong. A metaphor (A), is when one thing is described in terms of another, but this is not metaphorical. Onomatopeia (B) is when words sound like what they are (e.g., "slither"), but pens and pilferies don't make special sounds. A paradox (C) is something that sounds like a contradiction but turns out to be true in some deeper sense. An apostrophe (E) is when a poem directly addresses someone or something that can't hear the poem ("O Moon! You orb of wonder!"). If you don't know these terms, you should be sure to read over the glossary in this book before the exam.

11. **E** "Those" refers back to "the enemies of poetry." This is a straightforward grammar question that requires you to parse the complex opening sentence.

12. **A** "Divines" are preachers, here excoriated for giving boring rather than poetic sermons. Nashe is opposing divines to writers, whether great (B) or dead (C). He does say that the divines are fools (D) and Saturnists (E), but those are descriptions rather than definitions. (A) should strike you as the best answer.

13. **A** This is a pure definition question; you need to know what a tautology is. A tautology is unnecessary repetition, so (A) is the right answer. (B), (C), and (D) all sound like criticisms, and so seem to fit, but do not paraphrase the cited line. (E) merely says that the preachers have sermons, but sermons are not by definition ineloquent, as specified in the sentence cited.

14. **E** The selection specifically mentions all other options as functions of poetry: (A) is in line 40; (B) is in lines 34–37; (C) is in lines 40–42; and (D) is a direct quote from line 30. (E) is not a function of poetry, but is mentioned in the selection as a failure of boring preachers.

15. **D** This is a hard question asking for general knowledge. You could have reasoned it out if you realized that people have been questioning the necessity of poetry for millenia; this might have led you to choose the correct answer: Plato. (Actually, Plato decides that poets aren't really necessary in his *Republic*.) Nashe (A) is the author of this selection. Sidney (B) and Salustius (C) are other writers mentioned in the text. Milton (E) is the famous British poet who wrote *Paradise Lost*.

QUESTIONS 16–28

John Donne was a notable metaphysical poet of the seventeenth century, and remains one of the greatest English-language poets. His prodigious output of lyrics, satires, sermons, and meditations treat subjects both sacred and profane. He is also, however, notoriously difficult because of his ingeniously figurative language, which is why he tends to show up on English exams frequently.

   This poem, "A Valediction: Of Weeping," expresses feelings upon being separated from one's lover. Through kaleidoscopic shifts of perspective, it plays with the paradoxes of presence and absence, distance and proximity.

16. **C** If you are finding it difficult to tell precisely what this poem is about, you can use POE to answer this question. The easiest one to eliminate is (E), because there is far too much crying here for a pleasure cruise. Some of the images sound apocalyptic, so (D) might sound tempting, but you should have realized that this is a love poem and that the end of the world imagery is metaphorical. Likewise, though death is mentioned, it is probably also a metaphorical death, so (B) is wrong. That leaves (A) and (C). It is hard to tell if the relationship is ending or merely being interrupted by distance, but the lovers are definitely being separated. Hence, (C) is the correct answer.

17. **D** You should know the definition of "metaphysical conceit," because the AP Engish Literature Exam likes to use metaphysical poets. A metaphysical conceit is an elaborate metaphor or simile that occurs in a metaphysical poem. You should have recognized this as a metaphysical poem, since it is by John Donne. Check your literary movement overview in Chapter 2. Note that "metaphysical" here has little to do with philosophy, and much to do with depth of meaning. The metaphysical conceit in question is the comparison of tears to globes—each tear becomes an entire world once it reflects his beloved, just as round balls become globes

once someone pastes images of the continents on them. You may have been tempted to answer (C), recognizing that this is very metaphorical, but in this instance the lines are not literally a metaphor, but a simile: Note the use of "so doth" (line 14) to indicate the comparison.

18. **E** "O more than moon" is an address to the beloved. You should have realized this because the addressed entity has arms (line 21), which narrows your choices to either (E) or (D), the workman. It is obviously not (A) the moon. The world (B) has no arms. And nothing in this poem mentions the poet's soul (C).

19. **B** The tears in lines 14 and 15 are the speaker's tears, which "wear" the image of his beloved, and they are also the beloved's tears "worn" on her face. There is nothing here about clothing. Although seas and rain are mentioned in the poem, they are not specifically referenced in these two lines, and the comparison that is continuing from the previous lines is to globes, not to other waters. Therefore, the first and second choices are correct, as given in (B). (A) only gives the first choice, and is therefore incorrect. (C), (D), and (E) include incorrect choices.

20. **E** All of the stanzas contain images of roundness. The first stanza has coins and fruit, and even pregnancy, in a way. The second stanza has globes and worlds. The third stanza has the moon and the word "sphere."

21. **C** Many, many metaphysical poems contain circle imagery, because the iconography—or pictorial material—of seventeenth-century poetry interprets the circle as the perfect shape. Circles have no end and therefore indicate perfect wholeness and eternity. These qualities made circles especially popular in love poetry, of which this is an example. (A) is wrong because there isn't any imagery of worthlessness, nor is there a sense of hopelessness. (B) is half right, because there are globes and vast distances, but the whole point of the poem is to reduce the vast distances by containing them within the tiny spheres of tears, so choosing (B) is an incomplete reading of the poem. Furthermore, the globe imagery is really only prominent in the second stanza, rather than being sustained throughout the poem. (D) is wrong because there is no suggestion of faithlessness between the lovers. Eliminate (E) because there is little explicit sexuality in this poem.

22. **B** This is really a grammar question to see how well you can sort out the sentence structure in this poem. "Which" begins a dependent clause modifying "that." So "which" refers to whatever "that" is. "That" is the object of the verb "make." The subject of "make" is the workman. The workman is making globes out of the round balls that are blank in his workshop. Therefore, both "that" and "which" must refer to the round balls. Although the globes are copied from models, the "copies" are models the workman "hath by" in his shop; he refers to the copies but does not make them into anything, so (A) is wrong. "World" does not even show up in this stanza until several lines later when it is a metaphorized tear, so (C) is wrong. The workman is the subject of this independent clause, but the subject is not being modified by "which," so (D) is wrong. The listed continents are objects of the subject "workman" but are not modified by the dependent clause, so (E) is wrong.

23. **D** This is a tricky question because it requires both interpretation of the poem and some familiarity with the conventions of metaphysical poetry, but Process of Elimination can help you out here. Remember to read the question carefully; you are looking to identify the *wrong* association here, so you are looking for what *doesn't* fit in the answers. (B) fits the poem because there is an obvious connection between the moon, the sea, and tides. (C) obviously fits because the round imagery has been sustained throughout the entire poem, and you should remember that you have already been asked about round imagery. Remember to keep your answers consistent across questions. (E) probably fits because the poem certainly does describe unhappy feelings. That leaves us with (A) and (D); you must choose between a goddess and the man in the moon. There is no explicit reference to either a goddess or the man in the moon, but at least the idea of a goddess seems flattering to the beloved and fits the poem better. Therefore, (D) is the least likely association and the correct answer.

24. **D** "Diverse" here just means "different"; the phrase means "a different place." Heaven (A) and hell (B) have no place in the poem at all. Europe (C) is listed as a continent in the poem, but not specified as a destination. The ground (E) is just an answer for the truly desperate.

25. **A** Tears are found throughout all three stanzas, although you have to look closely at the final stanza to find the idea in the word "weep" (line 21). Globes (B) are only in the second stanza. Coins (C) are only in the first stanza. The moon (D) is only in the third stanza. The ocean (E) is in the second and third stanzas. Ocean is almost suggested by the mention of shores in the first stanza, but it is not as strong a suggestion as that of "weep" for tears in the third stanza, so tears (A) remains the best answer.

26. **B** Line 4 is "And by this mintage they are something worth." "They" refers back to "my tears" in line 2. The tears are said to be coined by the beloved's face (line 3), and the coin metaphor is carried forward into the use of "mintage" here; the process of being coined is the mintage that makes the tears worth something. The tears reflect her face the way that coins show a ruler's face. By showing the beloved's face, the tears become valuable, like coins. Therefore, (B) is the best paraphrase. (A) is contrary to the sense of the poem, because it says the beloved is worthless. (C) does not reflect the meaning of the line, although some readers might be confused if they don't know what "mintage" means. (D) is tempting, because it sounds nice and fits with the meaning of the poem, but it overstates—it goes beyond what the line means. Paraphrases are supposed to restate, not extend. (E) is both vague and sort of New Age, and is not the point.

27. **C** The speaker asks the lover to "forbear/ To teach the sea what it may do" (lines 21–22) and that she not let the wind "Example find" (line 24) in her behavior. He is saying that the natural elements are watching and learning from her, copying her behavior, an idea that is carried forward from the description of his lover as the moon influencing the tides. One would think, in the face of such great love, that she would have the power to break his heart (A), but that is not mentioned in the specified lines. He does mention dying in these lines (B), but mostly in the context of her power over the elements; he warns her against teaching the oceans and winds how to kill him, not against killing him herself. The lines assume that she has the power to restrain her grief (D), but just tell her to do so; they do not emphasize this power the way they do her power over nature. Nowhere in the poem is there anything mentioned about the right to take other lovers (E).

28. **A** The speaker flatters the beloved by exaggerating her powers over natural elements, by declaring the inestimable value of even the reflections of her image—in other words, through hyperbole.

Mary E. Wilkins Freeman (1852–1930) was a New England writer who was brought up in an impoverished and strictly religious household. As an adult, she wrote fiction that portrayed the psychological effects on women of a traditional and repressive culture. She was well-educated, but most profoundly influenced by her discussions with friends of literary classics. She is generally noted as an important early realist and regional writer, but her characters offer a psychological depth unusual in regional writers of her time. Freeman was also one of the few women of her time able to achieve economic independence through her earnings from her writing.

This selection is from the short story, "A New England Nun," published in 1891, about a woman who decides after a very long engagement that she really doesn't want to get married after all.

29. **D** This is a tricky question because the portrait of Louisa appeals to many popular stereotoypes about women. But this is also a question in which you can use POE. (A) is obviously wrong: Louisa is not bitter or domineering, but that was thrown in there in case you confused Louisa with her fears about her future mother-in-law. (B) is partly right, because Louisa is naive, but she is not shown doing anything childish. You might argue that her preconceptions about men are somewhat childish, but that would be overreading. (C) is also alluring, because "frightened" seems to relate to the end of the passage in which Louisa "trembles," but there are lots of reasons for trembling, and "foolish" doesn't really fit. You might find Louisa's ideas about men foolish, but her contemplation of how her upcoming marriage will change her life is certainly realistic enough, in its way. (E) might also appeal because of our sympathy for Caesar, but Louisa also loves the dog, and nothing in her behavior is deliberately cruel. Therefore, the only really acceptable answer is (D). Louisa is certainly sheltered, and knows it, and she is also innocent insofar as she believes what she is told about Caesar, Joe, and Joe's mother; but more important, she believes in the conventional wisdom regarding the difficulties of married life.

30. **B** Again, you can answer this question through POE and a careful reading of the selection. (A) is almost ridiculous: The only thing that comes close to a reference to farming in this selection is Louisa's distilling of herbs, and that doesn't seem to involve any seasonal harvest ritual. Besides, harvest rituals and their goddesses are usually sexual, which is precisely what Louisa's maidenly activities aren't. (C) is wrong because there is nothing to suggest that Louisa is mentally ill. (D) is wrong because, although Louisa has "almost the enthusiasm of an artist" while cleaning her house, there is nothing to suggest that she is a genius of any kind. (E) is tempting, because Louisa is engaged in many traditional tasks, but because she anticipates that her mother-in-law and husband will make her stop many of her less-productive activities, they are probably not the highest values of the town. This leaves (B). Note that (B) uses the phrase "feminine cultural sphere," which is a term widely used in feminist criticism to indicate traditionally feminine activities. The passage suggests this interpretation by its contrast between Louisa's activities and Joe's more masculine aura.

31. **A** We can examine each statement separately. Item I expresses the main idea of the passage, and is therefore true. II is an interesting idea, but is not relevant to the passage, because even if you disapprove of Caesar's treatment, there is no suggestion that society is cruel in this passage. III is there to confuse people who skimmed the passage and thought Caesar was an ancient Roman. IV is a theme suggested by the passage and supported by the reactions of the townspeople and by Louisa's reactions to her own life, and is therefore true. V is merely a flippant commonplace that sheds no real light on anything: No one is trying to teach anyone any tricks—the statement is false. Therefore, (A) is the only possible answer.

32. **C** There was for many centuries a well-regarded theory that said personalities were influenced by "humors" in the body: Warm humors in the body caused angry or passionate personalities, while cold humors caused unemotional or calm personalities. These humors were affected by diet and by environment. This is where you get the stereotype of the hot Latin lover who lives in a tropical region, eats spicy food, and is given to fits of violent temper. It is also where we get the idea of people being "in a good humor." The bitten neighbor is described as "choleric," which is another reference to the theory of humors. Louisa is deliberately feeding her dog bland food to discourage any further attacks on the neighbors. She is not poor or she would not be able to have such nice things in her house, so (A) is false. The passage does speak metaphorically of Caesar's imprisonment, but Louisa is not deliberately punishing her dog, certainly not for a decade, so (B) is wrong. There are many references to hermits and nuns in this story, but dogs do not practice celibacy as a religious practice, so (D) is wrong. (E) is wrong just from context, because the passage mentions that other kitchens give bones to dogs.

33. **B** "Redolent" means "smelling of," and because purity doesn't have a smell, its use here must be metaphorical. Irony (A) is tempting, but there is nothing opposed or contradictory here to indicate irony. There is no simile (C) because there is no direct comparison of two things. Because there is no contradiction, there cannot be an oxymoron (D). Nothing is alluded to, so (E) is wrong. If you do not know these terms, study the glossary in this book.

34. **A** The story of Caesar is a gentle satire on the minidramas of small-town life, which finds excitement in the vicious reputation of an old dog. Clues to the satirical tone are the many overwritten references to sin and danger, and especially Louisa's vision of Caesar on a rampage through the town. Freeman's treatment of this passage is too humorous to be either indignant (B) or pensive (C). Because it is clear to the reader, and even to Joe, that Caesar isn't really dangerous, there is nothing foreboding (D) or menacing (E) in this passage either. The selection does say that Louisa feels many "forebodings of disturbance," including worries about Caesar, but those are Louisa's feelings rather than the tone of the passage, which indicates the attitude of the author.

35. **E** "Sanguinary" means bloody, both in the sense of containing blood and of liking blood. (D), vegetarian, is obviously wrong because it contradicts the meaning of the sentence. The other answers draw on ideas raised in previous questions on this piece; remember to keep your answers consistent. We have already established that financial concerns do not dominate Caesar's diet, so (A) is wrong. (B) and (C) drag in the ideas of masculine and feminine traits that predominate in this selection, but they really have nothing to do with what the dog eats.

36. **C** This question tests how well you read Louisa's character, because the entire passage is about her attitude toward gender relations. Her meditations on the disorder her future husband will bring to her house and on the impending danger of Caesar's release are best summed up in (C). Louisa is living in a society that believes men and women belong together (A), but her worries show that she is not entirely convinced of this. On the other hand, she is not explicitly rejecting marriage, so (B) is not the right answer either. (D) introduces the idea of wildness that you might have associated with Caesar, but it is important to note that Louisa does not believe she has tamed Caesar, nor does she think she will have any influence over her husband, so (D) is wrong. Her belief that Joe's decision to release Caesar will prove disastrous shows that she does not think men are more intelligent than women, so (E) is also wrong.

37. **B** Caesar has a gentle face; he is mild-visaged. "Visage" means face. (E) might have misled some people because there is the suggestion that Caesar is vicious, and hence could be "masked," but we see Caesar differently than Louisa does. This adjective is just straightforwardly descriptive, not a clue to hidden depths. Don't over-read the passage.

38. **E** All the statements describe the narrative accomplishments of the Caesar vignette. Joe is shown to be kind and practical (A) when he urges Caesar's release; Louisa's fears (B) are demonstrated in her vision of Caesar on a rampage; Caesar's sad plight is an example of what happens when people refuse change (C); and the inflated terror of the townspeople is a satire of small-town life (D).

39. **B** "Indelicate" is a euphemism for "inappropriately sexual." Dirty jokes are indelicate; graphic sexual details are indelicate. The point here is that Louisa's concern about the chaos Joe may bring to her life is connected to her sexual concerns. Although this passage in general ponders the differences between Louisa and Joe, delicacy or lack thereof is not the primary concern of the passage, so (A) is wrong. There is nothing to suggest that Joe is especially coarse, nor that his belongings are shoddy, so (C) and (D) are wrong. (E) is another example of over-reading the passage. "Indelicate" does not refer to Caesar in any way, and so cannot foreshadow Louisa's vision of a rampaging dog.

QUESTIONS 40–54

Maxine Kumin is a revered contemporary poet who tends to examine the depths, such as they are, of comfortable suburban life. "Woodchucks" is from her 1972 collection *Up Country*.

40. **B** The poem literally describes the speaker's attempts to rid the garden of woodchucks. The final reference to Nazis (A) solidifies the subtext of the poem, and illuminates its underlying theme about violence, but is not the literal subject. There is a dream (D) mentioned in the final lines, but it is a minor detail rather than the main subject of the poem. Landscape design (E) and vegetarianism (C) may come to mind in the description of the garden, but neither is the subject of the poem.

41. **E** The theme of the poem is that the potential for violence and persecution are within everyone, even otherwise peaceful suburban gardeners. (D), the idea that the world is essentially violent, is tempting but too general. (A), (B), and (C) are not even close; note that (B), the idea that we must fight the battles of everyday life, might tempt people who misread the poem.

42. **E** The poem condemns all killing, even killing often justified as necessary, such as eliminating garden pests. Therefore, (E) is false, and the correct answer. In fact, (E) contradicts the entire sense of the poem. All of the other statements are true. Even if you did not know about the Nazi rhetoric of vermin extermination, you could recognize the presence of this rhetoric in the poem and would hesitate to eliminate (A). Likewise, you should notice the reference to Darwin, even if you are not clear on connections between Nazis and Social Darwinism; therefore, you would hesitate to eliminate (B). The third stanza demonstrates the truth of (C), that political beliefs are quite similar to religious beliefs, although recognizing this requires a sensitivity to tone in the poem. The very comparison of killing woodchucks with Nazi genocide should lead you to see Kumin's point that all violence is essentially similar (D).

43. **C** "Darwinian pieties" is an oxymoron because it is a contradiction in terms. Darwin's evolutionary theories are seen by many to be antireligious because they contradict the story of creation in the Bible. At the same time, "piety" means religious devotion. Kumin is suggesting that people are devoted to Darwin as blindly as they ever were to religion. However, Darwin is used here not so much to suggest evolution as to suggest the political beliefs associated with "Social Darwinism," which sees struggles between groups of people as a violent zero-sum contest for survival in which the winners are proven to be biologically superior. Social Darwinism is often a polite mask for racism and other social biases against groups perceived as inferior.

44. **D** The tone of the poem contradicts the speaker's attitudes, so nothing in the poem proves those attitudes correct. All the other statements about line 4 are true.

45. **C** The entire poem is an ironic satire against people who refuse to recognize the violence of their lives as part of the violence of the world. (A) and (D) are tempting because both Kumin and presumably the reader feel outrage over the violence in the world and would wish to protest it, but the poem itself remains ironic. There is a sense of triumph (E) in the fourth stanza, but its effectiveness is undercut by the pathetic references to mothers and babies. There is no helpless sorrow (B) anywhere in the poem.

46. **D** The entire point of the poem is the speaker's growing awareness of his or her own violent tendencies. The idea that all violence is related (B) is implied in the poem, but is not the main point of the final two lines. The other answers are all variously shallow misreadings of the poem.

47. **B** The garden, usually considered a peaceful place, is here the scene of violence, which is ironic, so choice I is true. The garden obviously symbolizes nature, which is the site of Darwinian struggle, so II is true. In this poem, the garden is very realistic and specific, suggesting that the issues discussed are specific and realistic as well, so IV is true. Item III is false, but tempting because gardens are often featured in pastoral poems. However, pastoral poems focus on the peacefulness of the countryside, which this poem obviously does not. Item V is obviously false, and contradicts the main theme of the poem.

48. **B** In the final line of the poem, "Nazi" is an allusion to the atrocities of genocide in World War II. The poem as a whole implies a comparison between the killing of woodchucks and genocide, but this is merely implied and does not become an outright simile (C) or metaphor (A) in the final line. Neither does the final line contain a paradox (D) or metonym (E). If you do not know what these terms mean, you should consult the glossary at the back of this book.

49. **C** "Beheading the carrots" is an example of personification because it applies a physical human quality to an inhuman object: Carrots don't have heads to lop off, but describing the woodchucks' actions in this way makes the woodchucks sound more sinister. Anthropomorphism (D) is a more involved form of personification, in which one ascribes human motivations to the nonhuman object.

50. **C** The speaker of a poem is not necessarily the poet, but is a narrator. That makes "the poet" (A) the wrong answer. The other answers are pretty ridiculous.

51. **A** This question is a little tricky. By switching from a setting of natural gardens to the idea of a staged scene, the poet is emphasizing the artificial cultural script influencing the speaker to act so brutally. There is even a suggestion that such scripts naturalize many brutal actions in human society and so render atrocities acceptable, as in the influence of Nazi ideologies. (B) is tempting because of the influence of ideology; social Darwinism holds that humans are naturally predatory, but the poem as a whole is arguing against exactly this point. (C) is partially true, because "killer" is a harshly clear word, but the effect is not unique to this line; equally harsh words have gone before in previous lines. (D) is wrong because although the line is alliterative, it is not especially onomatopoeic. (E) is just flat out wrong because the line isn't senseless and the speaker isn't confused.

52. **D** The way to answer this question is to evaluate each statement as true or false. Statement I is true; the first line tells you that you are going to hear a story about gassing the woodchucks. Statement II is true; "didn't turn out right" implies that things went "wrong," but what is wrong when you are gassing living creatures? Statement III uses a more academic discourse to say almost exactly the same thing as statement II and is also true. By the time you get to the end of the poem, you know that "didn't turn out right" is an understatement of what really happened, so IV is true. V is false, because the first line does not give enough information to be considered a summary of the poem. The first line still seems to be about woodchucks instead of about human nature, and no summary of this poem should focus on woodchucks. (D) is the only choice that correctly lists the true statements.

53. **C** "Airtight" is a pun, referring to the legal idea of an "airtight case" to show that the speaker felt justified in executing the woodchucks, but also referring to the physical process of gassing the woodchucks. It is not sustained enough to be a metaphor (A), and it does not symbolize anything (E). It might be read as an allusion (D) to the legal system, but it is not really specific enough to work as an allusion. It does not contradict itself, so it's not an oxymoron (B). If you don't know these terms, be sure to study the glossary in the back of this book. Incidentally, question 44 already told you that "airtight" is a pun.

54. **B** This question can be answered through POE. (A) is wrong because the final lines are certainly ironic. (C) is wrong because there is no contradiction at the end of the poem. (D) is wrong because the poem's strong moral point is about human violence, not about environmentalism. (E) is wrong because the dream mentioned is realistic rather than surreal, and therefore the verisimilitude of the poem is not abandoned. (Verisimilitude means "the quality of seeming real"—it's another good term to know for the exam.) That leaves only (B), which fits perfectly. Slant rhymes are imprecise rhymes, in this case "keeps/sleep" and "dream/unseen."

55. **B** This question is asking you to identify a figure of speech. There is no mention of winter (A), garbage (C), or woodchuck predators (E) in the poem, so those choices are incorrect. Answer (C) is incorrect, as it is understood that "the food from our mouths" should not be taken literally. It is figurative language, so answer (B) is correct.

HOW TO SCORE PRACTICE TEST 2

Section I: Multiple Choice

$$\underset{\text{number correct}}{\underline{\hspace{3cm}}} - (1/4 \times \underset{\text{number wrong}}{\underline{\hspace{3cm}}}) = \underset{\textbf{Multiple-Choice Score}}{\underline{\hspace{3cm}}}$$

Section II: Free Response

(See if you can find a teacher or classmate to score your essays using the guidelines in Chapter 7.)

$$\underset{\substack{\text{essay 1} \\ \text{(out of 9)}}}{\underline{\hspace{2cm}}} + \underset{\substack{\text{essay 2} \\ \text{(out of 9)}}}{\underline{\hspace{2cm}}} + \underset{\substack{\text{essay 3} \\ \text{(out of 9)}}}{\underline{\hspace{2cm}}} = \underset{\textbf{Free-Response Score}}{\underline{\hspace{3cm}}}$$

Composite Score

$$\underset{\textbf{Multiple-Choice Score}}{\underline{\hspace{3cm}}} \times 1.23 = \underset{\textbf{Weighted Section I Score}}{\underline{\hspace{3cm}}}$$

$$\underset{\textbf{Free-Response Score}}{\underline{\hspace{3cm}}} \times 3.06 = \underset{\textbf{Weighted Section II Score}}{\underline{\hspace{3cm}}}$$

$$\underset{\textbf{Weighted Section I Score}}{\underline{\hspace{3cm}}} + \underset{\textbf{Weighted Section I Score}}{\underline{\hspace{3cm}}} = \underset{\textbf{Composite Score}}{\underline{\hspace{3cm}}}$$

AP Grade Conversion

Composite Score	AP Grade
107–150	5
93–106	4
73–92	3
43–72	2
0–42	1

PART ◆ V

Glossary

THE GLOSSARY OF LITERARY TERMS FOR THE AP ENGLISH LITERATURE AND COMPOSITION EXAM

We've put an asterisk (*) beside the handful of terms that you *absolutely must know*.

Abstract An *abstract* style (in writing) is typically complex, discusses intangible qualities like good and evil, and seldom uses examples to support its points.

Academic As an adjective describing style, this word means dry and theoretical writing. When a piece of writing seems to be sucking all the life out of its subject with analysis, the writing is *academic*.

Accent In poetry, *accent* refers to the stressed portion of a word. In "To be, or not to be," accents fall on the first "be" and "not." It sounds silly any other way. But accent in poetry is also often a matter of opinion. Consider the rest of the first line of Hamlet's famous soliloquy, "That is the question." The stresses in that portion of the line are open to a variety of interpretations.

Aesthetic, Aesthetics *Aesthetic* can be used as an adjective meaning "appealing to the senses." Aesthetic judgment is a phrase synonymous with artistic judgment. As a noun, an aesthetic is a coherent sense of taste. The kid whose room is painted black, who sleeps in a coffin, and listens only to funeral music has an aesthetic. The kid whose room is filled with pictures of kittens and daisies but who sleeps in a coffin and listens to polka music has a confused aesthetic. The plural noun, *aesthetics*, is the study of beauty. Questions like *What is beauty?* or, *Is the beautiful always good?* fall into the category of aesthetics.

Allegory An *allegory* is a story in which each aspect of the story has a symbolic meaning outside the tale itself. Many fables have an allegorical quality. For example, Aesop's "The Ant and the Grasshopper" isn't merely the story of a hardworking ant and a carefree grasshopper, but is also a story about different approaches to living—the thrifty and the devil-may-care. It can also be read as a story about the seasons of summer and winter, which represent a time of prosperity and a time of hardship, or even as representing youth and age. True allegories are even more hard and fast. Bunyan's epic poem, *Pilgrim's Progress*, is an allegory of the soul, in which each and every part of the tale represents some feature of the spiritual world and the struggles of an individual to lead a Christian life.

Alliteration The repetition of initial consonant sounds is called *alliteration*. In other words, consonant clusters coming closely cramped and compressed—no coincidence.

Allusion A reference to another work or famous figure is an *allusion*. A classical allusion is a reference to Greek and Roman mythology or literature such as *The Iliad*. Allusions can be topical or popular as well. A topical allusion refers to a current event. A popular allusion refers to something from popular culture, such as a reference to a television show or a hit movie.

Anachronism The word *anachronism* is derived from Greek. It means "misplaced in time." If the actor playing Brutus in a production of Julius Caesar forgets to take off his wristwatch, the effect will be anachronistic (and probably comic).

Analogy An *analogy* is a comparison. Usually analogies involve two or more symbolic parts, and are employed to clarify an action or a relationship. *Just as the mother eagle shelters her young from the storm by spreading her great wing above their heads, so does Acme Insurers of America spread an umbrella of coverage to protect its policyholders from the storms of life.*

Anecdote An *anecdote* is a short narrative.

Antecedent The word, phrase, or clause that a pronoun refers to or replaces. In *The principal asked the children where they were going; they* is the pronoun and *children* is the antecedent.

Anthropomorphism In literature, when inanimate objects, animals, or natural phenomena are given human characteristics, behavior, or motivation, *anthropomorphism* is at work. For example, *In the forest, the darkness waited for me, I could hear its patient breathing....* Anthropomorphism is often confused with personification. But personification requires that the nonhuman quality or thing take on human shape.

Anticlimax An *anticlimax* occurs when an action produces far smaller results than one had been led to expect. Anticlimax is frequently comic. *Sir, your snide manner and despicable arrogance have long been a source of disgust to me, but I've overlooked it until now. However, it has come to my attention that you have fallen so disgracefully deep into that mire of filth which is your mind as to attempt to besmirch my wife's honor and my good name. Sir, I challenge you to a game of badminton!*

Antihero A protagonist (main character) who is markedly unheroic: morally weak, cowardly, dishonest, or any number of other unsavory qualities.

Aphorism A short and usually witty saying, such as: "'Classic'? A book which people praise and don't read."—Mark Twain.

*Apostrophe An address to someone not present, or to a personified object or idea.

Archaism The use of deliberately old-fashioned language. Authors sometimes use archaisms to create a feeling of antiquity. Tourist traps use archaisms with a vengeance, as in "Ye Olde Candle Shoppe"—Yeech!

Aside A speech (usually just a short comment) made by an actor to the audience, as though momentarily stepping outside of the action on stage. (See *soliloquy*.)

Aspect A trait or characteristic, as in "an aspect of the dew drop."

Assonance The repeated use of vowel sounds, as in, "Old king Cole was a merry old soul."

Atmosphere The emotional tone or background that surrounds a scene.

Ballad A long, narrative poem, usually in very regular meter and rhyme. A *ballad* typically has a naive folksy quality, a characteristic that distinguishes it from epic poetry.

Bathos, Pathos When the writing of a scene evokes feelings of dignified pity and sympathy, *pathos* is at work. When writing strains for grandeur it can't support and tries to elicit tears from every little hiccup, that's *bathos*.

Black humor This is the use of disturbing themes in comedy. In Samuel Beckett's *Waiting for Godot*, the two tramps, Didi and Gogo, comically debate over which should commit suicide first, and whether the branches of the tree will support their weight. This is *black humor*.

Bombast This is pretentious, exaggeratedly learned language. When one tries to be eloquent by using the largest, most uncommon words, one falls into *bombast*.

Burlesque A *burlesque* is broad parody, one that takes a style or a form, such as tragic drama, and exaggerates it into ridiculousness. A parody usually takes on a specific work, such as *Hamlet*. For the purposes of the AP exam, you can think of the terms *parody* and *burlesque* as interchangeable.

Cacophony In poetry, *cacophony* is using deliberately harsh, awkward sounds.

Cadence The beat or rhythm of poetry in a general sense. For example, *iambic pentameter* is the technical name for a rhythm. One sample of predominantly iambic pentameter verse could have a gentle, pulsing cadence, whereas another might have a conversational cadence, and still another might have a vigorous, marching cadence.

Canto The name for a section division in a long work of poetry. A *canto* divides a long poem into parts the way chapters divide a novel.

*Caricature A portrait (verbal or otherwise) that exaggerates a facet of personality.

Catharsis This is a term drawn from Aristotle's writings on tragedy. *Catharsis* refers to the "cleansing" of emotion an audience member experiences, having lived (vicariously) through the experiences presented on stage.

Chorus In drama, a *chorus* is the group of citizens who stand outside the main action on stage and comment on it.

Classic What a troublesome word! Don't confuse classic with classical. *Classic* can mean typical, as in *Oh, that was a classic blunder*. It can also mean an accepted masterpiece, for example, *Death of a Salesman*. But, classical refers to the arts of ancient Greece and Rome and the qualities of those arts.

Coinage (neologism) A *coinage* is a new word, usually one invented on the spot. People's names often become grist for coinages, as in, *Oh, man, you just pulled a major Wilson*. Of course, you'd have to know Wilson to know what that means, but you can tell it isn't a good thing. The technical term for coinage is *neologism*.

Colloquialism This is a word or phrase used in everyday conversational English that isn't a part of accepted "schoolbook" English. For example, *I'm toasted. I'm a crispy-critter man, and now I've got this wicked headache.*

Complex, Dense These two terms carry the similar meaning of suggesting that there is more than one possibility in the meaning of words (image, idea, opposition); there are subtleties and variations; there are multiple layers of interpretation; the meaning is both explicit and implicit.

*Conceit, Controlling Image In poetry, *conceit* doesn't mean stuck-up. It refers to a startling or unusual metaphor, or to a metaphor developed and expanded upon over several lines. When the image dominates and shapes the entire work, it's called a *controlling image*. A metaphysical conceit is reserved for metaphysical poems only.

Connotation, Denotation The *denotation* of a word is its literal meaning. The *connotations* are everything else that the word suggests or implies. For example, in the phrase *the dark forest*, *dark* denotes a relative lack of light. The connotation is of danger, or perhaps mystery or quiet; we'd need more information to know for sure, and if we did know with complete certainty that wouldn't be connotation, but denotation. In many cases connotation eventually so overwhelms a word that it takes over the denotation. For example, *livid* is supposed to denote a dark purple-red color like that of a bruise, but it has been used so often in the context of extreme anger that many people have come to use *livid* as a synonym for rage, rather than a connotative description of it.

Consonance The repetition of consonant sounds within words (rather than at their beginnings, which is alliteration). A flo*ck* of si*ck*, bla*ck*-che*ck*ered du*ck*s.

*Couplet A pair of lines that end in rhyme:

> But at my back I always *hear*
> Time's winged chariot hurrying *near*.
>
> —From "To His Coy Mistress" by Andrew Marvell

Decorum In order to observe *decorum*, a character's speech must be styled according to her social station, and in accordance with the occasion. A bum should speak like a bum about bumly things, while a princess should speak only about higher topics (and in a delicate manner). In Neoclassical and Victorian literature the authors observed decorum, meaning they did not write about the indecorous. The bum wouldn't even appear in this genre of literature.

*Diction, syntax The author's choice of words. Whether to use *wept* or *cried* is a question of *diction*. *Syntax* refers to the ordering and structuring of the words. Whether to say, *The pizza was smothered in cheese and pepperoni; I devoured it greedily*, or *Greedily, I devoured the cheese-and-pepperoni-smothered pizza*, is a question of syntax.

Dirge A song for the dead. Its tone is typically slow, heavy, and melancholy.

Dissonance The grating of incompatible sounds.

Doggerel Crude, simplistic verse, often in sing-song rhyme. Limericks are a kind of *doggerel*.

*Dramatic irony When the audience knows something that the characters in the drama do not.

Dramatic monologue When a single speaker in literature says something to a silent audience.

Elegy A type of poem that meditates on death or mortality in a serious, thoughtful manner. Elegies often use the recent death of a noted person or loved one as a starting point. They also memorialize specific dead people.

Elements This word is used constantly and with the assumption that you know exactly what it means—that is, the basic techniques of each genre of literature. For a quick refresher, here's a short and sweet list for each genre:

short story	poetry	drama	nonfiction (rhetorical)
characters	figurative language	conflict	argument
irony	symbol	characters	evidence
theme	imagery	climax	reason
symbol	rhythm	conclusion	appeals
plot	rhyme	exposition	fallacies
setting		rising action	thesis
		falling action	
		sets, props	

*Enjambment The continuation of a syntactic unit from one line or couplet of a poem to the next with no pause.

Epic In a broad sense, an epic is simply a very long narrative poem on a serious theme in a dignified style. Epics typically deal with glorious or profound subject matter: a great war, a heroic journey, the Fall from Eden, a battle with supernatural forces, a trip into the underworld, etc. The mock-epic is a parody form that deals with mundane events and ironically treats them as worthy of epic poetry.

Epitaph Lines that commemorate the dead at their burial place. An epitaph is usually a line or handful of lines, often serious or religious, but sometimes witty and even irreverent.

Euphemism A word or phrase that takes the place of a harsh, unpleasant, or impolite reality. The use of *passed away* for died, and *let go* for fired are two examples of *euphemisms*.

Euphony When sounds blend harmoniously, the result is *euphony*.

Explicit To say or write something directly and clearly (this is a rare happening in literature because the whole game is to be "implicit," that is, to suggest and imply).

Farce Today we use this word to refer to extremely broad humor. Writers of earlier times used *farce* as a more neutral term, meaning simply a funny play; a comedy. (And you should know that for writers of centuries past, *comedy* was the generic term for any play; it did not imply humor.)

Feminine rhyme Lines rhymed by their final two syllables. A pair of lines ending with *running* and *gunning* would be an example of feminine rhyme. Properly, in a feminine rhyme (and not simply a double rhyme) the penultimate syllables are stressed and the final syllables are unstressed.

First person narrator See *point of view*.

Foil A secondary character whose purpose is to highlight the characteristics of a main character, usually by contrast. For example, an author will often give a cynical, quick-witted character a docile, naive, sweet-tempered friend to serve as a *foil*.

Foot The basic rhythmic unit of a line of poetry. A *foot* is formed by a combination of two or three syllables, either stressed or unstressed.

*Foreshadowing An event or statement in a narrative that suggests, in miniature, a larger event that comes later.

Free verse Poetry written without a regular rhyme scheme or metrical pattern.

Genre A subcategory of literature. Science fiction and detective stories are *genres* of fiction.

Gothic, Gothic novel *Gothic* is the sensibility derived from gothic novels. This form first showed up in the middle of the eighteenth century and had a heyday of popularity for about sixty years. It hasn't really ever gone away. The sensibility? Think mysterious gloomy castles perched high upon sheer cliffs. Paintings with sinister eyeballs that follow you around the room. Weird screams from the attic each night. Diaries with a final entry that trails off the page and reads something like, *No, NO! IT COULDN'T BE!!*

Hubris The excessive pride or ambition that leads to the main character's downfall (another term from Aristotle's discussion of tragedy).

*Hyperbole Exaggeration or deliberate overstatement.

Implicit To say or write something that suggests and implies but never says it directly or clearly. "Meaning" is definitely present, but it's in the imagery, or "between the lines."

In medias res Latin for "in the midst of things." One of the conventions of epic poetry is that the action begins *in medias res*. For example, when *The Iliad* begins, the Trojan war has already been going on for seven years.

Interior monologue A term from novels and poetry, not dramatic literature. It refers to writing that records the mental talking that goes on inside a character's head. It is related, but not identical to *stream of consciousness*. Interior monologue tends to be coherent, as though the character were actually talking. Stream of consciousness is looser and much more given to fleeting mental impressions.

Inversion Switching the customary order of elements in a sentence or phrase. When done badly it can give a stilted, artificial, look-at-me-I'm-poetry feel to the verse, but poets do it all the time. This type of messing with syntax is called *poetic license. I'll have one large pizza with all the fixins*—presto chango instant poetry: *A pizza large I'll have, one with the fixin's all.*

*Irony This is one term you need to be very comfortable with for the AP test. Irony comes in a variety of forms, and you need to be able to recognize and be sensitive to it. Actually being able to name the specific type of irony involved is not important. ETS doesn't care if you can see an example of tragic irony and call it by name; they just want you to be able to see that it's irony. The reason irony shows up so much on the AP test is that it's a powerful verbal tool, and so good writers use it all the time. ETS also loves irony because ironic writing makes for good questions: Strong readers detect irony, weak readers do so less clearly.

One definition of irony is *a statement that means the opposite of what it seems to mean*, and although that isn't a bad definition, it doesn't get at the delicacy with which the authors on the AP test use irony. Simply saying the opposite of what one means is sarcasm. The hallmark of irony is an undertow of meaning, sliding against the literal meaning of the words. Jane Austen is famous for writing descriptions which seem perfectly pleasant, but to the sensitive reader have a deliciously mean snap to them. Irony insinuates. It whispers underneath the explicit statement, *Do you understand what I really mean?* Think of the way Mark Antony says again and again of Brutus, "But he is an honorable man." At first it doesn't seem like much, but with each repetition the undertone of irony becomes ever more insistent.

Lament A poem of sadness or grief over the death of a loved one or over some other intense loss.

Lampoon A satire.

Loose and periodic sentences A *loose* sentence is complete before its end. A *periodic* sentence is not grammatically complete until it has reached its final phrase. (The term *loose* does not in any way imply that the sentences are slack or shoddy.)

Loose sentence: *Jack loved Barbara despite her irritating snorting laugh, her complaining, and her terrible taste in shoes.*

Periodic sentence: *Despite Barbara's irritation at Jack's peculiar habit of picking between his toes while watching MTV and his terrible haircut, she loved him.*

Lyric A type of poetry that explores the poet's personal interpretation of and feelings about the world (or the part that his poem is about). When the word *lyric* is used to describe a tone it refers to a sweet, emotional melodiousness.

Masculine rhyme A rhyme ending on the final stressed syllable (a k a, regular old rhyme).

Means, Meaning This is the big one, the one task you have to do all the time. You are discovering what makes sense, what's important. There is literal meaning which is concrete and explicit, and there is emotional meaning.

Melodrama A form of cheesy theater in which the hero is very, very good, the villain mean and rotten, and the heroine oh-so-pure. (It sounds dumb, but melodramatic movies make tons of money every year.)

*Metaphor and Simile A *metaphor* is a comparison or analogy that states one thing *is* another. *His eyes were burning coals*, or *In the morning, the lake is covered in liquid gold*. It's a simple point, so keep it straight: a simile is just like a metaphor but softens the full-out equation of things, often, but not always, by using *like* or *as*. *His eyes were like burning coals*, or *In the morning the lake is covered in what seems to be liquid gold.*

Metaphysical conceit See *conceit*.

Metonym A word that is used to stand for something else that it has attributes of or is associated with. For example, a herd of 50 cows could be called 50 *head* of cattle.

Nemesis The protagonist's archenemy or supreme and persistent difficulty.

Neologism See *coinage*.

*Objectivity and Subjectivity An *objective* treatment of subject matter is an impersonal or outside view of events. A *subjective* treatment uses the interior or personal view of a single observer and is typically colored with that observer's emotional responses.

*Omniscient narrator See *point of view*.

Onomatopoeia Words that sound like what they mean are examples of onomatopoeia. *Boom. Splat. Babble. Gargle.*

*Opposition One of the most useful concepts in analyzing literature. It means that you have a pair of elements that contrast sharply. It is not necessarily "conflict" but rather a pairing of images (or settings or appeals, etc.), whereby each becomes more striking and informative because it's placed in contrast to the other one. This kind of *opposition* creates mystery and tension. Oppositions can be obvious. Oppositions can also lead to irony, but not necessarily so.

Oxymoron A phrase composed of opposites; a contradiction. *Bright black. A calm frenzy. Jumbo shrimp. Dark light. A truthful lie.*

Parable Like a fable or an allegory, a parable is a story that instructs.

*Paradox A situation or statement that seems to contradict itself, but on closer inspection, does not.

Parallelism Repeated syntactical similarities used for effect.

Paraphrase To restate phrases and sentences in your own words; to rephrase. Paraphrase is not analysis or interpretation, so don't fall into the thinking that traps so many students. Paraphrasing is just a way of showing that you comprehend what you've just read—that you can now put it in your own words. No more, no less.

Parenthetical phrase A phrase set off by commas that interrupts the flow of a sentence with some commentary or added detail. *Jack's three dogs, <u>including that miserable little spaniel</u>, were with him that day.*

Parody The work that results when a specific work is exaggerated to ridiculousness.

Pastoral A poem set in tranquil nature, or even more specifically, one about shepherds.

Pathos See *bathos*.

Periodic sentence See *loose sentence*.

Persona The narrator in a non-first-person novel. In a third person novel, even though the author isn't a character, you get some idea of the author's personality. However, it isn't really the author's personality because the author is manipulating your impressions there as in other parts of the book. This shadow-author is called the author's *persona*.

*Personification Giving an inanimate object human qualities or form. *The darkness of the forest became the figure of a beautiful, pale-skinned woman in night-black clothes.*

Plaint A poem or speech expressing sorrow.

*Point of view The perspective from which the action of a novel (or narrative poem) is presented, whether the action is presented by one character or from different vantage points over the course of the novel. Be sensitive to *point of view*, because ETS likes to ask questions about it, and they also like to you to mention point of view in your essays.

Related to point of view is the narrative form that a novel or story takes. There are a few common narrative positions:

- **The omniscient narrator** This is a third-person narrator who sees, like God, into each character's mind and understands all the action going on.

- **The limited omniscient narrator** This is a third-person narrator who generally reports only what one character (usually the main character) sees, and who only reports the thoughts of that one privileged character.

- **The objective, or camera-eye, narrator** This is a third-person narrator who only reports on what would be visible to a camera. The objective narrator does not know what the character is thinking unless the character speaks of it.

- **The first-person narrator** This is a narrator who is a character in the story and tells the tale from his or her point of view. When the first-person narrator is crazy, a liar, very young, or for some other reason not entirely credible, the narrator is *unreliable*.

- **The stream of consciousness technique** This method is like first-person narration but, instead of the character telling the story, the author places the reader inside the main character's head and makes the reader privy to all of the character's thoughts as they scroll through her consciousness.

Prelude An introductory poem to a longer work of verse.

*Protagonist The main character of a novel or play.

Pun The usually humorous use of a word in such a way to suggest two or more meanings.

Refrain A line or set of lines repeated several times over the course of a poem.

Requiem A song of prayer for the dead.

Rhapsody An intensely passionate verse or section of verse, usually of love or praise.

Rhetorical question A question that suggests an answer. In theory, the effect of a rhetorical question is that it causes the listener to feel she has come up with the answer herself. *Well, we can fight it out, or we can run—so, are we cowards?*

*Satire This is an important term for the AP test. ETS is fond of satirical writing, again because it lends itself well to multiple-choice questions. *Satire* exposes common character flaws to the cold light of humor. In general, *satire* attempts to improve things by pointing out people's mistakes in the hope that once exposed, such behavior will become less common. The great satirical subjects are hypocrisy, vanity, and greed, especially where those all-too-common characteristics have become institutionalized in society.

*Simile See *metaphor*.

Soliloquy A speech spoken by a character alone on stage. A soliloquy is meant to convey the impression that the audience is listening to the character's thoughts. Unlike an aside, a soliloquy is not meant to imply that the actor acknowledges the audience's presence.

*Stanza A group of lines in verse, roughly analogous in function to the paragraph in prose.

Stock characters Standard or clichéd character types: the drunk, the miser, the foolish girl, etc.

Stream of consciousness See *point of view*.

*Subjective See *objectivity*.

Subjunctive Mood *If I were you, I'd learn this one!* That's a small joke because the grammatical situation involves the words "if" and "were." What you do is set up a hypothetical situation, a kind of wishful thing: *if I were you, if he were honest, if she were rich.* You can also get away from the person and into the "it": *I wish it were true, would it were so* (that even sounds like Shakespeare and poetry). Go to page 64, question 15 for the perfect example: "Were one not already the Duke…"

Suggest To imply, infer, indicate. This is another one of those basic tools of literature. It goes along with the concept of *implicit*. As the reader, you have to do all the work to pull out the meaning.

Summary A simple retelling of what you've just read. It's mechanical, superficial, and a step beyond the paraphrase in that it covers much more material and is more general. You can summarize a whole chapter or a whole story, whereas you paraphrase word-by-word and line-by-line. Summary includes all the facts.

Suspension of disbelief The demand made of a theater audience to accept the limitations of staging and supply the details with imagination. Also, the acceptance on an audience's or reader's part of the incidents of plot in a play or story. If there are too many coincidences or improbable occurrences, the viewer/reader can no longer suspend disbelief and subsequently loses interest.

*Symbolism A device in literature where an object represents an idea.

Syntax See *diction*.

Technique The methods, the tools, the "how-she-does-it" ways of the author. The elements are not *techniques*. In poetry, *onomatopoeia* is a *technique* within the element of rhythm. In drama, *blocking* is a *technique*, as is *lighting*. Concrete details are not *techniques*, but tone is. Main idea is not a *technique*, but opposition is.

*Theme The main idea of the overall work; the central idea. It is the topic of discourse or discussion.

Thesis The main position of an argument. The central contention that will be supported.

Tragic flaw In a tragedy, this is the weakness of character in an otherwise good (or even great) individual that ultimately leads to his demise.

Travesty A grotesque parody.

Truism A way-too-obvious truth.

Unreliable narrator See *point of view*.

Utopia An idealized place. Imaginary communities in which people are able to live in happiness, prosperity, and peace. Several works of fiction have been written about *utopias*.

Zeugma The use of a word to modify two or more words, but used for different meanings. *He closed the door and his heart on his lost love.*

Completely darken bubbles with a No. 2 pencil. If you make a mistake, be sure to erase mark completely. Erase all stray marks.

1. YOUR NAME:
(Print)

Last   First   M.I.

SIGNATURE: _____ DATE: _____ / _____ / _____

HOME ADDRESS: _____
(Print)
                           Number and Street

_____
City   State   Zip Code

PHONE NO. : _____
(Print)

5. YOUR NAME
First 4 letters of last name

				FIRST INIT	MID INIT
Ⓐ	Ⓐ	Ⓐ	Ⓐ	Ⓐ	Ⓐ
Ⓑ	Ⓑ	Ⓑ	Ⓑ	Ⓑ	Ⓑ
Ⓒ	Ⓒ	Ⓒ	Ⓒ	Ⓒ	Ⓒ
Ⓓ	Ⓓ	Ⓓ	Ⓓ	Ⓓ	Ⓓ
Ⓔ	Ⓔ	Ⓔ	Ⓔ	Ⓔ	Ⓔ
Ⓕ	Ⓕ	Ⓕ	Ⓕ	Ⓕ	Ⓕ
Ⓖ	Ⓖ	Ⓖ	Ⓖ	Ⓖ	Ⓖ
Ⓗ	Ⓗ	Ⓗ	Ⓗ	Ⓗ	Ⓗ
Ⓘ	Ⓘ	Ⓘ	Ⓘ	Ⓘ	Ⓘ
Ⓙ	Ⓙ	Ⓙ	Ⓙ	Ⓙ	Ⓙ
Ⓚ	Ⓚ	Ⓚ	Ⓚ	Ⓚ	Ⓚ
Ⓛ	Ⓛ	Ⓛ	Ⓛ	Ⓛ	Ⓛ
Ⓜ	Ⓜ	Ⓜ	Ⓜ	Ⓜ	Ⓜ
Ⓝ	Ⓝ	Ⓝ	Ⓝ	Ⓝ	Ⓝ
Ⓞ	Ⓞ	Ⓞ	Ⓞ	Ⓞ	Ⓞ
Ⓟ	Ⓟ	Ⓟ	Ⓟ	Ⓟ	Ⓟ
Ⓠ	Ⓠ	Ⓠ	Ⓠ	Ⓠ	Ⓠ
Ⓡ	Ⓡ	Ⓡ	Ⓡ	Ⓡ	Ⓡ
Ⓢ	Ⓢ	Ⓢ	Ⓢ	Ⓢ	Ⓢ
Ⓣ	Ⓣ	Ⓣ	Ⓣ	Ⓣ	Ⓣ
Ⓤ	Ⓤ	Ⓤ	Ⓤ	Ⓤ	Ⓤ
Ⓥ	Ⓥ	Ⓥ	Ⓥ	Ⓥ	Ⓥ
Ⓦ	Ⓦ	Ⓦ	Ⓦ	Ⓦ	Ⓦ
Ⓧ	Ⓧ	Ⓧ	Ⓧ	Ⓧ	Ⓧ
Ⓨ	Ⓨ	Ⓨ	Ⓨ	Ⓨ	Ⓨ
Ⓩ	Ⓩ	Ⓩ	Ⓩ	Ⓩ	Ⓩ

IMPORTANT: Please fill in these boxes exactly as shown on the back cover of your test book.

2. TEST FORM

_____

6. DATE OF BIRTH

Month	Day		Year	
◯ JAN				
◯ FEB				
◯ MAR	⓪	⓪	⓪	⓪
◯ APR	①	①	①	①
◯ MAY	②	②	②	②
◯ JUN	③	③	③	③
◯ JUL		④	④	④
◯ AUG		⑤	⑤	⑤
◯ SEP		⑦	⑦	⑦
◯ OCT		⑧	⑧	⑧
◯ NOV		⑨	⑨	⑨
◯ DEC				

3. TEST CODE

4. REGISTRATION NUMBER

⓪	Ⓐ	⓪	⓪	⓪	⓪	⓪	⓪	⓪	⓪	⓪	⓪
①	Ⓑ	①	①	①	①	①	①	①	①	①	①
②	Ⓒ	②	②	②	②	②	②	②	②	②	②
③	Ⓓ	③	③	③	③	③	③	③	③	③	③
④	Ⓔ	④	④	④	④	④	④	④	④	④	④
⑤	Ⓕ	⑤	⑤	⑤	⑤	⑤	⑤	⑤	⑤	⑤	⑤
⑦	Ⓖ	⑦	⑦	⑦	⑦	⑦	⑦	⑦	⑦	⑦	⑦
⑧		⑧	⑧	⑧	⑧	⑧	⑧	⑧	⑧	⑧	⑧
⑨		⑨	⑨	⑨	⑨	⑨	⑨	⑨	⑨	⑨	⑨

7. SEX
◯ MALE
◯ FEMALE

The Princeton Review

© The Princeton Review, Inc.

FORM NO. 00001-PR

Practice Test 1

Start with number 1 for each new section.
If a section has fewer questions than answer spaces, leave the extra answer spaces blank.

1. Ⓐ Ⓑ Ⓒ Ⓓ Ⓔ
2. Ⓐ Ⓑ Ⓒ Ⓓ Ⓔ
3. Ⓐ Ⓑ Ⓒ Ⓓ Ⓔ
4. Ⓐ Ⓑ Ⓒ Ⓓ Ⓔ
5. Ⓐ Ⓑ Ⓒ Ⓓ Ⓔ
6. Ⓐ Ⓑ Ⓒ Ⓓ Ⓔ
7. Ⓐ Ⓑ Ⓒ Ⓓ Ⓔ
8. Ⓐ Ⓑ Ⓒ Ⓓ Ⓔ
9. Ⓐ Ⓑ Ⓒ Ⓓ Ⓔ
10. Ⓐ Ⓑ Ⓒ Ⓓ Ⓔ
11. Ⓐ Ⓑ Ⓒ Ⓓ Ⓔ
12. Ⓐ Ⓑ Ⓒ Ⓓ Ⓔ
13. Ⓐ Ⓑ Ⓒ Ⓓ Ⓔ
14. Ⓐ Ⓑ Ⓒ Ⓓ Ⓔ
15. Ⓐ Ⓑ Ⓒ Ⓓ Ⓔ

16. Ⓐ Ⓑ Ⓒ Ⓓ Ⓔ
17. Ⓐ Ⓑ Ⓒ Ⓓ Ⓔ
18. Ⓐ Ⓑ Ⓒ Ⓓ Ⓔ
19. Ⓐ Ⓑ Ⓒ Ⓓ Ⓔ
20. Ⓐ Ⓑ Ⓒ Ⓓ Ⓔ
21. Ⓐ Ⓑ Ⓒ Ⓓ Ⓔ
22. Ⓐ Ⓑ Ⓒ Ⓓ Ⓔ
23. Ⓐ Ⓑ Ⓒ Ⓓ Ⓔ
24. Ⓐ Ⓑ Ⓒ Ⓓ Ⓔ
25. Ⓐ Ⓑ Ⓒ Ⓓ Ⓔ
26. Ⓐ Ⓑ Ⓒ Ⓓ Ⓔ
27. Ⓐ Ⓑ Ⓒ Ⓓ Ⓔ
28. Ⓐ Ⓑ Ⓒ Ⓓ Ⓔ
29. Ⓐ Ⓑ Ⓒ Ⓓ Ⓔ
30. Ⓐ Ⓑ Ⓒ Ⓓ Ⓔ

31. Ⓐ Ⓑ Ⓒ Ⓓ Ⓔ
32. Ⓐ Ⓑ Ⓒ Ⓓ Ⓔ
33. Ⓐ Ⓑ Ⓒ Ⓓ Ⓔ
34. Ⓐ Ⓑ Ⓒ Ⓓ Ⓔ
35. Ⓐ Ⓑ Ⓒ Ⓓ Ⓔ
36. Ⓐ Ⓑ Ⓒ Ⓓ Ⓔ
37. Ⓐ Ⓑ Ⓒ Ⓓ Ⓔ
38. Ⓐ Ⓑ Ⓒ Ⓓ Ⓔ
39. Ⓐ Ⓑ Ⓒ Ⓓ Ⓔ
40. Ⓐ Ⓑ Ⓒ Ⓓ Ⓔ
41. Ⓐ Ⓑ Ⓒ Ⓓ Ⓔ
42. Ⓐ Ⓑ Ⓒ Ⓓ Ⓔ
43. Ⓐ Ⓑ Ⓒ Ⓓ Ⓔ
44. Ⓐ Ⓑ Ⓒ Ⓓ Ⓔ
45. Ⓐ Ⓑ Ⓒ Ⓓ Ⓔ

46. Ⓐ Ⓑ Ⓒ Ⓓ Ⓔ
47. Ⓐ Ⓑ Ⓒ Ⓓ Ⓔ
48. Ⓐ Ⓑ Ⓒ Ⓓ Ⓔ
49. Ⓐ Ⓑ Ⓒ Ⓓ Ⓔ
50. Ⓐ Ⓑ Ⓒ Ⓓ Ⓔ
51. Ⓐ Ⓑ Ⓒ Ⓓ Ⓔ
52. Ⓐ Ⓑ Ⓒ Ⓓ Ⓔ
53. Ⓐ Ⓑ Ⓒ Ⓓ Ⓔ
54. Ⓐ Ⓑ Ⓒ Ⓓ Ⓔ
55. Ⓐ Ⓑ Ⓒ Ⓓ Ⓔ

The Princeton Review

1. YOUR NAME: _____
(Print)

Last   First   M.I.

SIGNATURE: _____   **DATE:** ____ / ____ / ____

HOME ADDRESS: _____
(Print)

Number and Street

_____

City   State   Zip Code

PHONE NO. : _____
(Print)

IMPORTANT: Please fill in these boxes exactly as shown on the back cover of your test book.

2. TEST FORM

3. TEST CODE

4. REGISTRATION NUMBER

5. YOUR NAME

First 4 letters of last name | FIRST INIT | MID INIT

6. DATE OF BIRTH

Month	Day	Year
JAN		
FEB		
MAR	0 0	0 0
APR	1 1	1 1
MAY	2 2	2 2
JUN	3 3	3 3
JUL	4 4	4
AUG	5 5	5
SEP	7 7	7
OCT	8 8	8
NOV	9 9	9
DEC		

7. SEX
- MALE
- FEMALE

The Princeton Review

© The Princeton Review, Inc.

FORM NO. 00001-PR

Practice Test 2

Start with number 1 for each new section.
If a section has fewer questions than answer spaces, leave the extra answer spaces blank.

1. A B C D E
2. A B C D E
3. A B C D E
4. A B C D E
5. A B C D E
6. A B C D E
7. A B C D E
8. A B C D E
9. A B C D E
10. A B C D E
11. A B C D E
12. A B C D E
13. A B C D E
14. A B C D E
15. A B C D E

16. A B C D E
17. A B C D E
18. A B C D E
19. A B C D E
20. A B C D E
21. A B C D E
22. A B C D E
23. A B C D E
24. A B C D E
25. A B C D E
26. A B C D E
27. A B C D E
28. A B C D E
29. A B C D E
30. A B C D E

31. A B C D E
32. A B C D E
33. A B C D E
34. A B C D E
35. A B C D E
36. A B C D E
37. A B C D E
38. A B C D E
39. A B C D E
40. A B C D E
41. A B C D E
42. A B C D E
43. A B C D E
44. A B C D E
45. A B C D E

46. A B C D E
47. A B C D E
48. A B C D E
49. A B C D E
50. A B C D E
51. A B C D E
52. A B C D E
53. A B C D E
54. A B C D E
55. A B C D E

NOTES

NOTES

Our Books Help You Navigate the College Admissions Process

Find the Right School

Best 368 Colleges, 2009 Edition
978-0-375-42872-2 • $21.95/C$25.00
Previous Edition: 978-0-375-76621-3

Complete Book of Colleges, 2009 Edition
978-0-375-42874-6 • $26.95/C$32.00
Previous Edition: 978-0-375-76620-6

College Navigator
978-0-375-76583-4 • $12.95/C$16.00

America's Best Value Colleges, 2008 Edition
978-0-375-76601-5 • $18.95/C$24.95

Guide to College Visits
978-0-375-76600-8 • $20.00/C$25.00

Get In

Cracking the SAT, 2009 Edition
978-0-375-42856-2 • $19.95/C$22.95

**Cracking the SAT with DVD,
2009 Edition**
978-0-375-42857-9 • $33.95/C$37.95

Math Workout for the SAT
978-0-375-76433-2 • $16.00/C$23.00

**Reading and Writing Workout
for the SAT**
978-0-375-76431-8 • $16.00/C$23.00

**11 Practice Tests for the SAT and PSAT,
2009 Edition**
978-0-375-42860-9 • $19.95/C$22.95

12 Practice Tests for the AP Exams
978-0-375-76584-1 • $19.95/C$24.95

Cracking the ACT, 2008 Edition
978-0-375-76634-3 • $19.95/C$22.95

**Cracking the ACT with DVD,
2008 Edition**
978-0-375-76635-0 • $31.95/C$35.95

Crash Course for the ACT, 3rd Edition
978-0-375-76587-2 • $9.95/C$12.95

Fund It

**Paying for College Without
Going Broke, 2009 Edition**
978-0-375-42883-8 • $20.00/C$23.00
Previous Edition: 978-0-375-76630-5

Available at Bookstores Everywhere
www.PrincetonReview.com

AP Exams

Cracking the AP Biology Exam,
2009 Edition
978-0-375-42884-5 • $18.00/C$21.00

Cracking the AP Calculus AB & BC Exams,
2009 Edition
978-0-375-42885-2 • $19.00/C$22.00

Cracking the AP Chemistry Exam,
2009 Edition
978-0-375-42886-9 • $18.00/C$22.00

Cracking the AP Computer Science A & AB,
2006–2007
978-0-375-76528-5 • $19.00/C$27.00

Cracking the AP Economics Macro & Micro
Exams, 2009 Edition
978-0-375-42887-6 • $18.00/C$21.00

Cracking the AP English Language &
Composition Exam, 2009 Edition
978-0-375-42888-3 • $18.00/C$21.00

Cracking the AP English Literature &
Composition Exam, 2009 Edition
978-0-375-42889-0 • $18.00/C$21.00

Cracking the AP Environmental
Science Exam, 2009 Edition
978-0-375-42890-6 • $18.00/C$21.00

Cracking the AP European History Exam,
2009 Edition
978-0-375-42891-3 • $18.00/C$21.00

Cracking the AP Physics B Exam,
2009 Edition
978-0-375-42892-0 • $18.00/C$21.00

Cracking the AP Physics C Exam,
2009 Edition
978-0-375-42893-7 • $18.00/C$21.00

Cracking the AP Psychology Exam,
2009 Edition
978-0-375-42894-4 • $18.00/C$21.00

Cracking the AP Spanish Exam,
with Audio CD, 2009 Edition
978-0-375-76530-8 • $24.95/$27.95

Cracking the AP Statistics Exam,
2009 Edition
978-0-375-42848-7 • $19.00/C$22.00

Cracking the AP U.S. Government
and Politics Exam, 2009 Edition
978-0-375-42896-8 • $18.00/C$21.00

Cracking the AP U.S. History Exam,
2009 Edition
978-0-375-42897-5 • $18.00/C$21.00

Cracking the AP World History Exam,
2009 Edition
978-0-375-42898-2 • $18.00/C$21.00

SAT Subject Tests

Cracking the SAT Biology E/M Subject Test,
2009–2010 Edition
978-0-375-42905-7 • $19.00/C$22.00

Cracking the SAT Chemistry Subject Test,
2009–2010 Edition
978-0-375-42906-4 • $19.00/C$22.00

Cracking the SAT French Subject Test,
2009–2010 Edition
978-0-375-42907-1 • $19.00/C$22.00

Cracking the SAT U.S. & World History
Subject Tests, 2009–2010 Edition
978-0-375-42908-8 • $19.00/C$22.00

Cracking the SAT Literature Subject Test,
2009–2010 Edition
978-0-375-42909-5 • $19.00/C$22.00

Cracking the SAT Math 1 & 2 Subject Tests,
2009–2010 Edition
978-0-375-42910-1 • $19.00/C$22.00

Cracking the SAT Physics Subject Test,
2009–2010 Edition
978-0-375-42911-8 • $19.00/C$22.00

Cracking the SAT Spanish Subject Test,
2009–2010 Edition
978-0-375-42912-5 • $19.00/C$22.00